The Little Learner

The Little Learner

A Straight Line to Deep Learning

Daniel P. Friedman
Anurag Mendhekar

Drawings by Qingqing Su

Forewords by Guy L. Steele Jr. and Peter Norvig

The MIT Press
Cambridge, Massachusetts
London, England

This book was set in Computer Modern Unicode by the authors using LaTeX. Printed and bound in the United States of America.

Library of Congress Cataloging-in-Publication Data is available.

ISBN 978-0-262-54637-9

10 9 8 7 6 5 4 3 2 1

To Mary, from the title of the song
this is "Dedicated to the One I Love."
What a fabulous ride you have taken me on!
With all my love and admiration.
–Danny

To the shining stars in my life, Aruna, Rishma, and Aria Nina,
and my constant 4-legged companions Chikki and Heera.
Without you there would only be darkness.
–Anurag

We ran into each other on Friday, the 13th of April, 2018, at the overcrowded, official opening of the Luddy School of Informatics, Computing, and Engineering and we decided to write a book on machine learning based on this *very* deep conversation directly following the close of the event.

Anurag: I want to write a little book with you.
Dan: Let's do it!

⋮

a few seconds later

⋮

Dan: What's the topic?
Anurag: Machine learning
Dan: Now, that will be a worthy challenge!

And the rest of the time we reminisced ...

(**Contents**

Foreword

by Guy L. Steele Jr.

This book is *exactly* right.

Dan Friedman, with his able and expert co-authors, has been writing books in his unique "Little" style for over four decades. Every one is a gem, explaining deep and important ideas in computer science in bite-sized chunks. Dan and his co-authors have raised the "programmed learning" question-and-answer format to an art form, to a conversational style that seems almost breezy. This very volume introduces two innovations, *nuggets* and *revision charts*, that further streamline the presentation of chunks of program code and their behavior.

Regarding the fundamental ideas behind machine learning

> This book presents *exactly the right ideas*
>
> in *exactly the right format*
>
> and
>
> in *exactly the right order*
>
> All you need to do is read the book *in order* (don't skip ahead!)

The authors themselves remark:

> "Little" books are all about packaging ideas neatly into little boxes.

What ideas are in this book? The mathematics and computational techniques of machine learning, of course: you'll learn about successive approximation, stochastic gradient descent, neural networks, and automatic back-propagation. However, as a programming languages guy, I am also interested in how the authors use language to frame the mathematics. To me, a big overarching idea here is how the authors use *higher-order functions*—that is, functions that take other functions as arguments and/or return other functions as results—to explain the data structures and computations of machine learning.

The fundamental data structure is the *tensor*, which at first glance looks like an ordinary array or matrix; but the authors explain that tensor operations have the additional property of automatically using a higher-order mapping function when appropriate, and this—almost magically, it seems to me—enables a function apparently written for scalars (single numbers), or a tensor of a specific dimension, to be applied generally to all kinds and sizes of arrays, vectors, and matrices with no additional effort.

Another application of higher-order functions is *currying*, which allows you to give a function some of its arguments now and others later—when you give it some of its arguments now, it returns another function that can be applied to the other arguments later to get the final answer. The presentation in this book uses currying in a clear—and, to me, pleasantly surprising—way to explain the difference between *arguments* and *parameters* in machine learning, and why they need to be presented in a specific order, some now and some later. (A third sort of argument, *hyperparameters*, is also explained using yet another programming-language mechanism. If you're familiar with the buzzphrase "dynamic scoping" you are in for a treat; if you are not, no worries—hyperparameters and their behavior are clearly explained by example.)

The third use of higher-order functions in this book is to structure the *composition* of large neural networks from smaller building blocks, and to explain the behavior and training of these networks.

A fourth use of higher-order functions is to provide for *data abstraction.* At first, parameters are always simple numbers, but the code for processing them is so deftly defined using just a few interface functions—exactly the right ones—that the higher-order code does not need to be changed when the representation of parameters is extended. (A key idea is *projection*: provide two functions, one that projects data into an alternate representation that is easier to compute on, and another that pulls a computed result back into the original representation. Then a function that accepts two such functions as arguments can be used in a very general way.) Similarly, scalars are simple numbers throughout most of the book, but when it becomes necessary to generalize them to *duals* in appendix A, higher-order functions make the task simple.

So if you are interested in big-picture programming-language ideas
  Keep these applications of higher-order functions in mind as you read
  You may enjoy spotting them as they go by
but if you don't care about higher-order functions
  Please ignore everything I have just said
  Immerse yourself in the story of machine learning
This book needs no introduction; it is exactly right for its purpose.

I have read all the books in the "Little" series; each time I have said to myself, "This is the best one ever!" This time, Dan and Anurag have done it again—this is the best. It stands on its own; you don't need to have read earlier "Little" books to understand this one, and you don't need to understand Scheme or any other programming language ahead of time. The dozen or so programming-language ideas you need are explained along the way, each exactly when you need it, and with plenty of examples. Give it time and enjoy the journey.

Guy L. Steele Jr.
Lexington, Massachusetts
August 2022

Foreword

by Peter Norvig

Hi, I'm Peter Norvig, a long-time researcher and practitioner of machine learning.

I've had the pleasure of reading this book, and was asked to make some comments on it. I'm going to do that in the form of a dialog with my esteemed colleague, Typical Reader.

Welcome to this foreword Mx. Reader, how are you?

1 Thanks, I'm happy to be here, even if I am imaginary.

And please, call me Tipi.

Okay, Tipi.

I can say that I thoroughly enjoyed the book and appreciated the way it carefully developed the key concepts.

How did you find the book?

2 To be honest, I haven't read it all yet. So far I've only skimmed it. It looks interesting, but I'm trying to decide if it is worth the time and effort to work through the whole book.

You have a good point.

This book is more interactive than most, and asks more of the reader.

I can't tell you whether the book is right for you, but I can say that the best way to achieve expertise in any area is with deliberate practice, not just passive listening or reading.

3 It does seem to demand more effort than a typical book, because you have to work through the examples.

Working through the examples really helps the material stick with you!

I remember one time I was discussing a machine learning technique with a colleague, and they said they didn't see how a particular tricky part worked. I said that it seems tricky, but it is actually easy.

I remembered that Andrew Ng had a great video that was perfectly elegant in explaining how it worked. I then tried to duplicate what I learned from the video and—I couldn't do it.

Andrew's explanation was so clear when I watched it that I didn't bother actually learning it. My colleague did a quick search and said "This must be the video; let's watch it again," but I said no; this time I'm going to work the answer for myself, and then I'll remember it.

And I do remember it to this day.

4 Okay, you convinced me that practice makes improvement.

When I look around, however, I see machine learning tools mainly in Python, or maybe Java or R, but not so much in Scheme.

This book isn't about programming languages, and it isn't about machine learning toolkits.

It is about explaining the fundamental concepts of machine learning, and implementing them in the simplest possible way.

5 Is Scheme a good choice for that?

I think it is.

It is one of the simplest possible programming languages. Working with it is like sticking with basic mathematical notation, but it happens to be executable code, so there's no ambiguity about how it all works.

6 But will this book have me practicing the right things?

After you finish this book, are you going to take the Scheme code and run it in your next machine learning project?

Maybe, maybe not. But even if you use a machine learning toolkit like TensorFlow or PyTorch, what you will take away from this book is an appreciation for how the fundamentals work.

That appreciation will help you understand what to try next when TensorFlow or PyTorch is not behaving the way you thought it should.

7 Okay, I'm all for understanding the fundamentals. But is this book all theoretical? All mathy? I want a good understanding of the fundamentals, but I want that understanding to be useful in practice.

This book will give you that. It takes you through the key ideas of machine learning.

It is definitely not "mathy"; it has the minimum amount of math notation, and most topics are described with code and prose, not equations.

Personally, I'm the kind of person who is always more comfortable reading code than math, so this book filled me with cozy feelings, not with dread.

8 That sounds good. What are some of the key topics I will learn about? And how long does it take to get to them?

I think the topics are presented at just the right pace. It starts off introducing the absolute basics of Scheme and of lines and linear equations. By page 63 we get to L2 loss, learning rate, and gradient descent.

Often the topics are covered in a simple way first, and then in a full-blown practical way later; we come back to gradient descent on page 141 and get to Adam optimization (a state-of-the-art version of gradient descent) by page 173.

By the time we get to page 201, The Rule of Artificial Neurons, "An artificial neuron is a parameterized linear function composed with a nonlinear decider function" makes perfect sense, putting together the pieces that have been built up in the preceding pages.

We learn about the most commonly-used decider functions, like the "relu," and on page 209 there's a simple but deeply satisfying description of how any function can be approximated with the tools we have at hand.

The book continually builds on solid foundations like this to explore the issues that come up in practice; for example in the discussion of vanishing and exploding gradients on page 260.

9 Okay, you've convinced me; skimming wasn't enough, I'm going to work through the whole book.

By the way, was there anything in the book you disagree with?

I whole-heartedly agree with the pedagogical style of working through an issue, seeing the finished results that you have accomplished, and then enjoying a break.

I've used the Pomodoro Technique to help keep me focused on work intervals; this book is perfectly suited for such an approach.

I think, however, if you strictly followed the book's advice for the number of desserts to eat, you'd be overdoing it.

Take the functions, leave the cannoli!

[10] As a typical reader, I consume 77 grams of sugar per day.

I'll heed your warning and try to get closer to the daily recommended level of 24 grams per day.

Peter Norvig
Palo Alto, California
August 2022

Preface

> You can't skip chapters, that's not how life works. You have to read every line, meet every character. You won't enjoy all of it. Hell, some chapters will make you cry for weeks. You will read things you don't want to read, you will have moments when you don't want the pages to end. But you have to keep going. Stories keep the world revolving. Live yours, don't miss out.
>
> – Courtney Peppernell, a poem from *Pillow Thoughts II*, published by Andrews McMeel Publishing, © 2018.

Deep learning, an emerging area of artificial intelligence, has revolutionized the way problems are solved, be it winning at Go, recognizing cats in pictures, or asking a smart speaker to order pizza. The most beautiful thing about deep learning is how simple pieces come together to solve large, complex problems. How can we understand what makes these deep learning tools work? Our approach is to build them, a little bit at a time, and watch them work.

The ability to grapple with noisy data is what makes deep learning, which is a type of machine learning, tantalizing. Consequently, being 100% correct is no longer attainable. Our sense of exactness of solutions, which is common to many problems for which we write programs, disappears. While much of this lies with the problem domain itself, we can, and should, maintain a sense of exactness in the functions we define—to keep true to our intuition so we can be assured that these functions meet our expectations.

To learn these tools, we require only basic high-school mathematics along with some programming experience. The functions we define are intended to be run and experimented with. It is, of course, possible to read this book without running them, but each definition must be carefully understood.

How to read this book

Because you may find that either this topic or our exposition method is new, you should read each chapter until you fully understand it. This might lead to reading some chapters more than once. Do not move forward until the chapter being read is completely clear. Be determined. Work with others and discuss with them what has been unclear until each little piece falls into place.

It is futile to read ahead in a "Little" book because everything is structured in *exactly* the right order as a sequence of numbered *frames* separated by horizontal lines. Each chapter is fairly short and has lots of *white space*, so rereading an entire chapter carefully to regain a lost thread is not unreasonable.

We also have two appendices in *exactly* the right order. They explain how to build the underlying tools that help us with deep learning. These appendices also assume very little by way of the background knowledge necessary, but are a wee bit more demanding of the reader than the rest of the book.

How our programs are written

We package our ideas as little Scheme programs. Scheme allows our thoughts to be expressed clearly and directly, and with minimal fuss. It is a language that assumes very little and gets out of the way quickly, so that the code speaks for itself.

We use a very small subset of Scheme: **define** (or **let**) allows a global (or local) name to be given to a value, **lambda** creates a function as a value, and **cond** dispatches over a sequence of (*test value*) pairs. There are also primitive functions such as $+$, $-$, and $*$ that operate over numbers. This is explained in *Are you Schemish?*.

We use *little boxes* to hold the code and we explain how the programs in these boxes work. Once *Are you Schemish?* is understood, each subsequent frame, when read in order, is easily digestable. This book builds up a collection of concepts, with nearly all of them being functions. If we request a function definition (in the left part of a frame), take some time and produce a plausible one before looking at our answer (in the right part of the frame). Here is a simple example of a frame with little boxes:

1

This is a little box

```
(define a-function
  ... that fits nicely in a little box ...)
```

This is a red box

They don't get wider than this

The first memorable one is frame 26:25

and

that means frame 25 on page 26

```
(define another-function                    ●
  ... remember this one! ...)
```

We also categorize key properties as either *rules* or *laws*. Our rules are about the structure of entities, like their sizes. Our laws, on the other hand, are about the behavior of entities, like their equalities and invariants.

How to run the code

We have collected the functions and syntactic extensions necessary for the code in this book into a MAchine Learning Toolkit package, called *Malt*. Malt is a package in Racket, which is a superset of our small subset of Scheme. The package includes our code and examples as well as the tools necessary to experiment with them. Advice for its use is available at *www.thelittlelearner.com*.

How to eat desserts

Those familiar with "Little" books may miss the funny Scheme symbols that have been an opportunity to inject humor into the data. It is very difficult to find humor in numbers, though occasionally we find some elsewhere. So, we have included a cornucopia of desserts for consumption at a nearby outdoor café. Don't skip them! But don't overdo them either, and remember to eat your "peas and carrots" first.

We hope this little foray into deep learning will be fun for you, and we hope that it's as interesting to read as we have found it to write.

Bon appétit!

Daniel P. Friedman
Bloomington, Indiana

Anurag Mendhekar
Los Altos, California

Transcribing to Scheme

We write some of our functions using a more compact notation so that they are easier to read and to fit snugly in the little boxes. Before running a program, be sure to transcribe our notation into Scheme code. The table below shows how to write these directly in Scheme.

The *first* column in the table below refers to the earliest occurrence in the book of the notation shown in the *second* column. The *third* column shows how to transcribe our programs, (e.g. [5 (+ 10 2) 28] is transcribed as `(tensor 5 (+ 10 2) 28)`).

Page:Frame	Notation	Transcription
24:17	$[t\ ts\ \ldots]$	`(tensor` t ts $\ldots$`)`
26:24	l_i	`(ref` l i`)`
27:27	(**list** m $\ldots$)	`(list` m $\ldots$`)`
33:17	$\nmid t \nmid$	`(tlen` t`)`
36:24	$t\vert_i$	`(tref` t i`)`
41:42	$\vert l \vert$	`(len` l`)`
52:22	$(\langle op\rangle^{\langle rank\rangle}\ t)$	$(\langle op\rangle$`-`$\langle rank\rangle\ t)$
77:15	$(\nabla\ f\ \boldsymbol{\theta})$	`(gradient-of` f $\boldsymbol{\theta}$`)`
106:25	$(\bullet\ t\ u)$	`(dot-product` t u`)`
106:26	$(\langle op\rangle^{\langle rank_1\rangle,\langle rank_2\rangle}\ t)$	$(\langle op\rangle$`-`$\langle rank_1\rangle$`-`$\langle rank_2\rangle\ t)$
124:27	$t\Vert_b$	`(trefs` t b`)`
226:49	$l_{i\downarrow}$	`(refr` l i`)`

For example, on page 52, frame 22, we introduce a hyphen between *sum* and ^{1} to transcribe sum^1 to `sum-1` and on page 106, frame 26, we introduce a second hyphen to transcribe $\bullet^{1,1}$ to `dot-product-1-1`.

Greek letters and notational variants of variable names like $\hat{a}$, α, $\hat{\alpha}$, *an-*α, β, $\hat{c}$, ϵ, $\boldsymbol{\theta}$, Θ, λ, μ, and π are written, respectively, as `a-hat`, `alpha`, `alpha-hat`, `an-alpha`, `beta`, `c-hat`, `epsilon`, `theta`, `big-theta`, `lambda`, `mu`, and `pi`. Unicode can be used in names of formals, functions, and keywords.

The successful running of the code requires the installation of the Malt package for Racket v8.0 or later. Details on downloading and running the code can be found on *www.thelittlelearner.com.*

The Little Learner

0

Are You Schemish?

Psst. Psst. **Psst!**

1 Toto, I have a feeling we're not in Kansas anymore.[†]

[†]Thanks, Lyman Frank Baum (1856–1919) and thanks, Edgar Allan Woolf (1881–1943).

How about a quick review?

2 Of what?

Of the programming language we're using here.

3 Oh, that would be great.

Did you read the three-page preface?

4 Of course, no one should skip the preface
   it has a little poem for learning
and
   the desserts sound enticing
So, off to reread the preface.[†]

[†]Text laid out in this style, where punctuation is replaced by indentation, is a *nugget*.

Those who already know Scheme[†] can zip through this to the next chapter, *The Lines Sleep Tonight*, after briefly glancing at the table on page xxiii for perhaps a few familiar names.

5 Thanks.

[†]Thanks, John McCarthy (1927–2011), Gerald Jay Sussman (1947–), and Guy L. Steele Jr. (1954–).

Let's first learn how to give names to values

```
(define pie† 3.14)
```

[†]It's not the tastiest *pie* we could find; it's missing the meringue topping (i.e., more digits after the 4).

6 Does that give the name *pie* to the number 3.14?

Yes, it does.

Here are some more definitions

```
(define a-radius 8.4)

(define an-area
  (* pie
     (* a-radius a-radius)))
```

7 Assuming $*$ the multiplication function, does this mean *an-area* is

221.5584

Correct.

Functions are invoked with zero or more arguments

(⟨*function*⟩ ⟨*argument*⟩ ...)

Since all mathematical operations (such as $*$, $+$, etc.) are functions, they are also written in this way.

8 How can we make new functions?

Let's make a function of one *formal*

r

Formals are the names given to arguments that are passed in when the function is invoked

```
(λ (r)
  (* pie
     (* r r)))
```

In this expression, λ (also written **lambda**) marks the beginning of a new function. Then we have the formals. Here we have a single formal *r*. And then we have the *body* of the function, which is the expression for the value of the function.

What does this function produce?

9 It squares the argument *r* and multiplies it with *pie*. That looks like the area of a circle with radius *r*.

Does this function have a name?

No, it doesn't.

But we can give it one using **define**

```
(define area-of-circle
  (λ (r)
    (* pie
      (* r r))))
```

10 Aha.

λ is used to create a function and **define** is used to give it a name.

So, are functions also values?

Yes.

Functions are also values and they can be used like other values.

11 Does that mean that functions can result in other functions?

Yes, it does.

Here is an example

```
(define area-of-rectangle
  (λ (width)
    (λ (height)
      (* width height))))
```

What is

(*area-of-rectangle* 3.0)?

12 The function *area-of-rectangle* is a function with one formal. But it results in a function

```
(λ (height)
  (* width height))
```

Does it not?

Very close.

The extra bit of information we need to remember is that *width* inside this function already has a value of 3.0.

This is how to think about it

```
(λ (height)
  (* 3.0 height))
```

13 That is a neat trick.

The inner function *remembers* the argument passed in for the formal of the outer function.

Can we also pass functions in as arguments to other functions?

Indeed, we can.

Here is an example

```
(define double-result-of-f
  (λ (f)
    (λ (z)
      (* 2 (f z)))))
```

Explain how *f* is being used here.

14 Here *f* is a formal of *double-result-of-f*, and then *f* is later invoked on *z*.

This means *f* must be a function.

Correct.

Here's a function that adds 3 to its formal

```
(define add3
  (λ (x)
    (+ 3 x)))
```

What happens when we invoke *double-result-of-f* on the *add3* function?

(*double-result-of-f add3*)

15 When we invoke *double-result-of-f* on *add3*, we get the inner function.

We remember the argument passed in for the formal *f* from the outer function, which means that we remember that *f* must have been *add3*.

Very good.

We write it this way

```
(λ (z)
  (* 2 (add3 z)))
```

What happens when we invoke this function on the argument 4?

```
((λ (z)
   (* 2 (add3 z)))
 4)
```

16 The value of *z* inside this function is now 4, so we get

(* 2 (*add3* 4))

Great.

What about the rest of it?

17 The expression

```
(add3 4)
```

is the same as

```
((λ (x)
    (+ 3 x))
 4)
```

which gets us 7. Substituting this into our previous expression, we get

```
(∗ 2 7)
```

giving us 14.

Correct.

This way of remembering arguments passed in for formals of outer functions inside inner functions is known as β-substitution.†

This is a useful tool for understanding function invocation. Scheme, in reality, has better ways of doing β-substitution.

†Thanks, Alonzo Church (1903–1995).
Care also must be taken when doing β-substitution so that all the names in the definition are unique at every step. If not, formals of functions can be given new names to make sure they are always unique.

18 Is **define** also a function?

No, it is not.

It is a *keyword*. Expressions that begin with keywords are known as *special forms*. They are different from function invocations.

19 Is λ also a keyword?

Yes. Here is an example of another special form

```
(cond
  ((= pie 4) 28)
  ((< pie 4) 33)
  (else 17))
```

This expression results in 33.

Explain why.

20 The keyword here is **cond**[†].

Is **cond** short for *conditional*?

[†]Also known as McCarthy's **cond**.

Yes, it is.

21 So then

(= *pie* 4)

and

(< *pie* 4)

must be tests.

Yes, they are.

22 Since *pie* is not equal to 4, the first test fails[†] but the second test succeeds.[‡]

[†]It results in false, written in Scheme as #f.
[‡]It results in true, written in Scheme as #t.

Correct.

Each combination of test and value is known as a *clause*, where **else** is treated as true. The value of the **cond** expression is the value of the first clause with a true test, checking them from the top to the bottom.

23 The **cond** expression results in 33, because its associated test is the first one that is true.

Very good.

Let's combine these three special forms we have just learned

```
(define abs
  (λ (x)
    (cond
      ((< x 0) (- 0 x))
      (else x))))
```

Explain what *abs* does.

24 It is the absolute value function!

It takes a single number x and if the number is *less than* 0, it subtracts this negative number from 0, and it results in a positive number.

Else, it results in the nonnegative number

x

We also need a way to define *local names* inside our functions, where these names are not visible outside those functions.

25 Yes, that should be useful for defining readable functions.

We do that using a special form known as a **let**-expression. For example

```
(define silly-abs
  (λ (x)
    (let ((x-is-negative (< x 0)))
      (cond
        (x-is-negative (- 0 x))
        (else x)))))
```

26 It looks as if we are giving

(< x 0)

the local name

x-is-negative

Yes, we are.

The last expression of the **let** (in this example the **cond**) is known as the *body* of the **let**. Of course, it does not always have to be a **cond**. It can be any expression. The name *x-is-negative* can be used anywhere inside the body of the **let**-expression, but it has no value outside of it.

27 That's convenient.

Perfect.

We have everything we need.

28 No we don't. We still haven't seen loops.

Our language does not have loops.

29 What?

How can we define interesting functions without loops?

We use *recursive functions.*

30 Is that where the body of a function refers to the name given to the function itself?

Precisely.

Let's define a simple version of the remainder function.†

Here's an example of how it would work. Suppose we want to find the remainder where the two numbers are 13 and 4. The remainder is what's left over after removing as many 4s from 13 as possible.

What is the result here?

†It's simple because we assume its first argument to be a nonnegative number and its second argument to be positive.

31 The remainder is 1, since we can remove 4 three times from 13, to get 1.

Correct.

Let's do it step by step. Since 13 is larger than 4, we can remove 4 to get 9.

What is the next step?

32 The number 9 is also larger than 4, so we can remove it one more time to get 5.

Good.

The number 5 is still larger than 4, so we can remove it one last time to get 1.

33 Now it is smaller than 4, and we can no longer remove 4 from it.

So the remainder is 1.

Excellent.

Here is a skeleton for *remainder*, our simple remainder function

```
(define remainder
  (λ (x y)
    (cond
      ((< x y) X )
      (else            R            ))))
```

Find expressions that go inside the boxes labelled X and R.

34 To find the remainder, we must first check if we can remove y from x. This is possible only when x is greater than or equal to y.

If, however, x is less than y, then x must be the remainder. So, when

```
(< x y)
```

this function results in x. So, X is x.

What happens if x is not less than y?

Then, we can remove y from x once, and continue by finding the remainder of the result.

35 Ah, so we must find the remainder of

```
(- x y) and y
```

Correct.

We do this by recursively invoking *remainder*.

36 This means R is

```
(remainder (- x y) y)
```

Excellent.

Here, then, is *remainder*

```
(define remainder
  (λ (x y)
    (cond
      ((< x y) x)
      (else (remainder (- x y) y)))))
```

37 Is there a common pattern to help us define recursive functions?

Yes, there is.

Each recursive function tests its arguments to see if they meet a base test requirement. We refer to this test as the *base test*. We refer to the resultant value as the *base value*.

What are the base test and base value here?

38 The first clause in the **cond** is

(< x y), the base test

and

x, the base value

Is there a name for the second clause?

Yes.

It is known as the *recursive* case.

39 Could we see another example?

Sure.

Here is a skeleton for another recursive function *add* that without using +, adds two natural numbers[†]

```
(define add
  (λ (n m)
    (cond
      ( [    T    ] [V] )
      (else [          R          ] ))))
```

The argument n is the first number and the argument m is the second one.

We must find T, V, and R, but first describe what the base test of such a function would be.

[†] Another name for nonnegative integers, defined as having a 0 and *add1* defined on them.

40 The base test would be if one of the numbers is zero, since we're looking only at natural numbers.

Does this mean we have two base tests?

It could, but it is not necessary.

Since the order of the arguments to addition does not matter, we can, with no loss of generality, restrict our base test to just the second number.

What would the base value be?

41 The base value would be the first number, since adding any number to 0 gives us back that number.

That's a good start.

We can now fill in T and V.

Show the revised skeleton. Use the function *zero?*, which tests whether its argument is zero.

42 Here it is

```
(define add
  (λ (n m)
    (cond
      ((zero? m) n)
      (else [      R      ]))))
```

Correct.

Now let us look at R. If m is not zero, we can say that it is some number

$(k + 1)$

where k is a natural number.

What results when we add $k + 1$ and n?

43 We get

$(k + 1) + n$

Good.

We can rewrite this as

$(k + n) + 1$

44 How can that insight help us?

For natural numbers, we can always assume that a function *add1* exists that results in $k+1$ when given k.

And similarly, a function *sub1* exists that results in k when given $k+1$.

45 Where does that lead us?

R must, as in frame 44, result in

$$(k+n)+1$$

We already have n, so how do we get k from m?

46 Since m is $k+1$, we can get k using

(*sub1 m*)

Perfect.

And R must add 1 to the addition of k (which is (*sub1 m*)) and n.

47 So should R have this form?

(*add1 ... addition of n* **and** (*sub1 m*) ...)

Absolutely.

Now we have this insight.

Since n and (*sub1 m*) are also natural numbers, we can get their addition by invoking *add* on them!

48 Amazing!

So R must be

(*add1* (*add n* (*sub1 m*)))

Right!

Show the final *add*.

49 Here it is

```
(define add
  (λ (n m)
    (cond
      ((zero? m) n)
      (else (add1 (add n (sub1 m)))))))
```

Great.

Let's look at our example with 7 and 2

(*add* 7 2)

What happens next?

50 Since 2 is not *zero?*, we are in the recursive case. So, our result should be

(*add1* (*add* 7 (*sub1* 2)))

which is the same as the result of

(*add1* (*add* 7 1))

Correct.

Since the second argument to add in this recursive invocation is 1 (i.e., not zero), we can further rewrite this as

(*add1* (*add1* (*add* 7 (*sub1* 1))))

which is the same as

(*add1* (*add1* (*add* 7 0)))

51 Now our second argument is zero, so

(*add* 7 0)

gives us

7

Correct.

Now we can invoke the two wrapped *add1*s on 7

(*add1* (*add1* 7))

to get

(*add1* 8)

which is

9

52 And that is our result!

More succintly, we can describe this behavior in a same-as chart[†]

1. (*add* 7 2)
2. (*add1* (*add* 7 (*sub1* 2)))
3. (*add1* (*add* 7 1))
4. (*add1* (*add1* (*add* 7 (*sub1* 1))))
5. (*add1* (*add1* (*add* 7 0)))
6. (*add1* (*add1* 7))
7. (*add1* 8)
8. 9

So, there are seven steps besides the one that is the original problem

(*add* 7 2)

and by carefully going from one expression to the next, which always has the same value, we simplify the result to

9

Now try

(*remainder* 13 4)

[†]The same-as chart, introduced in *The Little Typer* (2018) p. 69, uses a *solid* vertical line on the left and shows expressions that are the same as one another.

53 These are fun, but not as much as a chocolate fudge banana split, right?

1. (*remainder* 13 4)
2. (*remainder* (− 13 4) 4)
3. (*remainder* 9 4)
4. (*remainder* (− 9 4) 4)
5. (*remainder* 5 4)
6. (*remainder* (− 5 4) 4)
7. (*remainder* 1 4)
8. 1

Debatable!

In both our examples, we have at least one argument *shrinking* and heading towards the base test.

54 Is this true of all recursive functions?

Yes, if we expect the recursive function to result in a value.

In general, when we're defining a recursive function, we should follow this sequence of steps

Figure out the base test

figure out the base value

find out how the arguments to the recursive invocation change, especially those that shrink

and

use the recursive invocation as part of a larger expression to obtain the overall result of the function.

We refer to the portion of the expression excluding the recursive invocation as its *wrapper*.†

† In the definition of *add*, this is the portion between "(*add1*" and the ")" that matches it.

55 Still, just a bit squeamish.

Did you *meet every character*?

56 Yes, and the ones in the framenotes.

Okay, then.

We have everything we need to get started.

The rest we'll learn along the way.

57 Exciting!

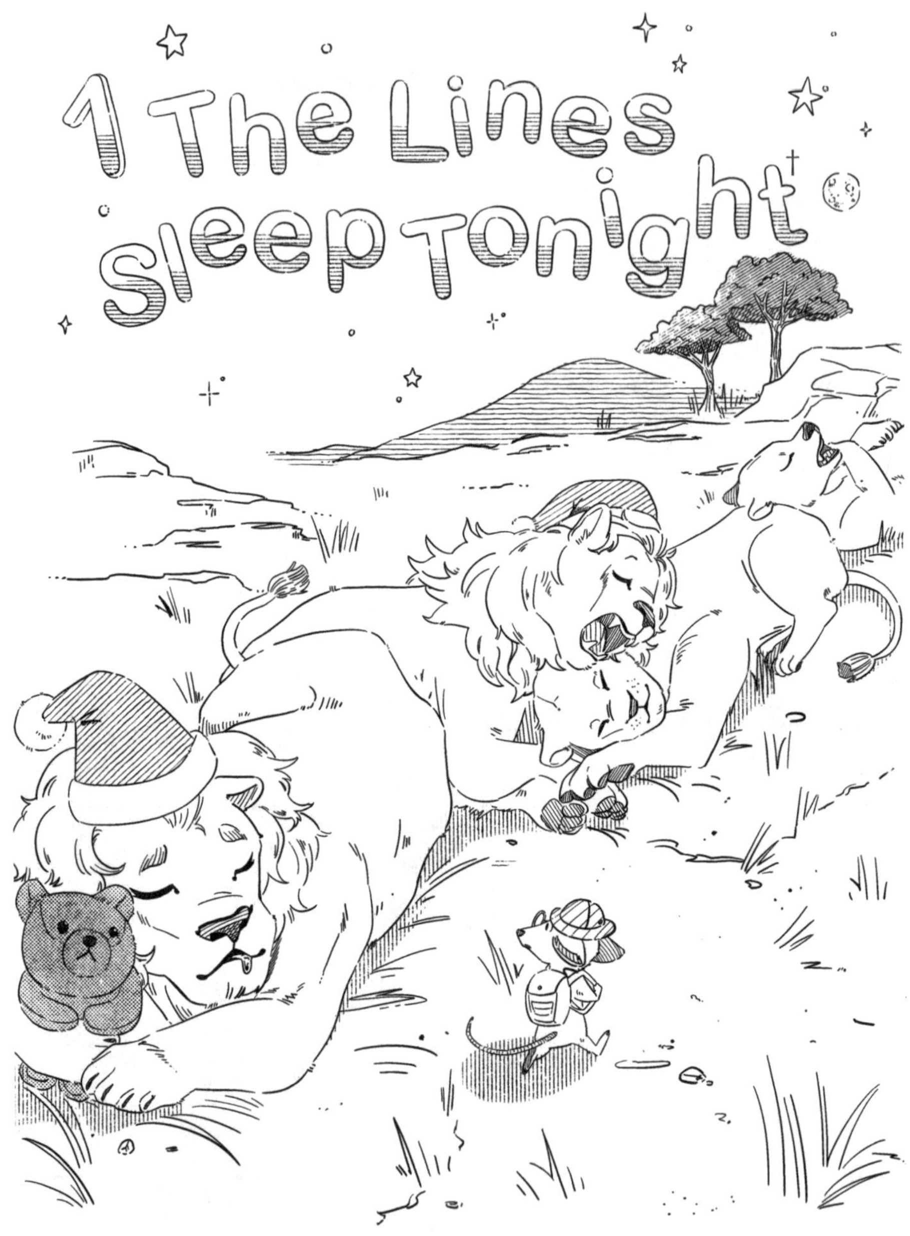

†With apologies and thanks to Solomon Ntsele (1909–1962).

Welcome back!

1 It's good to be here!

Indeed.

Remember this?

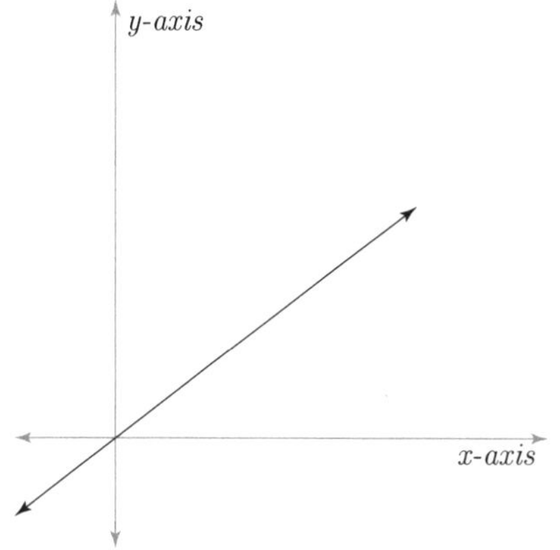

2 Yes.

That looks like a line in plane (2-dimensional) geometry along with two additional lines, the x-axis and the y-axis.†

†Thanks, René Descartes (1596–1650).

There is an *equation* that relates x with y for every point (x, y) on a line

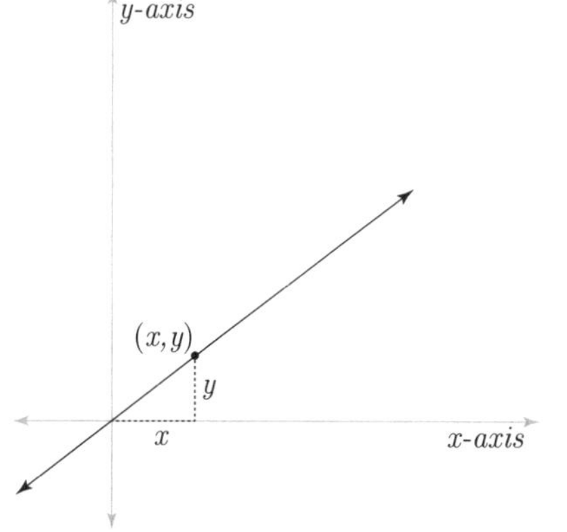

3 Does using arrows at both ends of the line mean that it extends indefinitely in both directions and does it follow that there is a corresponding y for every x?

Yes.

Our line passes through the *origin*.

4 What is the origin?

The point at which the x-axis and the y-axis meet is known as the *origin* and is the point (0, 0). The dark line in the picture passes through the origin.

5 So what is the equation of this line?

Because this line passes through the origin, y is a multiple of x by a constant factor w, which is known as the *slope* of the line

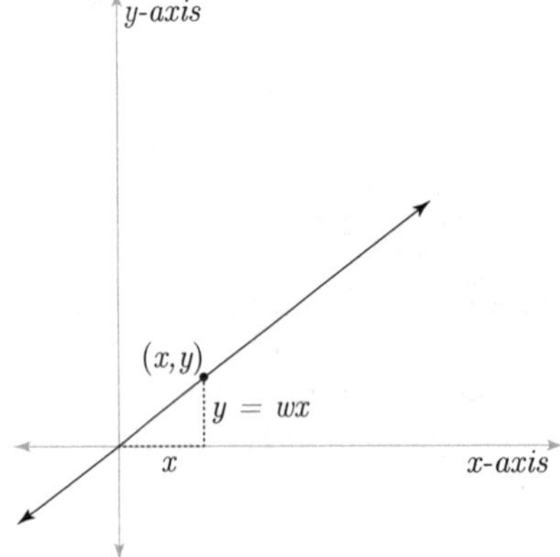

6 Does that mean $y = wx$?

Yes, it does.

7 What if the line does not go through the origin?

Good question. This is what it would look like

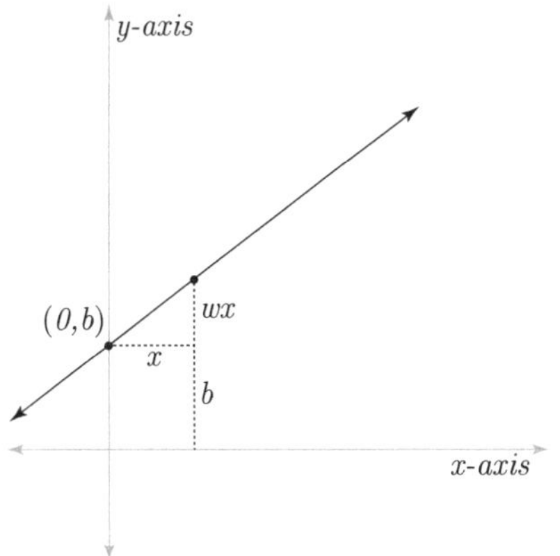

How can we determine y?

8 It appears that the whole line is lifted by b now.

We can determine y for any x using

$y = wx + b$[†]

[†] $y = mx + b$ might be more familiar.

Here is our first attempt at *line*[†]

```
(define line
  (λ (x)
    (λ (w b)
      (let ((y (+ (* w x) b)))
        y))))
```

[†] The dashes on the left indicate that this dashed definition of *line* is not yet final. As attempts are made, these dashes may never disappear or they may eventually turn into a final box, black or red.

9 This is a function of one argument that results in a function of two arguments?[‡]

This dashed definition of *line* seems backwards. Why don't we require ***w*** and ***b*** before x?

[‡] If this is confusing, consider rereading the chapter *Are You Schemish?*.

Great question!

That kind of definition assumes that $\boldsymbol{w}$ and $\boldsymbol{b}$ are known *prior to* the argument x.

Here, though, we deal with a different kind of problem, where x is known, but $\boldsymbol{w}$ and $\boldsymbol{b}$ must be figured out from a bunch of given values of x and y.

10 Why isn't *line* final?

That's because our next attempt can simplify *line* a little more. Since the body of the **let**, y, is only the name given to

```
(+ (* w x) b)
```

by the **let**, we get this *same-as* chart[†]

```
1. (let ((y (+ (* w x) b)))
     y)
2. (+ (* w x) b)
```

Even though there is no longer a y here, we sometimes refer to this value as the y associated with a given x.

11 So, this dashed definition should be our next attempt to finalize *line*

```
(define line
  (λ (x)
    (λ (w b)
      (+ (* w x) b))))
```

It looks correct, so why is *line* still dashed?

[†]Introduced in frame 16:53.

Good question.

This *line* is still dashed because we are going to make another attempt soon. But for now, it suffices.

Because $\boldsymbol{w}$ and $\boldsymbol{b}$ are used to determine the y corresponding to a given x, they are considered to be a special kind of formal. We name them *parameters* of *line*, and we use bold letters for them, whereas x is the *argument* of *line*.

12 How is the function *line* used?

Let's see an example.

What is

(*line* 8)?

13 (*line* 8) is a function that remembers that x is 8, and is waiting to accept arguments for its parameters ***w*** and ***b***

```
(λ (w b)
  (+ (* w 8) b))
```

That is correct.

When (*line* 8) is invoked on ***w*** and ***b***, we can determine y.

What is

((*line* 8) 4 6)?

14 Here are the steps with ***w*** being 4 and ***b*** being 6

```
1. ((line 8) 4 6)
2. ((λ (w b)
      (+ (* w 8) b))
    4 6)
3. (+ (* 4 8) 6)
4. (+ 32 6)
5. 38
```

This means that when x is 8, y is 38.

Excellent.

Functions that accept parameters *after* the arguments are known as

parameterized functions

Is *line* a parameterized function?

15 Yes.

It takes ***w*** and ***b*** as its parameters after it takes the argument x.

Why are parameterized functions special?

Good question.

Parameterized functions are used where we must figure out the right values for the parameters (here, ***w*** and ***b***) from given values of x and the corresponding values of y.

16 Could we see an example?

Sure.

Here *line-xs* are the *x*-coordinates and *line-ys* are the *y*-coordinates

```
(define line-xs
  [2.0 1.0 4.0 3.0])

(define line-ys
  [1.8 1.2 4.2 3.3])
```

For each *x*-coordinate in *line-xs*, there is a corresponding *y*-coordinate in *line-ys* and vice versa.

17 Do *line-xs* and *line-ys*, when taken together, give us these four *points*?

(2.0, 1.8)
(1.0, 1.2)
(4.0, 4.2)
(3.0, 3.3)

Yes.

Together, they form a *data set*.

18 Okay.

Here is how the data set

(*line-xs*, *line-ys*)

looks as points on a graph

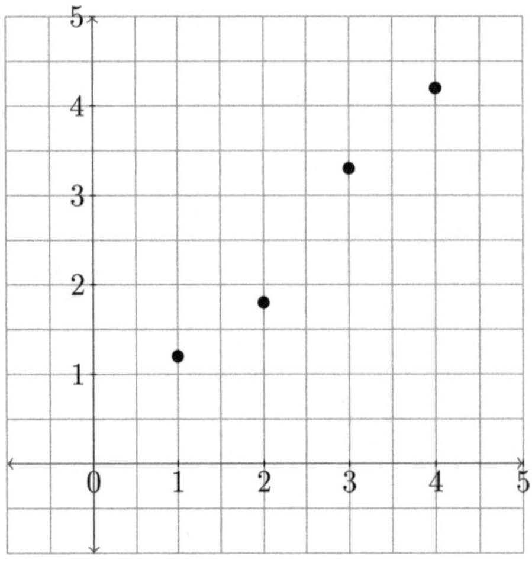

19 Those points look like they are *almost* on a straight line.

For good reason.

Draw a line that is close enough to these four points.

20 How about this?

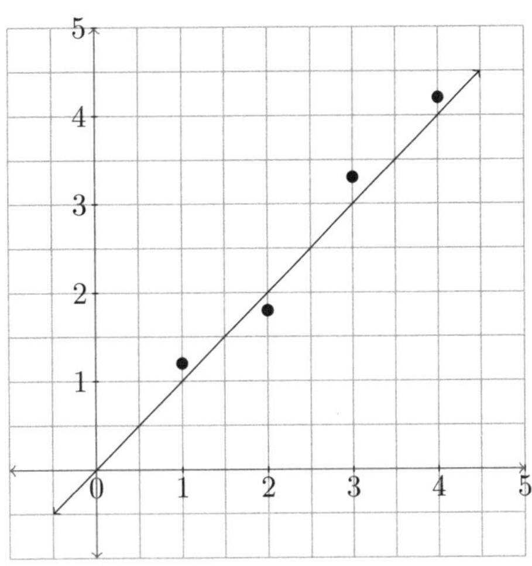

Yes, that is close enough.

Lines, as in frame 11, have two parameters, $\boldsymbol{w}$ and $\boldsymbol{b}$.

What are $\boldsymbol{w}$ and $\boldsymbol{b}$ for this line?

21 Since this line passes through the origin, $\boldsymbol{b}$ is 0.0.

And, the x and y coordinates of every point *on this line* are always equal. For example, (0.0, 0.0), (1.2, 1.2), etc. The points on this line look like $(a,\ a)$, for any x-coordinate a.

So, $\boldsymbol{w}$ must be 1.0.

That is correct.

This function is simply a line with parameters

$\boldsymbol{w} = 1.0$

and

$\boldsymbol{b} = 0.0$

How can we use this information?

22 If we are given a new x-coordinate, we can *predict* the corresponding y-coordinate from this line.

For example, if $x = 3.79$, then

$$y = 1.0 \times 3.79 + 0.0 = 3.79$$

The Rule of Parameters

(Initial Version)

Every parameter is a number.

Correct.

We refer to this as the *predicted y* for a given x.

Finding the parameters of a function from a data set is known as *learning.*

23 So we have *learned* a function that behaves approximately like the points given by the data set

(*line-xs*, *line-ys*)

The parameters $\boldsymbol{w}$ and $\boldsymbol{b}$ here are collectively known as the *parameter set*, which we refer to as $\boldsymbol{\theta}$.†

So, our $\boldsymbol{\theta}$ has two parameters. They are referred to as *members* of $\boldsymbol{\theta}$.

Then $\boldsymbol{w}$ is the first member of $\boldsymbol{\theta}$, which we write as $\boldsymbol{\theta}_0$.‡

†Pronounced "little theta."
‡Members are indexed beginning at 0.

24 Is $\boldsymbol{b}$ then $\boldsymbol{\theta}_1$?

It is.

Let's rewrite *line* to reflect this

```
(define line                    ●
  (λ (x)
    (λ (θ)
      (+ (* θ₀ x) θ₁))))
```

25 Why is this *line* in a red-colored box with a red-colored circle?

Good question.

We have chosen red boxes and circles to highlight final definitions that are *important* as well as sometimes being primitive.[†]

[†]The circle is for those who might have trouble distinguishing red lines from black lines.

26 Red is such a vibrant color for a toy.

How do we construct a $\boldsymbol{\theta}$ for $\boldsymbol{w}$ and $\boldsymbol{b}$?

Great question.

Here's an example. If $\boldsymbol{w}$ is 1.0 and $\boldsymbol{b}$ is 0.0, we construct it this way

(list 1.0 0.0)

27 So $\boldsymbol{\theta}$ is a *list* of members such that

$\boldsymbol{\theta}_0$

which is the same as $\boldsymbol{w}$ is

1.0

and

$\boldsymbol{\theta}_1$

which is the same as $\boldsymbol{b}$ is

0.0

Here's an example of how *line* is invoked with this $\boldsymbol{\theta}$

1. ((*line* 7.3) (list 1.0 0.0))
2. ((λ ($\boldsymbol{\theta}$)
      (+ (∗ $\boldsymbol{\theta}_0$ 7.3) $\boldsymbol{\theta}_1$))
    (list 1.0 0.0))

Complete this same-as chart.

28 Sure

3. (+ (∗ (list 1.0 0.0)$_0$ 7.3) (list 1.0 0.0)$_1$)
4. (+ (∗ 1.0 7.3) 0.0)
5. 7.3

Correct.

So far, we have examined our data set on a graph and estimated a $\boldsymbol{\theta}$.

29 And we used it to predict a

y-coordinate

for an

x-coordinate

that may not be in our data set.

In other words, we have *learned* from an existing data set how to make y-coordinate predictions for x-coordinates.

30 Yes, we have learned something!

Still, we have accomplished this by visually inspecting only the points on the graph.

31 Can we define a function that determines $\boldsymbol{\theta}$ for any data set?

An excellent question.

Yes, we can, and such a function is an example of what is known as *machine learning*.[†] But that's what the rest of the book is about!

[†] There are many forms of machine learning. Here we cover only one form.

32 It's a good time to take a break.

Toy Chest

(*line-xs*, *line-ys*) 24
line, 26
l_i (where l is a list and i is a zero-based index) 26
(**list** m ...) (where m ... are its members) 26

Let's take that break!
How about some butterscotch ice cream?

2 The More We Learn, the Tenser We Become

We can still taste the luxurious creamy butterscotch.

1 Mmm ... fantastic!

Is 5 a natural number?

2 Yes.

It is a nonnegative integer.

What about 0?

3 Yes.

It is a natural number.

Is −5 a natural number?

4 No.

Natural numbers cannot be negative.

What is 7.18?

5 That's a *real* number.

Is −13.713 also real?

6 Yes, it is.

Are all natural numbers also real numbers?

Yes, we consider them to be.

There is another name we use for all real numbers here. We refer to them as

scalars

7 Is 7.18 a scalar?

Yes.

What is π[†]?

[†]This π is much tastier than the *pie* from frame 3:6 because π has lots of meringue on it!

8 Like 3.141592653589793...? Then, π is also a scalar.

Correct.

The predicate *scalar?* tests whether something is a scalar and like all predicates is a function that *always* results in a Boolean—either false #f or true #t.†

†Thanks, George Boole (1815–1864).

9 Okay.

Here is a *tensor*^{1}.† A tensor^1 has only scalars

[5.0 7.18 π]

†Pronounced "tensor one."

10 Is that a superscript on the word *tensor*‡?

‡Thanks, Woldemar Voigt (1850–1919), Gregorio Ricci-Curbastro (1853–1925), Tullio Levi-Civita (1873–1941), and for popularizing, thanks, Albert Einstein (1879–1955).

Yes, it is.

A tensor^1 groups one or more scalars together†

[2.0 1.0 4.0 3.0]

†A tensor^1 can be thought of as a "*vector*" or a "*one-dimensional*" array.

Here, the empty tensor does not exist.

11 These bracketed scalars seem familiar!

They should be, that's *line-xs* from frame 24:17.

Here is another example

[8]

12 This tensor^1 contains the scalar 8.

Is there a tensor^2†?

†Pronounced "tensor two."

Yes, the *elements* of a tensor^2 are tensors^1.†

†A tensor^2 can be thought of as a "*matrix*" or a "*two-dimensional*" array.

13 What is an element?

For example

[[7 6 2 5] [3 8 6 9] [9 4 8 5]]

has 3 elements

[7 6 2 5]

[3 8 6 9]

and

[9 4 8 5]

14 Then if we have a tensor whose elements are tensors^m, does that make it a tensor^{m+1}?

Yes, but there's a condition.

All the tensors^m must have the same number of elements.

15 That seems reasonable.

What can we say about the 3 tensors^1 in frame 14?

16 Each has 4 elements and each of those elements is a scalar.

The number of elements in a tensor t can be found by invoking (from page xxiii)

↿t↾

For example

```
1. | ↿[17 12 91 67]↾
2. | 4
```

How about

↿[[3 2 8] [7 1 9]]↾

17 This is it

```
1. | ↿[[3 2 8] [7 1 9]]↾
2. | 2
```

Yes, it is.

18 Is this

[[[[8]]]]

also a tensor?

Yes, the tensor

[[[[8]]]]

is a tensor^{4} of an element

[[[8]]]

which is a tensor^{3} of an element

[[8]]

which is a tensor^{2} of an element

[8]

which is a tensor^{1} of an element

8

which is a scalar.

What is

[[5 6 4] [9 1 1] [0 6 2]]?

19 It looks like a tensor^{2} whose three elements are tensors^{1}.

Is this

[[[5] [6] [7]] [[8] [9] [0]]]

possible?

Yes, the tensor

[[[5] [6] [7]] [[8] [9] [0]]]

is a tensor^{3} of

2 tensor^{2} elements

each of those 2 elements has

3 tensor^{1} elements

each of those 3 elements has

1 single element

a scalar.

20 Since a tensor^{m+1} must have only tensors^{m} elements, a tensor^{1} should be made up of tensor^{0} elements.

Does that mean a scalar is a tensor^{0}?

Great question.

Yes, a scalar like 9 *is* a tensor^{0}.[†]

[†]But, "*zero-dimensional*" arrays are rarely, if ever, mentioned.

21 Does the superscript have a name?

Yes, it does.

It is known as the *rank* of the tensor.

22 What does the rank of a tensor mean?

The rank of a tensor tells us how deeply nested its elements are.

Here is a tensor^{3} because it has 1 tensor^{2} element that has 2 tensor^{1} elements of two scalars each

[[[8 9] [4 7]]][†]

[†]We can determine the rank of a tensor by counting the number of left square brackets before the leftmost scalar (here 8).

23 It appears we can define a function to determine the rank of a tensor.

The Rule of Rank

A tensor's rank is the number of left square brackets before its leftmost scalar.

Indeed, we can.

Before that, though, let's look at how to reach into a tensor to look at its elements. The operation†

$t|_i$

picks out the ith element of the tensor.

So, for example, $t|_0$ gets the 0th (first) element of the tensor.

†Pronounced "*tensor-ref t i*."

24 How do we use this to find the rank of a tensor?

Here is a function that finds the rank of a tensor

```
(define rank
  (λ (t)
    (cond
      ((scalar? t) 0)
      (else (add1 (rank t|0))†))))
```

Here, $t|_0$ is the 0th element of t, which always exists because we have already determined that t is not a scalar, and furthermore the 0th element is itself a tensor.

Now explain *rank*.

†The "(*add1*" and its matching ")" is a *wrapper* of the recursive invocation (*rank* $t|_0$).

This form of recursive function, where we follow the structure of its argument, is known as a *naturally recursive* function. See *The Little LISPer* (1974) p. 21 or *The Little Schemer* (1996) p. 45.

See frame 13:42 for *zero?*, and frame 14:45 for *add1* and *sub1*.

25 If the base test,‡ (*scalar?* t), succeeds then we know the rank of the tensor is 0.

In general, if the elements of a tensor are tensors^m, then the tensor has rank

$m + 1$

So, in the recursive case, we find

m

which is the rank of the 0th element of t

(*rank* $t|_0$)

and then *add1* to the result to get the rank of t.

Could we see how *rank* is 3 with the tensor in frame 23 using a same-as chart?

‡If this term is unfamiliar, see chapter 0.

Sure.

Given the same tensor from frame 23

[[[8] [9]] [[4] [7]]] here is a same-as chart that shows how its *rank* is 3

1. (*rank* [[[8] [9]] [[4] [7]]])
2. (*add1* (*rank* [[8] [9]]))
3. (*add1* (*add1* (*rank* [8])))
4. (*add1* (*add1* (*add1* (*rank* 8))))
5. (*add1* (*add1* (*add1* 0)))
6. (*add1* (*add1* 1))
7. (*add1* 2)
8. 3

26 That is so elegant and natural.

There's another observation here. We need look only at

$t|_0$

i.e., only the first element of the tensor.

27 Yes, why is that?

That is because in any given tensor, the nested tensors have the same number of elements. For example, the nested tensors of tensors^2 are all tensors^1, and each of those tensors^1 has the same number of tensors^0.

28 That's the requirement from frame 15.

Correct.

This means that the tensors^m that are elements of a tensor^{m+1} have the same *shape*.

29 What is the shape of a tensor?

The shape of

[[5.2 6.3 8.0] [6.9 7.1 0.5]]

is this list of positive natural numbers

(**list** $\underline{2}$ 3)[†]

Where do those natural numbers come from?

[†] We sometimes underline portions of an expression to draw attention to them.

30 This tensor is a tensor^2 of $\underline{2}$ tensors^1, each of which has 3 tensor^0 elements.

Exactly.

What is the shape of

[[[5] [6] [8]] [[7] [9] [5]]]?

31 The shape of

[[[5] [6] [8]] [[7] [9] [5]]]

is

(**list** $\underline{2}$ 3 1)

Right again.

[[[5] [6] [8]] [[7] [9] [5]]]
is a tensor^3 of
$\underline{2}$ tensor^2 elements
Each of those has
3 tensor^1 elements
Each of those has
1 tensor^0 element
which is a scalar.

What is the shape of

[9 4 7 8 0 1]?

32 [9 4 7 8 0 1] is a tensor^1 of $\underline{6}$ scalars.

So, is
(**list** 6)
the shape of
[9 4 7 8 0 1]?

That is correct.

33 Do scalars have a shape?

They do.

Since scalars have no parts, their shape is the empty list.

34 How do we write empty lists?

Like this

```
(list)
```

35 So the shape of the scalar 9 is

```
(list)?
```

Correct.

To find the shape of a tensor t, we need to know the number of elements it has.

36 So we use $\dagger t \dagger$ for it?

We do!

Here is the function *shape* that finds the shape of a given tensor t

```
(define shape                                    •
  (λ (t)
    (cond
      ((scalar? t) (list))
      (else (cons ⫯t⫯ (shape t|0))†))))
```

Explain this *shape*.

†The "(*cons* ⫯t⫯" and its matching ")" is a wrapper of (*shape* $t|_0$). Compare *rank*'s wrapper in frame 25.

37 But wait, what is *cons*?[‡]

‡Some might remember "CONS The Magnificent" on p. 17 of *The Little LISPer*.

The Rule of Members and Elements

Non-empty lists have members and non-scalar tensors have elements.

The function *cons* takes two arguments, a value v and a list l, and produces a new list by adding

v

to the front of

l

For example

```
(cons 3 (list 7 9))
(list 3 7 9)
```

Now, please explain *shape*.

38 When the argument to *shape*, t, is a scalar, its shape is simply the empty list.

Otherwise, it is a non-scalar tensor, so we find the 0th element's shape, which is a list, by recursively invoking *shape* thusly

(*shape* $t|_0$)

The shape of t is then ǂtǂ *cons*ed to the front of the resultant list.

Correct.

What is

(*shape* 9)?

39 (*shape* 9) is the empty list because 9 is a scalar.

What is

(*shape* [9 4 7 8 0 1])?

40 (*shape* [9 4 7 8 0 1]) is

(*cons* 6 (*shape* 9))

which is

(**list** 6)

The Rule of Uniform Shape

All elements of a tensor must have the same shape.

Using a same-as chart, determine (*shape* t) where t is

[[[5] [6] [8]] [[7] [9] [5]]]

from frame 31.

41 Here it is

1. (*shape* [[[5] [6] [8]] [[7] [9] [5]]])
2. (*cons* 2 (*shape* [[5] [6] [8]]))
3. (*cons* 2 (*cons* 3 (*shape* [5])))
4. (*cons* 2 (*cons* 3 (*cons* 1 (*shape* 5))))
5. (*cons* 2 (*cons* 3 (*cons* 1 (**list**))))
6. (*cons* 2 (*cons* 3 (**list** 1)))
7. (*cons* 2 (**list** 3 1))
8. (**list** 2 3 1)

The number of members in a list *ls* is

$|ls|$

How are *rank* and *shape* related?

42 Aha!

The number of members in the shape of a tensor† is also the rank of the tensor

(= |(*shape* t)| (*rank* t))

†We can also use a tensor's shape to determine its total number of scalars by taking the product of its shape's members.

The Law of Rank and Shape

The rank of a tensor is equal to the length of its shape.

There's one more definition we need to look at.

43 Can't wait.

Here's our final way to define *rank*, but this one is already *unwrapped*, i.e., no recursive invocation is wrapped!

```
(define rank                                  ●
  (λ (t)
    (ranked t 0)))

(define ranked
  (λ (t a)
    (cond
      ((scalar? t) a)
      (else (ranked t|0 (add1 a))))))
```

This *rank* definition uses a support function *ranked* that includes an additional formal *a* as an *accumulator*.

To see how it works, repeat the example in frame 26 but using this final *rank*.

44 Here it is

```
(rank [[[8] [9]] [[4] [7]]])
(ranked [[[8] [9]] [[4] [7]]] 0)
(ranked [[8] [9]] (add1 0))
(ranked [[8] [9]] 1)
(ranked [8] (add1 1))
(ranked [8] 2)
(ranked 8 (add1 2))
(ranked 8 3)
3
```

Instead of a wrapper around the recursive invocation of

rank

we

add1

to the accumulator

a

as we are going down into

$t|_0$

That is correct.

45 Thanks!

Seeing this way of using $t|_0$ as an argument in an unwrapped recursive invocation helps.

Unlike the dashed *rank* in frame 25, this new recursive function definition does *not* use a wrapper.

In fact, this matters so much that we have a law about it.

46 Let's see it.

The Law of Simple Accumulator Passing

In a simple accumulator passing function definition
every recursive function invocation is unwrapped,
and the definition has at most one argument that **does not change**;
an argument that **changes towards a true base test**;
and another that **accumulates** a result.

This Law of Simple Accumulator Passing is important.	47	Why?
This law enables us to handle very large tensors and lists.	48	How?
When combining simple accumulator passing function definitions, they could be thought of as one very big *loop*.	49	How is that possible?
Every Scheme system is required to support *tail call optimization* which makes each unwrapped recursive invocation behave the same as a loop.	50	How do the other requirements in the law help?
The other requirements ensure that we use a uniform pattern for our function definitions so that they are easy to read and understand.	51	These simple accumulator passing function definitions seem to offer great possibilities!
Now it is time for a break!	52	It is just what is needed. Things were getting intense.

Tensor Toys

Let’s line up for something delicious.
How about some boba tea?

Interlude I
The More We Extend, the Less Tensor We Get

The tea?

1 Boba with mango jelly, scrumptious!

How about an interlude?

2 What's an interlude?

It's where we temporarily shift our focus.

3 To what?

To have more fun with +.

4 That's addition, right?

Yes.

What is (+ 1 1)?

5 That's easy

(+ 1 1)

is

2[†]

[†]Thanks, Alfred North Whitehead (1861–1947) and Bertrand Arthur William Russell (1872–1970).

Thank goodness.

What is

(+ [2] [7])?

6 That's tricky. The arguments are tensors[1].

Is

(+ [2] [7])

the same as

[9]?

7

Yes, but why is that?

Here is a same-as chart to discover how the chart results in [9]

1.	(+ [2] [7])
2.	[(+ 2 7)]
3.	[9]

Why are those brackets turquoise?

8

When there is a function invocation like + on tensors, we use turquoise brackets to emphasize that we're going to look inside those tensors to help determine the invocation's final value.

What is

(+ [5 6 7] [2 0 1])?

Is

(+ [5 6 7] [2 0 1])

the same as

[7 6 8]?

9

Here is the same-as chart that shows how to get that result

1.	(+ [5 6 7] [2 0 1])
2.	[(+ 5 2) (+ 6 0) (+ 7 1)]
3.	[7 6 8]

It appears that + descends into its tensor^1 arguments to result in another tensor^1.

The last step results in the tensor^1 of the values of the three sums.

Yes.

What is

(+ [[4 6 7] [2 0 1]]
    [[1 2 2] [6 3 1]])?

10 We're adding two tensors[2] of the same shape. It is

1. [(+ [4 6 7] [1 2 2])
    (+ [2 0 1] [6 3 1])]
2. [[(+ 4 1) (+ 6 2) (+ 7 2)]
    [(+ 2 6) (+ 0 3) (+ 1 1)]]
3. [[5 8 9] [8 3 2]]

Must we have tensors of the same shape before we can add them?

Yes, we must.

Getting + to work on tensors of arbitrary rank is known as

the *extension*† of +.

Functions built using extension are known as *extended* functions. Can other functions that work on scalars be extended similarly?

†Also known as *pointwise* extension.

11 It would appear so.

There is nothing special about +. Other extended scalar functions should work in the same way.

Here's another way extension works. What is

(+ 4 [3 6 5])?

12 But these two tensors don't have the same shape!

Correct.

When that happens, we do this

1. (+ 4 [3 6 5])
2. [(+ 4 3) (+ 4 6) (+ 4 5)]

Finish this same-as chart.

13 Oh, we look inside the tensor^1 argument and repeatedly add 4 to each element.

The final answer is

3. [7 10 9]

Very good.

How about this?

1. (+ [6 9 1] [[4 3 8] [7 4 7]])

14 We can look inside the tensor^2 argument and add the tensor^1 argument to each element, just as we did in frame 13

2. [(+ [6 9 1] [4 3 8])
   (+ [6 9 1] [7 4 7])]
3. [[(+ 6 4) (+ 9 3) (+ 1 8)]
   [(+ 6 7) (+ 9 4) (+ 1 7)]]
4. [[10 12 9]
   [13 13 8]]

Excellent.

Let us now take an
extended version of *

This is *The Hadamard*† *multiplication.*

Now this one

1. (* [[4 6 5] [6 9 7]] 3)

†Thanks, Jacques Salomon Hadamard (1865–1963).

15 Here are the steps

2. [(* [4 6 5] 3) (* [6 9 7] 3)]
3. [[(* 4 3) (* 6 3) (* 5 3)]
   [(* 6 3) (* 9 3) (* 7 3)]]
4. [[12 18 15]
   [18 27 21]]

The first two steps use turquoise brackets because we are descending into those tensors^1. The last two steps don't have turquoise brackets because we have only scalars remaining, so we just multiply them without descending.

Let's look at another extended function
sqrt[†]

1. (*sqrt* 9)
2. 3

[†]The function *sqrt* must always result in a nonnegative square root.

16 Applying *sqrt* to the scalar 9 gets its square root, which is 3.

Now let's invoke *sqrt* on

[9 16 25]

This time the rank of the argument is 1. So *sqrt* descends into the tensor^1

1. (*sqrt* [9 16 25])
2. [(*sqrt* 9) (*sqrt* 16) (*sqrt* 25)]
3. [3 4 5]

17 The *sqrt* function has been invoked on each scalar in the tensor^1.

In these same-as charts, again, the tensor that is to be descended into is marked with turquoise brackets.

18 Could we see another example?

Sure.

Here is an example of how *sqrt* behaves on a tensor^2

1. (*sqrt* [[49 81 16] [64 25 36]])
2. [(*sqrt* [49 81 16]) (*sqrt* [64 25 36])]
3. [[(*sqrt* 49) (*sqrt* 81) (*sqrt* 16)]
   [(*sqrt* 64) (*sqrt* 25) (*sqrt* 36)]]
4. [[7 9 4]
   [8 5 6]]

19 It seems as if *sqrt* descends into each tensor^1 of the argument until it finds the tensors^0 and gets their square roots.

---

20 Yes, descending into a tensor is a trick we use often.

With a higher-rank tensor, the process would repeat itself until we encounter scalars and get their square roots.

That makes sense.

Can we treat functions of two arguments in a similar way?

---

21 Yes, we can.

We now know how extended functions of two arguments can be made to work when the two arguments have different ranks by descending into the higher-ranked tensor.

Do extended functions always descend until they find scalars?

---

22 Some don't.

To see that, let's look at a new function

sum^1

And this is how we expect it to behave

```
(sum¹ [10.0 12.0 14.0])
36.0
```

It looks as if it is summing the scalars in a tensor^1.

But why do we have a superscript 1 on *sum*?

---

23 The superscript is a reminder that sum^1 expects a tensor^1.[†]

Now that we know that sum^1 *always* takes a tensor^1, let's define it.

[†] We use this superscript convention for other functions, too.

That sounds interesting.

Here is sum^1

```
(define sum¹                                   ●
  (λ (t)
    (summed t (sub1 ∤t∤) 0.0)))

(define summed
  (λ (t i a)†
    (cond
      ((zero? i) (+ t|₀ a))
      (else
        (summed t (sub1 i) (+ t|ᵢ a))))))
```

Explain sum^1.

†Here is how we place our formals for a simple accumulator passing function definition. If there is one that **does not change**, like *t*, it is the first formal; the one that **accumulates**, like *a*, is the last formal; and the one that **changes towards a true** base test, like *i*, is to the accumulator's left. See, for example, *rank* on page 42.

24

We invoke the support function *summed* with the tensor

t

the last index in *t*

(*sub1* ∤*t*∤)

and an accumulator starting at

0.0

The function *summed* counts the index *i* down to zero. At each step it adds the *i*th element in the tensor *t* to the accumulator, and recursively invokes *summed*.

And finally, when we reach the 0th element in the tensor, we add that element to the accumulator which results in the sum of the entire tensor.

We refer to the extended version of sum^1 as *sum*, which descends into its argument until it finds a $tensor^1$ instead of a $tensor^0$.

25

How does *sum* work?

Here is *sum* working on a $tensor^3$

```
1. (sum
     [[[1 2] [3 4]] [[5 6] [7 8]]])
2. [(sum [[1 2] [3 4]])
    (sum [[5 6] [7 8]])]
3. [[(sum¹ [1 2]) (sum¹ [3 4])]
    [(sum¹ [5 6]) (sum¹ [7 8])]]
4. [[3 7]
    [11 15]]
```

What can we say about the rank of this result?

26

This is a $tensor^2$, so its rank is 2, which means that the rank is 1 less than the rank of the input, which is also true for sum^1.

The Law of Sum

For a tensor t with rank $r > 0$, the rank of (*sum* t) is $r - 1$.

Yes.

This is a useful property of *sum* that we rely on later.

27 What about functions that are constructed from these extended functions?

A great question.

If we use extended functions to form new functions, then the new functions also automatically work in an extended fashion.

28 Could we see an example of this?

Sure.

Here is such an example.

What is

((*line* [2 7 5 11]) (list 4 6))?

29 We're invoking *line* on a tensor[1] argument.

Does that mean the functions + and ∗ in *line* are extended functions?

It does!

Here, we want to find y values for many (here, four) x values on the line with $\boldsymbol{\theta}_0$ being 4 and $\boldsymbol{\theta}_1$ being 6.

30 Magnificent!

Finish the same-as chart to determine the corresponding four predicted *ys*

1. ((*line* [2 7 5 11]) (list 4 6))

31 Here goes

2. ((λ (**θ**)
   (+ (∗ $\boldsymbol{\theta}_0$ [2 7 5 11]) $\boldsymbol{\theta}_1$))
   (list 4 6))
3. (+ (∗ 4 [2 7 5 11]) 6)
4. (+ [(∗ 4 2) (∗ 4 7) (∗ 4 5) (∗ 4 11)] 6)
5. (+ [8 28 20 44] 6)
6. [(+ 8 6) (+ 28 6) (+ 20 6) (+ 44 6)]
7. [14 34 26 50]

This interlude is about how it is possible to extend functions that operate on fixed ranks of tensors into functions that also accept tensors of different ranks. We use the concept of *descending* into the higher-ranked tensors to accomplish this.

32 And we have learned that by doing this, we descend into the higher-ranked tensor while repeating the lower-ranked tensor until the one- or two-argument operation can proceed.

Extendy Toys

sum 53

How about some cappuccino? With some beignets?

3 Running Down a Slippery Slope

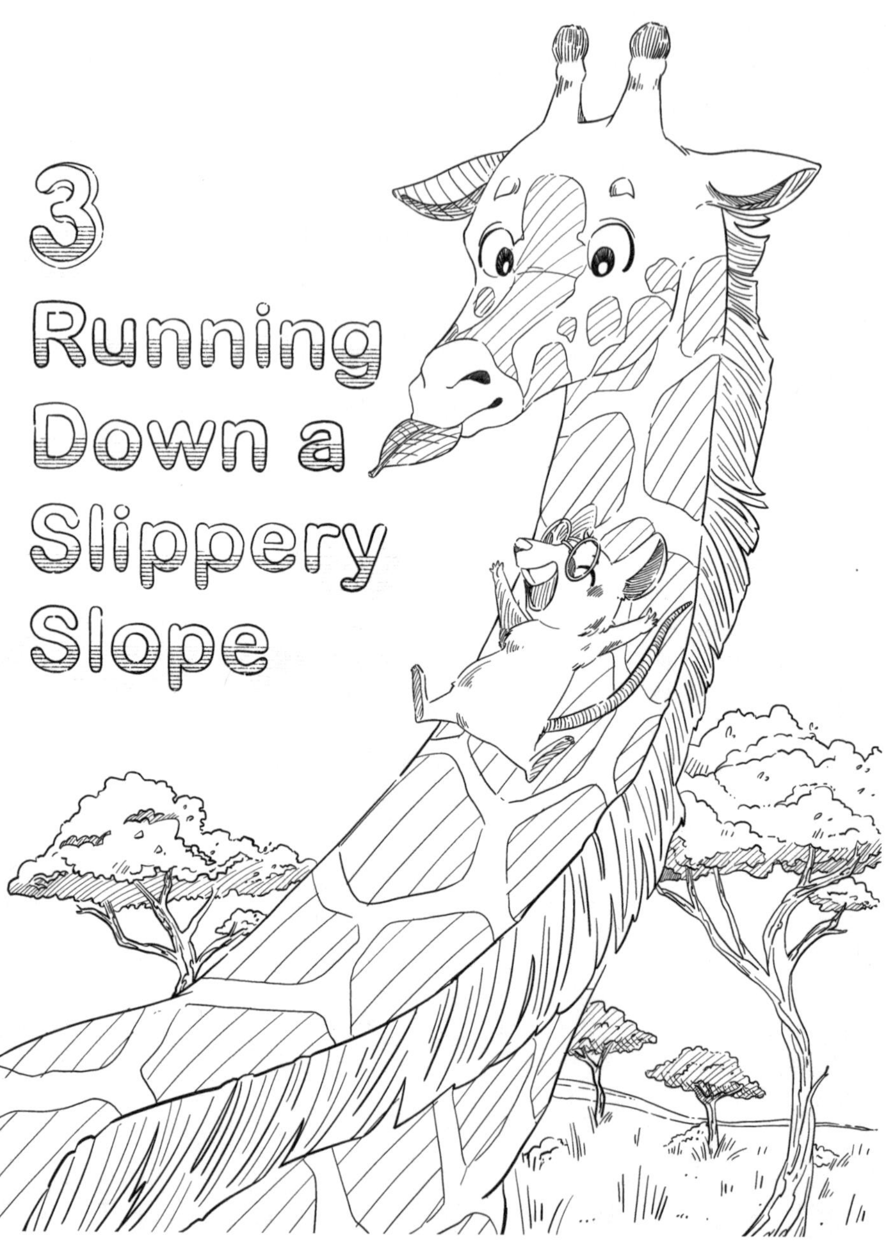

1 How was the cappuccino?

The beignets went great with it.[†]

[†]Thanks, *Café du Monde* (1862–), New Orleans.

---

2 Let us now return to defining a function to automatically find the $\boldsymbol{\theta}$ that best fits (from frame 27:29) the given data set in 24:17. We refer to this $\boldsymbol{\theta}$ as *well fitted.*

Just as we visually fit a line to match our points from frame 25:20?

---

3 Exactly.

Here we introduce

successive approximations[†]

[†]Thanks, Joseph Raphson (c.1648–c.1715).

Are successive approximations a way to find a well-fitted $\boldsymbol{\theta}$?

---

4 Yes.

We determine $\boldsymbol{\theta}_0$ and $\boldsymbol{\theta}_1$ by arbitrarily starting them at 0.0. We then repeatedly revise $\boldsymbol{\theta}$ to bring it as close as we wish to what it must finally be.[†]

[†]Successive approximation is a family of methods in mathematics, another one of which may be familiar to some as being a method to determine the roots of a polynomial such as a square root. Thanks, Sir Isaac Newton (1643–1727) and Joseph Raphson.

An example, please.

Sure.

Here is the data set from frame 24:17

line-xs is [2.0 1.0 4.0 3.0]

and

line-ys is [1.8 1.2 4.2 3.3]

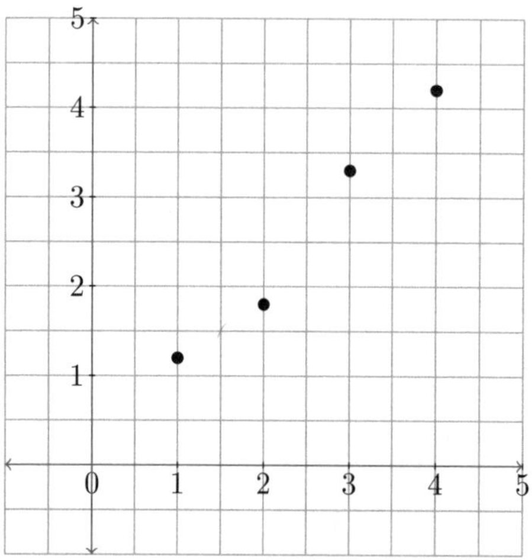

5 So then do we start with

$\boldsymbol{\theta}_0 = 0.0$

and

$\boldsymbol{\theta}_1 = 0.0$?

That is a fine place to start.

What line does this $\boldsymbol{\theta}$ give us?

6 We can find out by using

(**list** 0.0 0.0) as $\boldsymbol{\theta}$

1. ((*line line-xs*) $\boldsymbol{\theta}$)
2. ((*line* [2.0 1.0 4.0 3.0]) (**list** 0.0 0.0))
3. (+ (∗ 0.0 [2.0 1.0 4.0 3.0]) 0.0)
4. [0.0 0.0 0.0 0.0]

The y-coordinates produced for the x-coordinates in *line-xs* are all 0.0. So this $\boldsymbol{\theta}$ represents the x-axis!

7 Indeed it does.

Those values, which we refer to as the *predicted ys* from frame 26:23, are very different from the given *line-ys*!

What does this mean?

---

8 It means that $\boldsymbol{\theta}_0$ and $\boldsymbol{\theta}_1$ do not yet *fit* our data set.

Do we have to revise $\boldsymbol{\theta}_0$ and $\boldsymbol{\theta}_1$ to bring the predicted *ys* closer to the given *line-ys*?

---

9 Yes, we do.

But, in order to do that, we need to know how far away we are from the well-fitted $\boldsymbol{\theta}$.

We need a *single* scalar that tells us how close or how far away we are. This scalar is known as the *loss.*[†] The well-fitted $\boldsymbol{\theta}$ would be the one where this loss is as close to 0.0 as possible.

When the loss *is* 0.0, it is *ideal.*

[†]This is also known as *cost.*

Why can't it be a tensor[1]?

---

10 With a scalar, it is simpler to decide how to revise $\boldsymbol{\theta}$.

How is this scalar used?

---

11 We determine this scalar, or loss, every time we revise $\boldsymbol{\theta}$. Since the loss shows us how far away we are from the well-fitted $\boldsymbol{\theta}$, we use it as a guide for revising $\boldsymbol{\theta}$.

How do we find the loss for a given $\boldsymbol{\theta}$?

We'll define a function for it, of course!

But we'll do it in two steps. First we determine a tensor representing how far away we are and then reduce this tensor down to a scalar.

The simplest way to determine how far away we are is to find the difference between the given *line-ys* and the predicted *ys* as we see in this skeleton

(− *line-ys* [*P*])

Find *P*.

12 *P* must be the predicted *ys*. So, *P* must be

((*line line-xs*) (list $\boldsymbol{\theta}_0$ $\boldsymbol{\theta}_1$))

Correct.

This gives us

(− *line-ys* ((*line line-xs*) (list $\boldsymbol{\theta}_0$ $\boldsymbol{\theta}_1$)))

It, however, is not yet a scalar. It is still a tensor^1, so we must turn it into a scalar.

What function, which we have already defined, derives a scalar from a tensor^1?

13 That function is *sum* from frame 53:25.

Is this

(*sum*
  (− *line-ys* ((*line line-xs*) (list $\boldsymbol{\theta}_0$ $\boldsymbol{\theta}_1$))))

how we find the scalar?

Almost, but it is not good enough.

Here's why. Suppose we had another data set and another $\boldsymbol{\theta}$ that would have given us a difference of

[4.0 −3.0 0.0 −4.0 3.0]

What would be the result of

(*sum*
  [4.0 −3.0 0.0 −4.0 3.0])?

14 It would be 0.0, the ideal loss, which it clearly is *not*!

So, even though the individual differences are very high, the sum of 0.0 suggests that the $\boldsymbol{\theta}$ is a *perfect fit.*

Aha! This problem arises from having negative values in the argument to *sum*.

So what should we do?

15 We solve this by squaring each element.[†] This turns the negative elements of the difference to positive, and the positive elements stay positive

```
(sum
  (sqr
    (− line-ys ((line line-xs) (list θ₀ θ₁)))))
```

Here, the (extended −) descends into the two tensors[1] resulting in a tensor[1] of differences, then *sqr* squares the resultant tensor[1] of differences, yielding a tensor[1] for *sum* to produce a scalar.

Now the sum of the squares is positive if *at least* one of the elements in the difference is non-zero.

That's a promising strategy.

How should we define our loss function?

[†]Other functions, such as *abs* (i.e., absolute value) from frame 9:24 work, but we use only squaring here because it works better in most situations.

16 Here is a function that does this

```
(define l2-loss
  (λ (xs ys)
    (λ (θ)
      (let ((pred-ys† ((line xs) θ)))
        (sum
          (sqr
            (− ys pred-ys)))))))
```

[†]The predicted *ys* is named *pred-ys*.

Why is this function named *l2-loss*?

17 It is an instance of a family of functions that use exponents to find the loss. Here, since we use *sqr* (i.e., raised to the power of 2), this loss function is *l2-loss*.[†]

[†]In mathematics, the square root of the sum of the squares of a tensor[1] is known as *L2-norm*. The *L2-norm* is also known as *Euclidean* distance. Thanks, Euclid of Alexandria (325BCE–270BCE).

Why is this definition dashed?

When used as a loss function, however, the square root is typically left out. Another variant of this loss function divides the sum of the squares by the number of elements in the tensor to produce a *mean squared error* (or *MSE*) loss function.

Because we're going to generalize *l2-loss*.

This *l2-loss* relies on *line*. But, as far as this *l2-loss* is concerned, *line* is just some function that results in a predicted *ys*, *pred-ys*, when given *xs* and $\boldsymbol{\theta}$.

18 How can we use this observation?

We can make *l2-loss* less specific to *line*, so we can use it with other functions as well. We redefine *l2-loss* to take *line* as an argument

```
(define l2-loss
  (λ (line)
    (λ (xs ys)
      (λ (θ)
        (let ((pred-ys ((line xs) θ)))
          (sum
            (sqr
              (- ys pred-ys))))))))
```

19 Why is *this l2-loss* dashed?

This *l2-loss* is dashed because the name *line* is too specific.

Since we have made *line* into a formal, the name no longer represents the original *line* function. So, we should rename the formal *line* to something more meaningful.

20 So what name should we pick?

Here, the function *line* is referred to as a *target* function because that is the function whose $\boldsymbol{\theta}$ we are trying to find for a given data set.

So, instead of the name *line*, let's use the name *target*.†

21 Sounds better.

†This process, briefly touched upon in frame 7:18, is known as α-substitution and dictates how the formals of a λ-expression may be properly renamed. Thanks, Alonzo Church.

Here is how we define the final *l2-loss* to use the name *target* instead of *line*

```
(define l2-loss                              •
  (λ (target)
    (λ (xs ys)
      (λ (θ)
        (let ((pred-ys ((target xs) θ)))
          (sum
            (sqr
              (− ys pred-ys))))))))
```

22 Aha!

The dashed *l2-loss* in frame 19 before we generalized it is specific to the function *line*. If we want to use it for the function *line* again, how can we use this generalized form of *l2-loss*?

23 We should invoke *l2-loss* with *line*

```
(l2-loss line)
```

Correct.

Here's the same-as chart for this

1. (*l2-loss line*)
2. ```
   (λ (xs ys)
     (λ (θ)
       (let ((pred-ys ((line xs) θ)))
         (sum
           (sqr
             (− ys pred-ys))))))
   ```

This function, which is produced when *l2-loss* is invoked with a target function, is referred to as an *expectant* function.

24 Why do we refer to

```
(λ (xs ys) ...)
```

as an

expectant function?

That's because it is *expecting* a data set as arguments.

25 That makes sense.

What does an expectant function produce when it receives a data set?
```

Let's find out

```
1. ((l2-loss line) line-xs line-ys)
2. (λ (θ)
     (let ((pred-ys ((line line-xs) θ)))
       (sum
         (sqr
           (− line-ys pred-ys)))))
```

This function, which awaits a $\boldsymbol{\theta}$ as its argument, is known as an

objective function

26 What does the objective function do?

When provided with a $\boldsymbol{\theta}$, the objective function produces a scalar representing the loss, which is a measure of how far away we are from the well-fitted $\boldsymbol{\theta}$.

27 So, it is going to help us achieve our objective of finding a well-fitted $\boldsymbol{\theta}$!

Let's try it with our current $\boldsymbol{\theta}_0$ and $\boldsymbol{\theta}_1$ which are still 0.0

```
(((l2-loss line) line-xs line-ys)
 (list 0.0 0.0))
```

Looking at the final *l2-loss* in frame 22, we must first determine *pred-ys*, which is

```
((target xs) θ)
```

Use the ideas in the same-as chart from frame 55:31 to help find *pred-ys* for *line-xs* and our $\boldsymbol{\theta}$.

28 Since the value of *target* here is the function *line*, *pred-ys* is determined by

```
1. ((target xs) θ)
2. ((line line-xs) θ)
3. ((line [2.0 1.0 4.0 3.0])
    (list 0.0 0.0))
4. (+ (∗ 0.0 [2.0 1.0 4.0 3.0])
      0.0)
5. [0.0 0.0 0.0 0.0]
```

Great.

29 Here it is

Keeping this value of *pred-ys* in mind, we find the *loss* for this $\boldsymbol{\theta}$

```
1. (((l2-loss target) xs ys) θ)
2. (((l2-loss line) line-xs line-ys)
    (list 0.0 0.0))
3. (((l2-loss line)
     [2.0 1.0 4.0 3.0]
     [1.8 1.2 4.2 3.3])
    (list 0.0 0.0))
4. (sum
     (sqr
       (− [1.8 1.2 4.2 3.3] pred-ys)))
```

Complete this same-as chart.

```
5. (sum
     (sqr
       (− [1.8 1.2 4.2 3.3]
          [0.0 0.0 0.0 0.0])))
6. (sum
     (sqr
       [1.8 1.2 4.2 3.3]))
7. (sum
     [(sqr 1.8) (sqr 1.2) (sqr 4.2) (sqr 3.3)])
8. (sum
     [3.24 1.44 17.64 10.89])
9. 33.21
```

The loss tells us how far away we are and 33.21 tells us we are quite far away.

How do we revise our $\boldsymbol{\theta}$ to get the scalar loss 33.21 closer to the ideal loss, 0.0?

We begin by testing the behavior of $\boldsymbol{\theta}_0$ to see how we should revise it; we'll worry about $\boldsymbol{\theta}_1$ later.

30 Okay

We change $\boldsymbol{\theta}_0$ by increasing it by a small amount, for testing purposes, so that

$$\boldsymbol{\theta}_0 = 0.0099$$

Find the new *pred-ys* for this new $\boldsymbol{\theta}$.

```
1. ((target xs) θ)
2. ((line line-xs) θ)
3. ((line [2.0 1.0 4.0 3.0])
    (list 0.0099 0.0))
4. (+ (* 0.0099 [2.0 1.0 4.0 3.0])
      0.0)
5. [0.0198 0.0099 0.0396 0.0297†]
```

†Scheme systems sometimes produce answers like 0.029700000000000004 due to limitations in the implementation of floating-point numbers. While using same-as charts, we shall round these numbers appropriately.

Perfect.

31 Here it is

Here is the same-as chart to find the new loss for this new $\boldsymbol{\theta}_0$

```
1. (((l2-loss line) line-xs line-ys)
     (list 0.0099 0.0))
2. (((l2-loss line)
      [2.0 1.0 4.0 3.0]
      [1.8 1.2 4.2 3.3])
     (list 0.0099 0.0))
```

Now, complete this same-as chart.

```
3. (sum
     (sqr
       (- [1.8 1.2 4.2 3.3] pred-ys)))
4. (sum
     (sqr
       (- [1.8 1.2 4.2 3.3]
          [0.0198 0.0099 0.0396 0.0297])))
5. 32.59
```

The loss has gone down.

In other words, we are slightly closer to the ideal loss!

We changed the loss by

$(32.59 - 33.21) = -0.62$

by revising $\boldsymbol{\theta}_0$ from 0.0 to 0.0099.

Our test has succeeded.

32 So should we *continue* to revise $\boldsymbol{\theta}_0$ in increments of 0.0099 until we come as close as possible to the ideal loss?

It could mean that.

Revising $\boldsymbol{\theta}_0$ every time by 0.0099 may require too many revisions to get to the well-fitted $\boldsymbol{\theta}$.

There is a way, however, that takes fewer revisions.

33 Show us the way!

Remember that increasing $\boldsymbol{\theta}_0$ by 0.0099 has changed our loss by -0.62. So our *rate of change*[†] is

$$\frac{-0.62}{0.0099} = -62.63$$

34 How do we use this rate of change?

[†] Thanks, Gottfried Wilhelm Leibniz (1646–1716) and thanks, Sir Isaac Newton.

The rate of change is also known as the *derivative*.

35 The rate of change of a function (here, of the objective function), determines how its result changes when its argument (i.e., $\boldsymbol{\theta}$) is revised.

By using the rate of change *cautiously*, we can get to the well-fitted $\boldsymbol{\theta}$ with fewer revisions.

What does using it cautiously mean?

---

36 This rate of change has a large *absolute value*.[†] This means that a small *increase* in $\boldsymbol{\theta}_0$ causes a relatively large *decrease* in its loss.

We can use this idea to determine how much to further revise $\boldsymbol{\theta}_0$ so that we can make an even bigger reduction in loss. But, we must be careful.

What should we be wary of?

[†] The absolute value of a scalar, defined as a function in frame 9:24, is its value without its sign. For example, here the absolute value of both -62.63 and 62.63 is 62.63.

---

37 We have to be wary that our revision of $\boldsymbol{\theta}_0$ always moves us closer to, but does not *overshoot*, the ideal loss.

One choice, for example, is to revise $\boldsymbol{\theta}_0$ by 62.63, which is the absolute value of the whole rate of change. When we do this, however, we end up with a

loss of 113763.027

This is far bigger than 32.59, which is our previous loss, and much greater than the ideal loss.

That is something to be wary of indeed.

How do we solve this problem?

---

38 We take a small scalar (like 0.01), and multiply the rate of change by it, and revise $\boldsymbol{\theta}_0$ by that amount.

So we get

$$0.01 \times -62.63 = -0.6263$$

Is this a small enough revision that won't overshoot the ideal loss?

Yes, it should be.

This small scalar is known as the

learning rate

Since we use this scalar often, we have a special symbol for it

$\alpha^{\dagger}$

We rewrite our example thusly

$\alpha \times -62.63 = -0.6263$

39 Okay.

† The learning rate (usually a very small number between 0.0 and 0.01) is also known as the *step size*. We'll see more of how to find an appropriate learning rate in later chapters.

The step size is sometimes written as λ, but because we already have a meaning for λ, we prefer to use a different Greek letter.

Since we need to *increase* $\boldsymbol{\theta}_0$ to reduce the loss, we must *subtract* this negative value from our current $\boldsymbol{\theta}_0$. So the new $\boldsymbol{\theta}_0$ is

$0.0 - -0.6263 = \underline{0.6263}.$

40 But, didn't we set $\boldsymbol{\theta}_0$ to 0.0099?

That was just to find the rate of change.

Once we find the rate of change, we forget about 0.0099.

41 Okay.

So we revise by multiplying the learning rate and the rate of change and then subtracting the result from our current

$\boldsymbol{\theta}_0$?

The Law of Revision

(Initial Version)

$$\text{new } \boldsymbol{\theta}_0 = \boldsymbol{\theta}_0 - (\alpha \times \text{rate of change of loss with respect to } \boldsymbol{\theta}_0)$$

Exactly!

We proceed, as before, by finding the new *pred-ys* for the new $\boldsymbol{\theta}_0$

1. ((*line line-xs*) $\boldsymbol{\theta}$)
2. ((*line* [2.0 1.0 4.0 3.0])
   (**list** 0.6263 0.0))
3. (+ (∗ 0.6263 [2.0 1.0 4.0 3.0])
   0.0)
4. [1.2526 0.6263 2.5052 1.879]

Now find the loss.

42 We use this new *pred-ys* to find the loss

1. (((*l2-loss line*) *line-xs line-ys*)
   (**list** 0.6263 0.0))
2. (*sum*
     (*sqr*
       (− *line-ys pred-ys*)))
3. (*sum*
     (*sqr*
       (− [1.8 1.2 4.2 3.3]
          [1.2526 0.6263 2.5052 1.879])))
4. 5.52

We have gone from a loss of 33.21 to a loss of 5.52. That is so much better than just increasing $\boldsymbol{\theta}_0$ by 0.0099 as we did in frame 30!

Amazing. We've taken a big step closer to the ideal loss now.

We repeat this process to get our next revision.

43 Can we subtract −0.6263 from $\boldsymbol{\theta}_0$ again?

No, we cannot!

Let's find out what the rate of change of loss is with $\boldsymbol{\theta}_0$ at 0.6263. Let us give

((*l2-loss line*) *line-xs line-ys*)

the temporary name *obj*. Then the rate of change is

1. (÷ (− (*obj* (**list** (+ 0.6263 0.0099) 0.0))
         (*obj* (**list** 0.6263 0.0)))
      0.0099)
2. −25.12

44 It's different from the rate of change we found in frame 34.

Does this mean that the rate of change depends on the *current* $\boldsymbol{\theta}_0$?

45 That is exactly what it means.

So do we determine the rate of change again using $\boldsymbol{\theta}_0 + 0.0099$?

---

46 We could.

But there is a much better way—one that is simpler and more precise.

That sounds exciting.

What is this new way?

---

47 That's what we'll discover in the next chapter, where we also find out how to revise $\boldsymbol{\theta}_1$!

What's the best snack to help prepare for that next chapter?

Lossy Toys

How about a chocolate chip cookie?
Be sure to cautiously dust the crumbs away!

4 Slip-slidin' Away†

†Thanks, Paul Frederic Simon (1941–).

1

And the cookie?

Ready?

That's the way it crumbles.

Let's roll!

2

We start with a picture

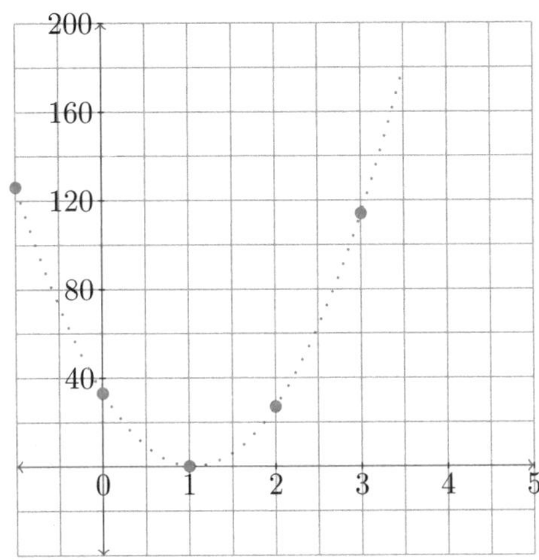

This graph looks different, what is it?

3

It is a graph of the loss in our example against $\boldsymbol{\theta}_0$ while keeping $\boldsymbol{\theta}_1$ at 0.0. The y-axis here represents the loss, and the x-axis represents $\boldsymbol{\theta}_0$, which we also refer to as *weight*.

So, for any possible value of the weight, this graph shows the corresponding value of the loss.

What are the big orange dots?

4

To draw this picture, we choose five weights −1.0, 0.0, 1.0, 2.0, and 3.0.

For each weight, we determine its corresponding loss, while keeping $\boldsymbol{\theta}_1$ at 0.0 and using the data set

(*line-xs*, *line-ys*)

The orange dots represent the losses at each of these weights.

How can we find these five losses?

First, let's take a deeper look at our objective function

((*l2-loss line*) *line-xs line-ys*)

Show a same-as chart that expands it.

5 Here it is

```
1. ((l2-loss line) line-xs line-ys)
2. ((l2-loss line) [2.0 1.0 4.0 3.0]
                   [1.8 1.2 4.2 3.3])
3. (λ (θ)
     (let ((pred-ys
             ((line [2.0 1.0 4.0 3.0]) θ)))
       (sum
         (sqr
           (- [1.8 1.2 4.2 3.3]
              pred-ys)))))
```

Great.

Let us name this λ-expression *obj*, for objective function, from frame 64:26.

Explain how we can use *obj* to determine the losses.

6 The λ-expression *obj* takes the parameters of a line as its argument and results in a scalar representing how closely that line fits the data set (i.e., the loss).

So we must construct a $\boldsymbol{\theta}$ with each of those five weights as $\boldsymbol{\theta}_0$ and 0.0 as $\boldsymbol{\theta}_1$. The corresponding losses would be

(*obj* (**list** −1.0 0.0)), which is 126.21
(*obj* (**list** 0.0 0.0)), which is 33.21
(*obj* (**list** 1.0 0.0)), which is 0.21
(*obj* (**list** 2.0 0.0)), which is 27.21
(*obj* (**list** 3.0 0.0)), which is 114.21

Correct.

We use this orange style of graph to show quantities that are *not* part of our data set.

What is our initial estimate for $\boldsymbol{\theta}_0$?

7 It is 0.0.

The loss when $\boldsymbol{\theta}_0$ is 0.0 (and keeping $\boldsymbol{\theta}_1$ at 0.0) is 33.21 from frame 65:29.

The point (0.0, 33.21) is circled in this graph

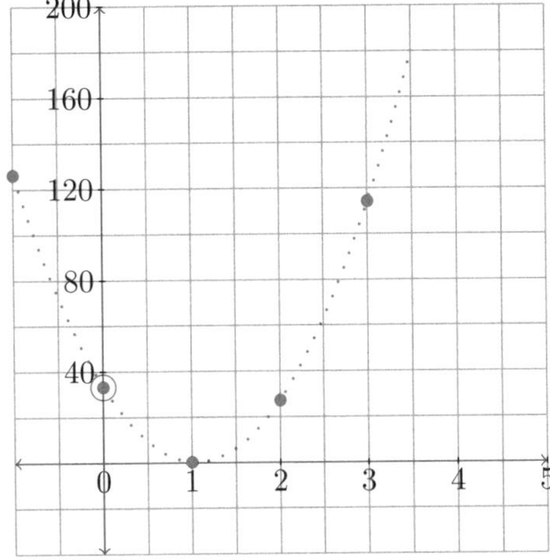

8 Aha!

So the loss seems to be the lowest at the bottom of this curve.†

†The bottom of this curve in this graph visually appears to be at 0.0 of the y-axis, but this rarely happens. Depending upon the data set, the bottom is usually higher than 0.0.

Correct.

We need to "roll" down this incline to get to its bottom, and from frame 67:37, we have discovered that we can use the rate of change to roll down faster than we could before without overshooting.

9 How can we represent rates of change on this graph?

Here is how we do it for our initial estimate with $\boldsymbol{\theta}_0$ being 0.0

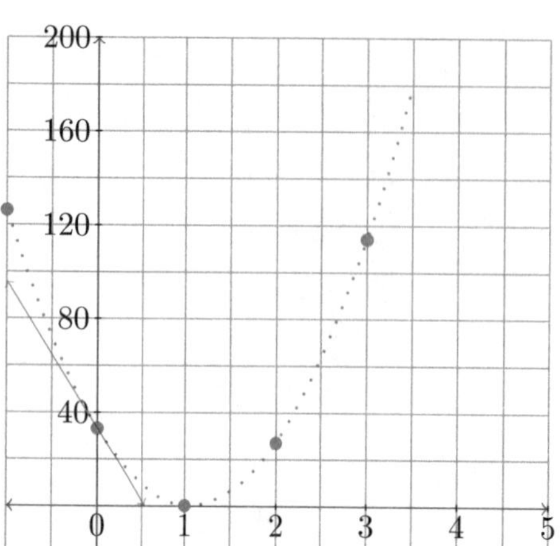

10 What is the turquoise colored line?

That turquoise line is different from the line for which we are trying to find $\boldsymbol{\theta}_0$ and $\boldsymbol{\theta}_1$. This line is known as a *tangent.*

A tangent touches the *loss* curve at exactly one point.

11 Is that point (0.0, 33.21)?

Yes, it is.

The rate of change that we have determined is the

slope of the tangent

This slope has a different name so we don't confuse it with $\boldsymbol{\theta}_0$. It is known as the

gradient

12 Could we see the tangent for our next $\boldsymbol{\theta}_0$ at 0.6623?

Here are the tangents for our first two estimates of $\boldsymbol{\theta}_0$

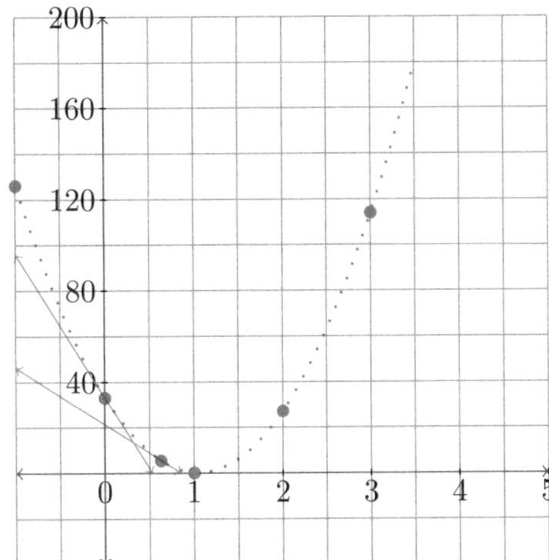

Describe what's interesting about this graph.

13 We see that the tangent for our second $\boldsymbol{\theta}_0$ is less steep than the tangent for our first $\boldsymbol{\theta}_0$. Thus, the gradient of the second is lower than the gradient of the first.

These are only for $\boldsymbol{\theta}_0$, but we must also have them for $\boldsymbol{\theta}_1$.

Is there something similar for $\boldsymbol{\theta}_1$?

Well done.

A gradient is a general way of understanding the rate of change of a parameterized function with respect to *all* its parameters.

14 How can we find this gradient?

To find the gradient of a function at given values of its arguments, we need to use a new function ∇. The first argument to ∇ is a function f that takes a list of tensors, including $\boldsymbol{\theta}$s. The second argument to ∇ is *the list* for which we need gradients of f.

15 Does this function then result in the gradients?

Yes.[†]

The result of ∇ is a list of gradients of f with respect to each parameter in $\boldsymbol{\theta}$, and is referred to as the *gradient list*.

So, for example, if we want the gradient of f with respect to parameters u and v, we write it

$(\nabla\ f\ (\textsf{list}\ u\ v))$

16 How about an example?

[†]Those familiar with *automatic differentiation* may recognize that the (partial) derivatives of the function with respect to a given set of arguments are automatically determined.

Thanks, William Kingdon Clifford (1845–1879), thanks, Robert Edwin Wengert (1922–2001), and thanks, Lev Nikolayevich Korolev (1926–2016), L. M. Beda, T. S. Frolova, and N. V. Sukhikh.

That's a great idea.

Let's find the gradient of *sqr* with respect to its argument at 27.0

1. $(\nabla\ (\lambda\ (\boldsymbol{\theta})\ (sqr\ \boldsymbol{\theta}_0))\ (\textsf{list}\ 27.0))$
2. $(\textsf{list}\ 54.0)$

The first argument to ∇ is a function that expects a $\boldsymbol{\theta}$ containing a single parameter, and it squares that single tensor using *sqr*. The second argument is the $\boldsymbol{\theta}$ containing the parameter 27.0. This expresses the gradient of *sqr* at the scalar 27.0.[†]

17 Instead of these lists, couldn't we directly use scalars here?

[†]Those familiar with gradients should recognize that the gradient of x^2 at any value x, is $2x$.

The inner workings of ∇ can be found in the appendix *Ghost in the Machine* on page 351.

Some may observe that if ∇ were to take arguments one at a time (in other words, were we to *Curry* it), then $(\nabla\ f)$ would be equivalent to the mathematical definition of the gradient of f. Here, however, we define it with two arguments for simplicity.

Thanks, Moses Schönfinkel (1889–1942) and Haskell Brooks Curry (1900–1982)

A great question.

While using scalars directly without packaging them in a list would make sense for simple examples, more complex learning problems require a very large collection of parameters.

It is easiest to package them in a list, so we have designed ∇ to work exclusively with lists.

18 So, does ∇ always accept a function and a list of parameters and result in a list of gradients, one for each parameter?

Yes, that is correct.

∇ always results in a list of gradients—one for each parameter provided in $\boldsymbol{\theta}$.

19 How can we use ∇ to determine the gradient of *l2-loss* with respect to

$\boldsymbol{\theta}_0$ and $\boldsymbol{\theta}_1$

where each parameter starts out as

0.0?

Here is the gradient of *obj*, which is the objective function

((*l2-loss line*) *line-xs line-ys*)

at $\boldsymbol{\theta}_0$ and $\boldsymbol{\theta}_1$ equal to 0.0

1. (∇ *obj* (**list** 0.0 0.0))
2. (∇ ((*l2-loss line*) *line-xs line-ys*) (**list** 0.0 0.0))
3. (**list** −63.0 −21.0)

20 So the gradient of *obj*

with respect to $\boldsymbol{\theta}_0$ is -63.0

and the gradient of *obj*

with respect to $\boldsymbol{\theta}_1$ is -21.0

But why is this value

-63.0

different from the rate of change

-62.63

of

$\boldsymbol{\theta}_0$

from frame 66:34?

An excellent question.

Our way of finding the rate of change in frame 66:34 is an approximation.

∇ yields more precise results and also yields the gradient with respect to $\boldsymbol{\theta}_1$ at the same time.

21 Now that we have a way to find the rate of change, should we use it repeatedly as we did in frame 69:43 to find the well-fitted $\boldsymbol{\theta}$ for *obj*?

Indeed! We revise our $\boldsymbol{\theta}$ using ∇ a little bit at a time, over many revisions.

To do that, let's define an *iteration* function that makes things easier for us.

22 Does an iteration function help us repeat a function invocation over and over again?

It does.

Here is a skeleton of a function *revise* that takes a *revision function* f, which does not change, a natural number *revs*, and an accumulator $\boldsymbol{\theta}$. It revises $\boldsymbol{\theta}$ *revs* times, each time yielding a new value for $\boldsymbol{\theta}$ by invoking f on the current value of $\boldsymbol{\theta}$

```
(define revise
  (λ (f revs θ)
    (cond
      ((zero? revs) θ)
      (else
        [ R ]))))
```

Here, *revs* is the number of revisions of $\boldsymbol{\theta}$ remaining and $\boldsymbol{\theta}$ is the value accumulated so far. When *revs* reaches 0, it results in the accumulated $\boldsymbol{\theta}$. When *revs* has not counted down to 0, we have R, which must revise $\boldsymbol{\theta}$ once.

Find R.

23 R should recursively invoke *revise* with the new values of *revs* and $\boldsymbol{\theta}$. We need to provide a new $\boldsymbol{\theta}$ by invoking the revision function f on $\boldsymbol{\theta}$

```
(f θ)
```

Similarly, since we have finished a revision, the new value of *revs* must be

```
(sub1 revs)
```

Thus, R must be

```
(revise f (sub1 revs) (f θ))
```

Here's *revise*

```
(define revise                                  ●
  (λ (f revs θ)
    (cond
      ((zero? revs) θ)
      (else
       (revise f (sub1 revs) (f θ))))))
```

24 Can we try it out?

Sure.

Using *revise*, write a same-as chart with this revision function *f*

```
(λ (θ)
  (map (λ (p)
         (− p 3))
    θ))
```

this starting *revs*

```
5
```

and this initial **θ**

```
(list 1 2 3)
```

The final **θ** is

```
(list −14 −13 −12)
```

25 What is *map*?

Well-timed question!

In its most specific form *map* accepts a function and a list, and it invokes the function on every member of that list, to produce a new list that is the result of *map*. For example

```
1. (map (λ (x)
          (add1 x))
     (list 5 7 3))
2. (list (add1 5) (add1 7) (add1 3))
3. (list 6 8 4)
```

26 If this is the most specific form, is there a more general form of *map*?

In the more general form *map* accepts more than one list and invokes its function on corresponding members of each list

1. | (*map* (λ (x y)
   | (+ x y))
   | (list 12 17 32)
   | (list 8 3 11))
2. | (list (+ 12 8) (+ 17 3) (+ 32 11))
3. | (list 20 20 43)

27 So, in frame 25, invoking *map* on the revision function f and $\boldsymbol{\theta}$ produces a new list where every member is 3 less than the corresponding member of the $\boldsymbol{\theta}$.

Here's the start of the same-as chart

1. | (*revise* f 5 (list 1 2 3))
2. | (*revise* f 4 (f (list 1 2 3)))
3. | (*revise* f 4 (list −2 −1 0))
4. | (*revise* f 3 (f (list −2 −1 0)))
5. | (*revise* f 3 (list −5 −4 −3))

Now complete the same-as chart.

28 Thanks for the hint

6. | (*revise* f 2 (f (list −5 −4 −3)))
7. | (*revise* f 2 (list −8 −7 −6))
8. | (*revise* f 1 (f (list −8 −7 −6)))
9. | (*revise* f 1 (list −11 −10 −9))
10. | (*revise* f 0 (list −14 −13 −12))
11. | (list −14 −13 −12)

Now let's get back to defining a function that guides us from one $\boldsymbol{\theta}$ to the next.

The third argument to *revise* must be a list containing the initial values of $\boldsymbol{\theta}_0$ and $\boldsymbol{\theta}_1$, in that order.

What would this initial $\boldsymbol{\theta}$ look like?

29 Since we're initializing $\boldsymbol{\theta}_0$ and $\boldsymbol{\theta}_1$ at 0.0, the initial $\boldsymbol{\theta}$ should be

(list 0.0 0.0)

Could we see what f, this revision function, looks like?

Sure.

Here is a skeleton for this, where *revs* is 1000 and the learning rate α is 0.01

```
(let ((α 0.01)
      (obj ((l2-loss line) line-xs line-ys)))
  (let ((f (λ (θ)
             (let ((gs (∇ obj θ)))
               (list
                 [     W     ]
                 [     B     ])))))
    (revise f 1000 (list 0.0 0.0))))
```

Explain how the invocation of *revise* in this example works.

30 We carry out 1000 revisions, starting with (**list** 0.0 0.0) and invoking f for each revision.

The revision function accepts an initial $\boldsymbol{\theta}$ and then produces a different $\boldsymbol{\theta}$, and repeats this for 1000 revisions.

Very good.

In the revision function, we determine the gradient of the objective function with respect to $\boldsymbol{\theta}_0$ and $\boldsymbol{\theta}_1$, which are packaged into a $\boldsymbol{\theta}$.

We use ∇ to get the gradient list *gs*, which is a list of two scalars.

The first is the

gradient of the loss with respect to $\boldsymbol{\theta}_0$

and the second is the

gradient of the loss with respect to $\boldsymbol{\theta}_1$

Now find the expressions for W and B.

31 Since the revision function must produce a new $\boldsymbol{\theta}$

W should be the new $\boldsymbol{\theta}_0$

and

B should be the new $\boldsymbol{\theta}_1$

Correct.

And how do we determine these new members of $\boldsymbol{\theta}$ i.e., the new parameters?

32 We multiply the gradient for a given parameter by the learning rate α and subtract it from that parameter.

The gradient with respect to $\boldsymbol{\theta}_0$ is given by the 0th member of the gradient list gs, which is gs_0. So the expression W is

$$(-\ \boldsymbol{\theta}_0\ (*\ \alpha\ gs_0))$$

Similarly, because the gradient with respect to $\boldsymbol{\theta}_1$ is given by gs_1, the expression B is

$$(-\ \boldsymbol{\theta}_1\ (*\ \alpha\ gs_1))$$

Yes, well done.

Here is the completed revision function *f* with *W* and *B* filled in. We show the invocation of *revise* using this new *f* in a *revision* chart.

We use revision charts to show the results after multiple revisions

```
▷ (let ((f (λ (θ)
              (let ((gs (∇ obj θ)))
                (list
                  (− θ₀ (* α gs₀))
                  (− θ₁ (* α gs₁)))))))
    (revise f 1000 (list 0.0 0.0)))
▶ (list 1.05 1.87e−06†)
```

†In Scheme, 1.87e−06 is 1.87×10^{-6}, which we consider small enough to be practically 0.0.

33 So, this means that after 1000 revisions, we get a reasonably well-fitted $\boldsymbol{\theta}$.

What does this line

(**list** 1.05 1.87e−06)

look like?

The Law of Revision

(Final Version)

$$\text{new } \boldsymbol{\theta}_i = \boldsymbol{\theta}_i - (\alpha \times \text{rate of change of loss w.r.t. } \boldsymbol{\theta}_i)$$

Here's the line fitted to our original points

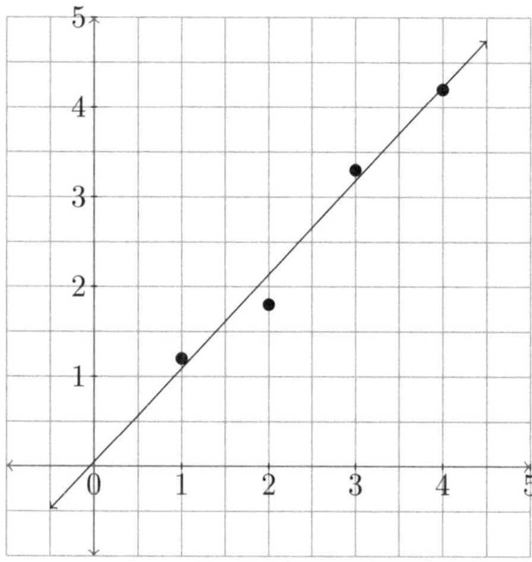

34 That's exciting! It is almost identical to the visually estimated line from frame 25:20.

Another question, though. Why do we have *revs* at 1000? Are we certain we'll reach a well-fitted $\boldsymbol{\theta}$ by then?

A very good question.

We pick a high enough number for *revs* that we know gets us close enough to the well-fitted $\boldsymbol{\theta}$.

Depending upon the kind of function we are optimizing, we can pick an appropriate *revs* (usually through a combination of the size of the data set and experimentation).

35 That sounds a little ad hoc. Is there a better approach?

---

30 Yes, but for only certain kinds of problems.

As we encounter problems with $\boldsymbol{\theta}$s that have much larger tensors and target functions that do much more interesting things, a fixed number for *revs* is usually a good approach.

Does this way of finding $\boldsymbol{\theta}_0$ and $\boldsymbol{\theta}_1$ have a name?

---

37 Yes, it does.

This algorithm is known as

optimization by gradient descent[†]

[†]Thanks, Augustin-Louis Cauchy (1789–1857).

Who knew sliding down a slippery slope would be this much fun!

---

38 It sure is!

There is one more simplification we can make to our revision function

f

Let's look at the expression in our revision function that produces a new $\boldsymbol{\theta}$

```
(list
  (− θ0 (∗ α gs0))
  (− θ1 (∗ α gs1)))
```

What about it?

---

39 This expression is specific to a $\boldsymbol{\theta}$ that contains exactly two parameters.

Oh, so it works for target functions (like *line*) that need exactly two parameters in their $\boldsymbol{\theta}$s.

Exactly.

In general, we must produce a new $\boldsymbol{\theta}$ independent of the length of $\boldsymbol{\theta}$, and correspondingly of the length of *gs*.

40 Can we use *map* here?

Yes, we can.

At each member of $\boldsymbol{\theta}$ and *gs*, we have to subtract α times that member of *gs* from a member of $\boldsymbol{\theta}$. We can write this as a function of two arguments where *p* is a member in $\boldsymbol{\theta}$ and *g* is the corresponding member in *gs*

```
(λ (p g)
  (- p (* α g)))
```

41 Oh, now we *map* this function over

$\boldsymbol{\theta}$

and

gs

Correct.

We now rewrite the invocation of *revise*

```
(let ((f (λ (θ)
           (let ((gs (∇ obj θ)))
             (map (λ (p g)
                    (- p (* α g)))
               θ
               gs)))))
  (revise f 1000 (list 0.0 0.0)))
```

42 So we have replaced the lines

```
(list
  (- θ₀ (* α gs₀))
  (- θ₁ (* α gs₁)))
```

with a similar invocation using *map* from frame 25

```
(map (λ (p g)
       (- p (* α g)))
  θ
  gs)
```

Yes, correct.

43 Okay.

The parameterized function given by

((*l2-loss line*) *line-xs line-ys*)

is the objective function from frame 64:26 because our objective is to find the $\boldsymbol{\theta}$ that minimizes this function, i.e., that rolls us down the incline to the lowest point, representing the lowest loss.

We now express the complete gradient descent for our data set

```
(let ((α 0.01)
      (obj ((l2-loss line) line-xs line-ys)))
  (let ((f (λ (θ)
             (map (λ (p g)
                    (- p (* α g)))
               θ
               (∇ obj θ)))))
    (revise f 1000 (list 0.0 0.0))))
```

We are going to make a temporary adjustment. Except for the initial value of $\boldsymbol{\theta}$, we have two "*constant* scalars" in this expression

The number of revisions *revs*

and

the learning rate α

For now, let's **define** these names

```
(define revs 1000)

(define α 0.01)
```

How should we now express gradient descent?

44 Like this?

```
(let ((obj ((l2-loss line) line-xs line-ys)))
  (let ((f (λ (θ)
             (map (λ (p g)
                    (- p (* α g)))
               θ
               (∇ obj θ)))))
    (revise f revs (list 0.0 0.0))))
```

Excellent!

45 Okay.

In this expression, the value of *obj*

((l2-loss line) line-xs line-ys)

and the initial value of $\boldsymbol{\theta}$

(**list** 0.0 0.0)

become arguments to a function named

gradient-descent

We now define this algorithm as the function *gradient-descent*. The Θ[†] is a *renaming* of the formal of *f* from page xxiii

```
(define gradient-descent
  (λ (obj θ)
    (let ((f (λ (Θ)
               (map (λ (p g)
                      (- p (* α g)))
                 Θ
                 (∇ obj Θ)))))
      (revise f revs θ))))
```

This function *gradient-descent* gives us the ability to find the well-fitted $\boldsymbol{\theta}$s of many different objective functions with their own $\boldsymbol{\theta}$s.

[†]Prounounced "big theta."

46 And it is what we started out looking for!

What is Θ here?

The Θ is a formal of *f*, the revision function.[†]

[†]Again, we have consistently renamed $\boldsymbol{\theta}$ to Θ, as in frame 62:21.

47 Why have we introduced Θ?

48 Now it seems frivolous, but in fact we have

grate expectations[†]

for

Θ

But for now, Θ is simply a name we use for the formal of the revision function.

[†] Thanks, Charles Dickens (1812–1870) for your *Great Expectations*.

Okay, for now.

---

49 Where can the *initial* $\boldsymbol{\theta}$ and Θ be found?

$\boldsymbol{\theta}$ appears only where we invoke *revise*.

Θ appears only in the revision function.

---

50 Here is how we use a revision chart with *gradient-descent* to learn $\boldsymbol{\theta}_0$ and $\boldsymbol{\theta}_1$ with their initial estimates at 0.0

```
▷ (gradient-descent
    ((l2-loss line) line-xs line-ys)
    (list 0.0 0.0))
▶ (list 1.05 1.87e−06)
```

It's the same as the result in frame 33.

We now have a new learning toy!

---

51 Yes, we do!

We'll play with it in the upcoming interlude.

Whew! That's a relief.

Slippery Toys

That was quite a slippery slide.
Pull yourself up with a tiramisu!

Interlude II.

Too Many Toys Make Us Hyperactive

How was the tiramisu?

1 Could not get enough of it.

This interlude is about *hyperparameters.*

2 What are hyperparameters?

The temporarily-**define**d names like *revs* and α that control the behavior of *gradient-descent* are known as hyperparameters.

Hyperparameters are *always* names associated with *scalars* like these.

3 Why are they important?

These scalars vary by the problem under consideration and must be selected after some thought and experimentation.

4 So the scalars that we have picked for α and *revs* in *gradient-descent* from chapter 4 may not necessarily work in other situations?

That is correct.

There are other hyperparameters we encounter later.

To make our lives easier when using them, we introduce a new construct.

5 Interesting.

Can we pack them all up into a list as we did for $\boldsymbol{\theta}$?

No, a better way would be to treat them as a special kind of name.

6 What makes them special?

Once these names are declared as hyperparameters, they are available to be used in *any* function.

7 Okay.

Here is a nonsensical example

```
(declare-hyper smaller)

(declare-hyper larger)
```

Now, what is

(+ *smaller* *larger*)?

8 Because neither *smaller* nor *larger* is associated with a scalar, it has no value.

The Rule of Hyperparameters

Every hyperparameter either is a scalar or has no value.

Yes, that is correct.

What is the value of this expression?

```
(with-hypers
  ((smaller 1)
   (larger 2000))
  (+ smaller larger))
```

9 That should be 2001.†

Will either *smaller* or *larger* still be a scalar outside **with-hypers**?

†Thanks, Arthur C. Clarke (1917–2008).

No, they won't.

These hyperparameters have scalars associated with them only during **with-hypers** expressions.

10 Is **with-hypers** similar to **let**?

No, it is not.

A **let**-expression creates a new local name for a value, but a **with-hypers** provides a new value for a pre-existing name that has been declared as a hyperparameter.

11

That clarifies it!

Once these hyperparameters have scalars associated with them by **with-hypers**, those scalars are available to *all* functions using them.

After the *body*

(+ *smaller larger*)

if **with-hypers** has yielded a result, the hyperparameters would no longer have values.[†]

[†]This does not show the generality of **with-hypers**. In fact, **with-hypers** can be nested, so that coming out of the inner **with-hypers** still maintains the scalars associated with hyperparameters in the outer **with-hypers**.

12

So the hyperparameters are like our **define**d names, but they can be associated with scalars only when set up using **with-hypers**?

Yes, correct.

Now it gets more interesting. Suppose we define *nonsense?*, this mostly useless function

```
(define nonsense?
  (λ (x)
    (= (sub1 x) smaller)))
```

What is (*nonsense?* 6)?

13

Again, it has no value for the very same reason as before. The hyperparameter *smaller* has not yet been provided a scalar.

We discover, by providing a scalar for the hyperparameters in use

```
(with-hypers
  ((smaller 5))
  (nonsense? 6))
```

that the result is #t. To see how this works, imagine that the definition of *nonsense?* is also inside the **with-hypers**, and work it out from there.

14 Is (*nonsense?* 6) the body of this **with-hypers**?

Yes!

Explain how we get this result.

15 When *nonsense?* is invoked within **with-hypers**, the scalar *smaller* is 5, so (*nonsense?* 6) results in #t.

So why is *nonsense?* dashed?

That's because it is silly to use the name

nonsense?

16 Are we going to use hyperparameters in a new

gradient-descent?

Indeed, but that is for the next chapter.

17 Can't wait!

Hyperactive Toys

This diversion was too short for a break!
Grab another piece of tiramisu!

5
Target Practice

Are we all set to resume?

1 Can't wait!

It's time to generalize what we have learned so far.

2 Is this where we find out how Θ meets our g**rate** expectations?

No, we are not there yet, but we are getting closer.

3 Where should we start?

Now, we declare two sensible hyperparameters

```
(declare-hyper revs)

(declare-hyper α)
```

We have seen *revs* and α before, but not as hyperparameters.

4 How do we use these hyperparameters for *gradient-descent*?

Here's the dashed *gradient-descent* from frame 89:46. It repeats a single revision *revs* number of times, and for each revision it refines the result of the previous revision

```
(define gradient-descent
  (λ (obj θ)
    (let ((f (λ (Θ)
               (map (λ (p g)
                      (- p (* α g)))
                 Θ
                 (∇ obj Θ)))))
      (revise f revs θ))))
```

Now, remember *l2-loss*?

5 Here is *l2-loss* from frame 63:22

```
(define l2-loss
  (λ (target)
    (λ (xs ys)
      (λ (θ)
        (let ((pred-ys ((target xs) θ)))
          (sum
            (sqr
              (- ys pred-ys))))))))
```

This definition of *gradient-descent* uses the two hyperparameters

revs

and

α

Using *l2-loss* and **with-hypers** from frame 94:9, provide a scalar for each hyperparameter and show how to invoke *gradient-descent* in a revision chart.

6 Here is the revision chart

```
▷ (with-hypers
    ((revs 1000)
     (α 0.01))
    (gradient-descent
      ((l2-loss line) line-xs line-ys)
      (list 0.0 0.0)))
▶ (list 1.05 1.87e−06)
```

We have gotten the same result from frame 90:49, and we have cleanly separated out our hyperparameters.

The definitions of *gradient-descent* and *l2-loss* in frame 5 take functions as arguments and are not tied to a particular target function (like *line*).

7 This means that we can use these two functions for learning the $\boldsymbol{\theta}$ for *arbitrary* target functions.

That is liberating!

Here is a new data set

```
(define quad-xs
  [−1.0 0.0 1.0 2.0 3.0])

(define quad-ys
  [2.55 2.1 4.35 10.2 18.25])
```

Draw its corresponding graph.

8 These points are not on a line

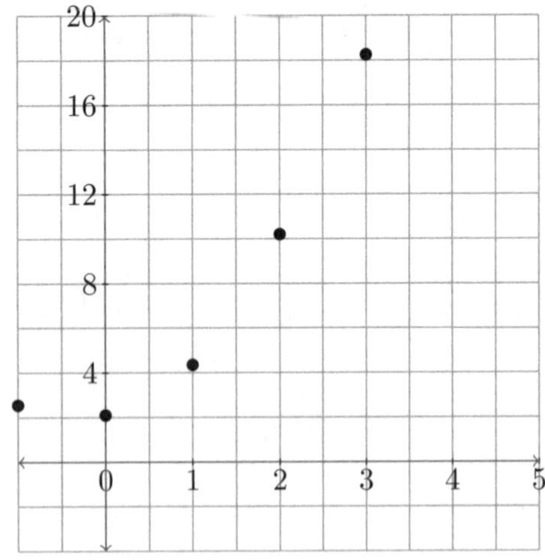

---

9 Indeed, they are not. So, we must learn the $\boldsymbol{\theta}$ of a different target function.

For this example, we use a simple *nonlinear* function.

What is a nonlinear function?

---

10 A nonlinear function is not *linear* in its arguments.

And ...

---

11 A linear function is one that uses only addition and *scaling* to find its result.

What is scaling?

---

12 Scaling multiplies its argument by a fixed value or by a parameter. For example

(* 5.0 x)

scales the value of x by 5.0.

And if we have a parameter

$\boldsymbol{\theta}_0$

then

(* $\boldsymbol{\theta}_0$ x)

scales the value of x by $\boldsymbol{\theta}_0$.

So, this is why *line* is a linear function. It scales its argument x with $\boldsymbol{\theta}_0$ and adds $\boldsymbol{\theta}_1$ to it.

What nonlinear function does the data set in frame 8 represent?

---

13 A very good question.

Let's make the assumption that this data set is *quadratic*.

What does *quadratic* mean?

---

14 It means that it can be predicted by a quadratic function.

What is a quadratic function?

15

Here is a general definition of a quadratic function[†]

```
(define quad                                  ●
  (λ (t)
    (λ (θ)
      (+ (* θ0 (sqr t))
         (+ (* θ1 t) θ2)))))
```

The function *quad* has three scalar parameters provided in a $\boldsymbol{\theta}$.

[†]This might look more familiar as the quadratic equation with t replaced by x

$$ax^2 + bx + c = 0$$

Could we see an example of how *quad* works?

16

Sure.

Let's take

t to be 3.0

and

$\boldsymbol{\theta}$ to be (**list** 4.5 2.1 7.8)

Show a same-as chart for this example.

Here it is

1. ((*quad* 3.0) (**list** 4.5 2.1 7.8))
2. (+ (∗ 4.5 (*sqr* 3.0))
   (+ (∗ 2.1 3.0) 7.8))
3. (+ 40.5
   (+ 6.3 7.8))
4. 54.6

Does the use of *sqr* make *quad* nonlinear?

17

Indeed it does.

Now we use *gradient-descent* with *l2-loss* as the loss function to learn the $\boldsymbol{\theta}$ for this data set with *quad* as the target function.

And what is the new expectant function from frame 63:24?

The expectant function is the loss function invoked on the target

(*l2-loss quad*)

And what is the objective function?

18 The objective function from frame 64:26 is the function obtained by invoking the expectant function on the new data set

((*l2-loss quad*) *quad-xs quad-ys*)

Great.

We invoke *gradient-descent* on this objective function and an initial $\boldsymbol{\theta}$.

What should this initial $\boldsymbol{\theta}$ be?

19 Can we use 0.0's

(**list** 0.0 0.0 0.0)

as we did before?

Yes, we can.

Now let's consider the hyperparameters.

20 That's right.

We are now finding the $\boldsymbol{\theta}$ for a different target function.

What scalars should we provide for the hyperparameters *revs* and α?

Since our target is a quadratic function that squares its argument, which here is *quad-xs*, it is likely that our gradients could get really large.

To avoid overshooting with large jumps between revisions, we guess a lower learning rate.

Experience tells us that 0.001 should be reasonable.

21 What about the scalar for *revs*?

For now, let's keep it at 1000, so our invocation of *gradient-descent* should be the body of the **with-hypers** in this revision chart

```
▷ (with-hypers
    ((revs 1000)
     (α 0.001))
    (gradient-descent
      ((l2-loss quad) quad-xs quad-ys)
      (list 0.0 0.0 0.0)))
▶ (list 1.48 0.99 2.05)
```

22 So, the result of *gradient-descent* with these hyperparameters and its target is

```
(list 1.48 0.99 2.05)
```

We have learned that the three values of the parameters for *quad* are 1.48, 0.99, and 2.05. This is similar to how we previously learned the values of $\boldsymbol{\theta}_0$ and $\boldsymbol{\theta}_1$ for *line*!

We have used *gradient-descent* with a target function other than *line*!

Indeed!

Now we let go of some more assumptions in how we use *gradient-descent* and *l2-loss*.

Here's a new data set

```
(define plane-xs
  [[1.0 2.05]
   [1.0 3.0]
   [2.0 2.0]
   [2.0 3.91]
   [3.0 6.13]
   [4.0 8.09]])

(define plane-ys
  [13.99
   15.99
   18.0
   22.4
   30.2
   37.94])
```

23 This data set is different since *plane-xs* is a tensor^{2} made up of

6 2-element tensors^{1}

whereas *plane-ys* is a tensor^{1} made up of

6 scalars

24 Yes, that is correct.[†]

In the data sets

(*line-xs*, *line-ys*)

and

(*quad-xs*, *quad-ys*)

the *xs* and *ys* have always been tensors^1 of the same shape.

Now we expand this. We allow the *xs* and *ys* to be of different shapes, but both must have the same number of nested tensors. In other words, we would require that

⸢*xs*⸣

and

⸢*ys*⸣

be the same.

To refresh our understanding of how ⸢*xs*⸣ and ⸢*ys*⸣ would behave, see frame 33:17.

[†]Just as a line is a linear relationship between the two coordinates of a point in 2 dimensions, a plane is a linear relationship between the coordinates of a point in 3 dimensions.

How does this generalization impact *gradient-descent* and *l2-loss*?

25 Great question.

Here is a target function similar to *line*

```
(define plane                                    ●
  (λ (t)
    (λ (θ)
      (+ (• θ₀ t) θ₁))))
```

Here *t*, the argument to *plane*, is a tensor^1. This is different from *line*, which expects a scalar instead.

And what is •[†]?

[†]Pronounced "dot product."

Thanks, Josiah Willard Gibbs (1839–1903) and Edwin Bidwell Wilson (1879–1964).

The function $\bullet^{1,1}$ is defined

```
(define •^{1,1}                                    •
  (λ (w t)
    (sum^1
      (* w t))))
```

where w and t are tensors of rank 1, and both must have the same shape.

26 Could we see an example of what it does?

Sure.

Here, for example, $\bullet^{1,1}$ takes two tensors[1]

1. $(\bullet^{1,1}$ [2.0 1.0 7.0] [8.0 4.0 3.0])
2. (sum^1
   (∗ [2.0 1.0 7.0] [8.0 4.0 3.0]))

Complete the same-as chart.

27 Here it is

3. (sum^1
   [(∗ 2.0 8.0) (∗ 1.0 4.0) (∗ 7.0 3.0)])
4. (sum^1
   [16.0 4.0 21.0])
5. 41.0

We multiply the scalars pairwise yielding a new tensor[1] and then finally we produce the *sum* of the new tensor.

Using the $\bullet^{1,1}$ function is a way of multiplying two tensors[1] and producing a single scalar.

We get the extended function • by extending this definition of $\bullet^{1,1}$ to include tensors of rank higher than 1.

28 Okay.

The rank of the resulting tensor is then one lower than its arguments.

29 Isn't this because of the law from page 54?

The Rule of Data Sets

In a data set (*xs*, *ys*)
both *xs* and *ys* must have the same number of elements.
The elements of *xs*, however, can have a different shape from the elements of *ys*.

Indeed.

Now we learn the well-fitted $\boldsymbol{\theta}$ for *plane* from this data set using

l2-loss

and

gradient-descent

We begin by trying to find the initial estimate for $\boldsymbol{\theta}$.

What should it be?

30 But to do that we need to know the shapes of $\boldsymbol{\theta}_0$ and $\boldsymbol{\theta}_1$ in frame 25.

How do we find them?

We determine them using the shape of the tensors from our data set

(*plane-xs*, *plane-ys*)

knowing that they will be used as arguments to *plane*.

We know that each element in *plane-xs* is a tensor[1], and that each element in *plane-ys* is a scalar.

31 Aha!

So when we invoke *plane* on an element from *plane-xs*, a well fitted $\boldsymbol{\theta}$ must produce a result that is the same shape as an element of *plane-ys*.

Correct.

Since • behaves exactly like *sum*, and produces a result that is one rank lower than its arguments, in order to produce a scalar, its arguments must both be tensors^{1} of the same length.

So, what should the shape of $\boldsymbol{\theta}_0$ be?

32 The first argument to • is

$\boldsymbol{\theta}_0$

The second argument, in frame 26, is a tensor^{1} from

plane-xs

So, the shape of $\boldsymbol{\theta}_0$ must be the same shape as a tensor^{1} from *plane-xs*, which is

(**list** 2)

Correct.

And what about the shape of $\boldsymbol{\theta}_1$?

33 The tensor

$\boldsymbol{\theta}_1$

should have the same shape as the result of the function

plane

from frame 25, which must be the shape of every scalar drawn from

plane-ys

and so $\boldsymbol{\theta}_1$ must be a scalar, thus its shape is

(**list**)

In other words, $\boldsymbol{\theta}_1$ is a scalar.

Correct, again.

Now determine the initial list of parameters $\boldsymbol{\theta}$, using shapes that are based on how they are used inside the target function, for example, in frames 25 and 26:25.

34 How about this

(**list** [0.0 0.0] 0.0)

where

$\boldsymbol{\theta}_0$ is initialized to a tensor^{1} [0.0 0.0]

and

$\boldsymbol{\theta}_1$ is initialized to the scalar 0.0

The Rule of Parameters

(Final Version)

Every parameter is a tensor.

Perfect.

Here, $\boldsymbol{\theta}_0$ and $\boldsymbol{\theta}_1$ have different shapes. Because $\boldsymbol{\theta}$ is a list, its members, unlike the elements of a tensor, can have different shapes.

35 Does having different shapes mean we have to rewrite some of our functions?

No, not at all.

36 That's a relief.

The Rule of θ

$\boldsymbol{\theta}$ is a list of parameters that can have different shapes.

We need just one more thing!

We need to decide what scalars to provide for hyperparameters *revs* and α.

For a first guess, let's keep the same scalars as for *quad* in frame 22.

37 Okay.

Now show the revision chart using **with-hypers** for the data set in frame 23.

38 Here it is

```
▷ (with-hypers
    ((revs 1000)
     (α 0.001))
    (gradient-descent
      ((l2-loss plane) plane-xs plane-ys)
      (list [0.0 0.0] 0.0)))
▶ (list [3.98 2.04] 5.78)
```

Excellent.

We have found the

well-fitted $\boldsymbol{\theta}$

39 How do we know it is the correct one?

We'll test it on one of the points from the data set given in frame 23.

Let's pick

plane-xs$|_3$

```
1. ((plane [2.0 3.91])
    (list [3.98 2.04] 5.78))
2. (+ (• [3.98 2.04] [2.0 3.91])
      5.78)
3. 21.71
```

40 That's reasonably close to *plane-ys*$|_3$, the given value 22.4.

Why aren't they exactly the same?

Because data sets are often noisy and target functions usually don't fit them exactly. A close enough match is typically all we can expect.

41 Now it's time for a break!

Toys for Target Practice

That was some heavy lifting!

Time for a *besan laddoo* (बेसन लड्डू)!

Interlude III

The Shape of Things to Come[†]

[†]Thanks, Herbert George Wells (1866–1946).

Target practice is over.

1 Whew!

At least we got to enjoy some *laddoos*.

What is the shape of this tensor^2

```
[[2 4 5]
 [6 7 9]]?
```

2 It is

```
(list 2 3)
```

Let's annotate this tensor^2 with its shape

$$\begin{matrix}[[2\ 4\ 5] \\ \ [6\ 7\ 9]]_{(2\ 3)}\end{matrix}$$

3 That makes it a little easier to understand its shape.

We now drop the nested square brackets and write it[†]

$$\begin{bmatrix}2 & 4 & 5 \\ 6 & 7 & 9\end{bmatrix}_{(2\ 3)}$$

[†] We write tensors^2 the same way that matrices are normally written. Furthermore, we annotate the tensor with a shape.

4 It appears that each inner tensor^1 is written as a separate row, without the enclosing brackets.

This is a less cluttered notation, but when defining functions we assume that these tensors are written in their nested form as in frame 2.

Yes, that is correct.

An important instance of this is a tensor^2 where every row is a tensor^1 of exactly one scalar.

5 Could we see an example?

Here is a tensor^2

[[5] [7] [8]]

which is written like this[†]

$$\begin{bmatrix}5\\7\\8\end{bmatrix}_{(3\ 1)}$$

[†] This is known as a *column matrix*.

6 So, we can understand the rank and shape of the tensor without counting brackets as in the law on page 35.

How can we write the tensor^2

[[5 7 8]]?

Tricky question!

The tensor^2

[[5 7 8]]

has the shape

(**list** 1 3)

So we write it[†]

$$\begin{bmatrix}5 & 7 & 8\end{bmatrix}_{(1\ 3)}$$

[†] This is known as a *row matrix*.

7 This looks troublingly similar to

[5 7 8]

But that is a different tensor since its shape is

(**list** 3)

Indeed

[5 7 8]

is a tensor^1 that has the shape

(**list** 3)

so we could have written it

$$\begin{bmatrix}5 & 7 & 8\end{bmatrix}_{(3)}$$

To keep things simple, however, we'll drop the shape annotation for all tensors^1.

8 So

[5 7 8]

is simply a tensor^1 with 3 scalars, whereas

$$\begin{bmatrix}5 & 7 & 8\end{bmatrix}_{(1\ 3)}$$

is a tensor^2 with 1 tensor^1.

It's time for some apples!

Honey Crisp?

6
An Apple a Day

Are we ready for some apples?

1 Yes, we are! Do apples have anything to do with our burning desire to learn how Θ meets our gr**ate** expectations?

No, but we are at the penultimate moment. Just wait a little longer. We've been setting the table a little bit at a time.

2 Waiting with bated breath.

Good.

Let's move on to them apples!

The data sets so far contain very few points. Real data sets, however, have thousands, millions, or even billions of points.

3 Why is that a problem?

Here, again, is *l2-loss* from frame 63:22

```
(define l2-loss
  (λ (target)
    (λ (xs ys)
      (λ (θ)
        (let ((pred-ys ((target xs) θ)))
          (sum
            (sqr
              (− ys pred-ys))))))))
```

This *l2-loss* uses the entire data set (i.e., the tensors *xs* and *ys*) each time it is invoked. That's because it is finding the difference between the *ys* in the data set and the corresponding *pred-ys*, those predicted by the target.

4 So, *gradient-descent* invokes *l2-loss*, this *loss* function, *revs* times and at each revision it uses the entire data set.

Is that a problem?

It is, but more importantly, it is unnecessary.

There's a better way that does not require traversing the entire data set thousands of times.

5 What is this better way?

We'll get to that very soon.

We first need to understand *sampling*.

6 What is sampling?

Imagine an apple-grower, say Maria,[†] who has picked 1000 apples to sell at a market.

[†]Thanks, Maria "Granny" Ann Smith née Sherwood (1799–1870) for first cultivating the Granny Smith variety from a chance seedling.

7 What do apples have to do with anything?

They're delicious, and they keep the doctor away.

Actually, they may not be delicious, unless Maria has made sure they are of high quality.

8 So what is she to do?

A very good question, indeed.

Maria can't take a bite of *every* apple! That would make every apple completely worthless.

9 What can she do to avoid tasting *every* apple?

Maria randomly picks a small number of apples to taste.

10 Aha!

She *samples* a few apples.

That is correct.

By tasting enough apples, Maria gets a very good approximation of how delicious all the apples are and how much they can sell for at the market.

What is Maria's problem similar to?

11 It is similar to what's happening in frame 4. If we visit every point with each revision, it is a lot like tasting *every* apple.

Can we use sampling to solve this problem?

Yes, we can!

Using a small random sample of a few points from the data set produces a good enough approximation of loss, which can be used to revise $\boldsymbol{\theta}$. We refer to this sample as a *batch* and its generation as *sampling a batch* from the data set.

12 So each revision examines only a small fraction of the whole data set.

Yes, and we repeat this over many revisions, with new samples for each revision, to get as close to the ideal loss as possible.

13 How do we accomplish this?

We start with our still-dashed *gradient-descent* from frame 99:5

```
(define gradient-descent
  (λ (obj θ)
    (let ((f (λ (Θ)
               (map (λ (p g)
                      (− p (∗ α g)))
                 Θ
                 (∇ obj Θ)))))
      (revise f revs θ))))
```

What can we say about the objective function *obj*, and the *xs* and *ys* from a data set?

14 We get an objective function when an expectant function is invoked with *xs* and *ys*.

For example, for the expectant function

(*l2-loss line*)

and the data set from frame 24:17, the objective function is

((*l2-loss line*) *line-xs line-ys*)

The objective function produces the loss for a given $\boldsymbol{\theta}$ and our objective is to make this loss as close to the ideal as possible.

Yes.

In general terms, we can write

((*l2-loss target*) *xs ys*)

where

target is the target function

and

(*xs*, *ys*) is a given data set

15 And *l2-loss* is a loss function.

If we want to invoke the expectant function

(*l2-loss target*)

with batches sampled only from *xs* and *ys*, we must randomly sample paired tensors from *xs* and *ys* at each revision, and pass those sampled tensors to the expectant function.

16 That suggests we need to create a support function!

It does, indeed! But we need some basics first.

If i is a natural number less than $\nmid xs \nmid$, which is the same as $\nmid ys \nmid$, what is the ith point in the data set?

17 The ith point is made up of

the ith element from *xs*

and

the ith element from *ys*

Correct. We use i as an index as we did in frame 53:24.

So, to sample a batch, we generate a few random indices, and then select the corresponding elements from *xs* and *ys*. We refer to these random indices as

a *batch* of *indices*

18 How do we generate a batch of indices?

The Rule of Batches

A batch of indices consists of random indices that are natural numbers smaller than $\nmid xs \nmid$.

We use the function *samples*. It takes two arguments. The first, n, is the number of points in the data set. The second, s, is the size of the sample set. Both are natural numbers greater than one, and s is less than or equal to n.

19 Why do we name the function *samples*?

That's because it picks a batch of indices in the same way that Maria picks random apples to taste.

20 Okay.

Invoking *samples* results in a list with s members, each being a randomly chosen index less than n. Here, we find a batch of 3 indices from a data set of length 20

(*samples* 20 3)

And here is an example of what it might return, since the indices are random

(list 18 2 11)

21 How is *samples* defined?

---

22 To define *samples*, we first need to learn how to randomly generate natural numbers for indices.

Okay.

We do that using *random*, which accepts one argument, n, a positive natural number, and generates a randomly selected index from 0 to $n - 1$. For example

(*random*† 45)

might produce

31

or any other index from 0 to 44.

†Every time *random* is invoked, it probably generates a different random natural number from its previous invocation.

How do we use *random* to generate a list of indices?

---

23 Here is a skeleton for *samples*

```
(define samples
  (λ (n s)
    (sampled n s (list))))

(define sampled
  (λ (n i a)
    (cond
      ((zero? i) a)
      (else
       (sampled n (sub1 i)
         (cons [    R    ] a))))))
```

Here we use the support function *sampled*, where we are counting down from s to 0, and at each step we accumulate a randomly generated index.

Find R.

Since we are accumulating randomly generated indices, R must be

(*random n*)

Great.

This is the final version of *samples*

```
(define samples                          •
  (λ (n s)
    (sampled n s (list))))

(define sampled
  (λ (n i a)
    (cond
      ((zero? i) a)
      (else
       (sampled n (sub1 i)
         (cons (random n) a))))))
```

Does *sampled* meet the requirements of simple accumulator passing on page 43?

24 Indeed it does.

The invocation of *sampled* is not wrapped, so we need look at only the formals of *sampled*

n does not change

i changes towards passing a base test

and

a accumulates a result[†]

[†]Since each number in *a* is chosen randomly, their order in the batch of indices does not matter.

Perfect.

Since *samples* picks indices randomly, does

(*samples* 20 3)

give the same answer at each revision?

25 It shouldn't.

That's correct, most of the time.[†]

At each revision, *samples* results in a new batch of indices. So, provided the size of the data set *n* is large enough, the chances of it producing the same *s* indices at every revision are very small.

[†]A single invocation of *samples* might also have repeated indices since each index is picked independently of the others.

26 So, now that we know how to randomly sample indices, how do we use these indices to get a batch from the data set?

We need a new toy for this!

Once again, $t|_i$ selects the ith element from a tensor t where i is the *index*.

Now we show how to select more than one element from the tensor t. Here, the elements to select are given by a batch b, of indices. We pick these elements from t

$t\|_b$

This results in a tensor of the same rank as t, but containing only those elements in t that correspond to the batch b of indices.

27 Could we see an example?

Sure.

Let's take t to be a tensor[1] with 7 elements

[5.0 2.8 4.2 2.3 7.4 1.7 8.1]

Here is a list b of 4 indices

(**list** 6 0 3 1)

28 How do we use this list of indices?

This way

1. $t\|_b$
2. $[5.0\ 2.8\ 4.2\ 2.3\ 7.4\ 1.7\ 8.1]\|_{(\textsf{list}\ 6\ 0\ 3\ 1)}$
3. [8.1 5.0 2.3 2.8]

29 Can t have a rank higher than 1?

Yes, t's rank can be higher than 1.

Here's an example where t is a tensor[2], and b is the list from the previous example

1. $t\|_b$
2. $\begin{bmatrix} 5.0 & 1.0 & 2.1 \\ 2.8 & 3.3 & 7.4 \\ 4.2 & 6.7 & 8.2 \\ 2.3 & 3.4 & 5.1 \\ 7.4 & 8.0 & 9.1 \\ 1.7 & 3.0 & 2.7 \\ 8.1 & 9.3 & 5.4 \end{bmatrix}_{(7\ 3)} \|_{(\textsf{list}\ 6\ 0\ 3\ 1)}$
3. $\begin{bmatrix} 8.1 & 9.3 & 5.4 \\ 5.0 & 1.0 & 2.1 \\ 2.3 & 3.4 & 5.1 \\ 2.8 & 3.3 & 7.4 \end{bmatrix}_{(4\ 3)}$

30 This looks like a useful toy.

Are we now ready to define the support function we suggested in frame 16?

We are, indeed!

Here is a skeleton of a function *sampling-obj* that takes three arguments. The first, *expectant*, is an expectant function and the other two, *xs* and *ys*, form a data set

```
(define sampling-obj
  (λ (expectant xs ys)
    (let ((n |xs|))
      (λ (θ)
        (let ((b [         B         ]))
          ((expectant [X] [Y]) θ))))))
```

31 This function seems to be returning another function

(λ (θ) ...)

Correct.

It returns an objective function that samples the data set instead of using the entire data set.

Find the expressions for B, X, and Y.

32 In this skeleton, b should be a batch of indices (which is a list), and X and Y must correspond to the samples extracted from the data set using those indices.

So, B should result in a list of sampled indices. But we're missing some information.

How large should our batch of indices be?

A very good question.

The batch size usually varies depending upon the data set and the kind of target function we are dealing with.

33 So should we just declare it as a hyperparameter?

Yes

```
(declare-hyper batch-size) ●
```

Now, what is B in frame 31?

34 B should generate a batch of indices using

samples

with the number of points we have in the data set

$|xs|$

as the first argument, and

batch-size

as the second argument. But in the body of the **let**-expression, $|xs|$ is associated with n. So, B should be

(*samples n batch-size*)

Perfect.

What about X and Y?

35 Those expressions should use b to select the corresponding tensor from the formals *xs* and *ys*.

So X should be

$xs\|_b$

and Y should be

$ys\|_b$

Correct.

Here's *sampling-obj*

```
(define sampling-obj                              ●
  (λ (expectant xs ys)
    (let ((n ⫳xs⫳))
      (λ (θ)
        (let ((b (samples n batch-size)))
          ((expectant xs‖b ys‖b) θ))))))
```

36 How do we use *sampling-obj*?

When we invoke *gradient-descent*, we now give it a *sampling-obj*.

For example

```
(with-hypers
  ((revs 1000)
   (α 0.01)
   (batch-size 4))
  (gradient-descent
    (sampling-obj
      (l2-loss line) line-xs line-ys)
    (list 0.0 0.0)))
```

Here our new hyperparameter *batch-size* is given the scalar 4.

37 This means that at each revision, we use only a batch of size 4 from the data set to measure the loss. So, we examine a mere

(∗ 4 1000)

points in total, instead of running through the entire data set at each revision.

And even if our data set has billions of points, each revision looks at only 4, right?

100% correct!

At each revision a new batch with only *batch-size* points is selected.

This kind of gradient descent where the objective function uses sampling is known as

stochastic gradient descent

38 What does *stochastic* mean?

The Law of Batch Sizes

Each revision in stochastic gradient descent uses only a batch of size *batch-size* from the data set and the ranks of the tensors in the batch are the same as the ranks of the tensors in the data set.

An excellent question.

Stochastic is another way of saying we use random numbers to determine our results. Using *samples* as part of our objective function is what makes it stochastic.

39 Does stochastic gradient descent work for different targets?

It does! Let's return to our example from frame 105:25 using *plane* as our target function.

What does our expectant function look like?

40 Since our target function is *plane*, the expectant function must be

(*l2-loss plane*)

Correct.

Let us take

revs to be 15000

α to be 0.001

and

batch-size to be 4

41 Then our hyperparameters should look like

```
(with-hypers
  ((revs 15000)
   (α 0.001)
   (batch-size 4))
  ...)
```

From frame 108:34, the initial $\boldsymbol{\theta}$ is

(list [0.0 0.0] 0.0)

How is *gradient-descent* invoked?

42 Using this revision chart

```
▷ (with-hypers
    ((revs 15000)
     (α 0.001)
     (batch-size 4))
    (gradient-descent
      (sampling-obj
        (l2-loss plane) plane-xs plane-ys)
      (list [0.0 0.0] 0.0)))
▶ (list [3.98 1.97] 6.16)
```

Great. That's enough for now.

43 Good! A break would be wonderful.

Random Toys

Go have a slice of apple pie!

Preferably à la mode!

7 The Crazy
"ates"

How was the pie?

1 Warm and smothered with a dollop of vanilla ice cream.

Mmm. Delicious.

Here we teach our new toy
gradient-descent
some new tricks.

2 What kinds of tricks?

Tricks that make it more flexible, so we can change its behavior.

3 Why would we want to change its behavior?

So that it gets to its well-fitted $\boldsymbol{\theta}$ with fewer revisions (i.e., a smaller value for *revs*).

4 That's a good reason.

So how do we make it more flexible?

One of the reasons why *gradient-descent* from frame 99:5 is unable to get to its well-fitted $\boldsymbol{\theta}$ with fewer revisions is because it has very little information to work from.

5 What other information does it need?

Before we get to the details of that, what matters here is that we must find a way to hold this information and bring it up to date as the parameter is revised.

The first thing to remember is that this extra information is associated with each parameter in $\boldsymbol{\theta}$.

We'll build up to this one step at a time.

6 Okay.

We start with our most recent and still dashed *gradient-descent*

```
(define gradient-descent
  (λ (obj θ)
    (let ((f (λ (Θ)
               (map (λ (p g)
                      (- p (* α g)))
                 Θ
                 (∇ obj Θ)))))
      (revise f revs θ))))
```

7 Are we finally going to reveal how Θ meets our gr**ate** expectations from frame 90:48?

Indeed, this is the ultimate moment!

What does *map* do in this function?

8 It invokes this function

```
(λ (p g)
  (- p (* α g)))
```

on every member of

Θ

and

(∇ *obj* Θ)

in a pairwise fashion.

Correct.

In this dashed *gradient-descent*, we use *revise* to repeatedly revise a *list of parameters.*

Much like *map*, the function *revise* is a general-purpose function. We can use it to revise any kind of value.

As long as we're careful to make sure that *gradient-descent* accepts a **θ** and ultimately results in a well-fitted **θ**, it doesn't matter how we transform **θ** along the way.

9 Could we see an example revising a different kind of value?

The Law of Revisions

As long as we make sure that *gradient-descent* accepts an initial $\boldsymbol{\theta}$ and results in a well-fitted $\boldsymbol{\theta}$, any reasonable way of revising it from the first to the last revision is okay.

Sure, here is a mostly useless example but it serves to illustrate a trick for transforming our parameters by first wrapping them up and then unwrapping them later.†

What is the value of this expression?

```
(map (λ (p)
        (list p))
  θ)
```

†This use of the terms wrapp*ing* (*ed*) and unwrapp*ing* (*ed*) for parameters is different from their use describing recursive definitions in chapter 2.

10 It wraps each parameter p in $\boldsymbol{\theta}$ into a singleton‡ and therefore produces a list of singletons.

‡A list with one member.

Yes.

Whenever a parameter is wrapped in a list, we refer to it as

an accompanied parameter†

†From 1964, *The Miles Davis Quintet* would have been *The Miles Davis Singleton* were it not for his accompaniments of
Tony Williams (1945–1997).
Wayne Shorter (1933–),
Ron Carter (1937–), and
Herbie Hancock (1940–),
Its parameter, however, would have been
Miles Davis (1926–1991).
Thanks to all.

11 But here nothing is accompanying the parameter in this list, correct?

That's correct. The parameter is keeping itself company.

This is our *lonely representation.*[†]
Θ is a list of accompanied parameters, but in this lonely representation, there are no accompaniments.

12 How do we use this lonely representation?

[†]The lonely representation simply shows an example where the list has no accompaniments. We'll be adding information to accompany parameters to get more meaningful representations.

We are going to use it for revisions within *gradient-descent.*

But first, we make sure we can convert back and forth between Θ and ***θ***. So we need two support functions. Here's the first one. It takes a ***θ*** and converts it to a Θ.

We refer to it as *lonely-i*, with *i* for *inf*late

```
(define lonely-i
  (λ (θ)
    (map (λ (p)
           (list p))
      θ)))
```

Explain *lonely-i.*

13 It takes a ***θ*** and it wraps each parameter in ***θ*** in a list, giving us a Θ.

Correct.

Now define *lonely-d*, with *d* for *def*late, that does the opposite. It takes a Θ and results in a ***θ***.

14 So, we can *map* over Θ and pick the *revised* parameter out of each accompanied parameter

```
(define lonely-d
  (λ (Θ)
    (map (λ (P)
           P₀)
      Θ)))
```

Here P is an accompanied parameter, correct?

Yes.

15 How can we tell P from p?

Θ is a list of P and $\boldsymbol{\theta}$ is a list of p!

16 Oh! It's pretty obvious now!

Since we are now revising Θ and not $\boldsymbol{\theta}$, we define a function that does the revision for us

```
(define lonely-u
  (λ (Θ gs)
    (map (λ (P g)
           (list (− P₀ (∗ α g))))
      Θ
      gs)))
```

The *u* in *lonely-u* stands for *upd*ate, because this function is an instance of what are referred to as *update functions.*

Explain *lonely-u*.

17 This function maps over Θ and the gradients *gs* in a pairwise fashion. Since each member of Θ is a singleton, we extract the parameter from the accompanied parameter and use the gradient and the learning rate to produce the revised parameter.

But why does it wrap the result in a list?

That's because *lonely-u* must result in a revised Θ rather than a revised $\boldsymbol{\theta}$.

18 Ah!

Wrapping the result in a list ensures that the well-fitted Θ is still a list of singletons.

We use these three functions

lonely-i

lonely-d

and

lonely-u

to generalize *gradient-descent*.

19 How can we do that?

Rather than scattering the three "ates" throughout the *gradient-descent*, we pass them to a more general *gradient-descent*

```
(define gradient-descent
  (λ (inflate deflate update)
    (λ (obj θ)
      ...)))
```

Now define *lonely-gradient-descent* using this new

gradient-descent

20 Here it is!

```
(define lonely-gradient-descent
  (gradient-descent
    lonely-i lonely-d lonely-u))
```

And we see that those "ates" rhyme!

Interesting, right.

Let's now use this more general skeleton of *gradient-descent*

```
(define gradient-descent
  (λ (inflate deflate update)
    (λ (obj θ)
      (let ((f (λ (Θ)
                 ([ U ]
                   Θ
                   (∇ obj
                     [ D ])))))
        ([ R ]
          (revise f revs
            [ I ]))))))
```

Find I, D, U, and R.

21 Since we are revising a list of singletons, that means we must invoke *revise* with an initial Θ. So, I must be

(inflate **θ***)*

D is the second argument to ∇, so it has to be a list of parameters. This means we must convert the Θ back to a **θ**. So, D must be

(deflate Θ*)*

U must be invoked to update Θ, so U must be

update

Finally, *gradient-descent* must result in a **θ**. The invocation of *revise*, however, results in a Θ. So when we're done, we must convert the well-fitted Θ back to the well-fitted **θ**. So R must be

deflate

Excellent.

Here is our penultimate *gradient-descent*

```
(define gradient-descent
  (λ (inflate deflate update)
    (λ (obj θ)
      (let ((f (λ (Θ)
                 (update
                   Θ
                   (∇ obj
                     (deflate Θ))))))
        (deflate
          (revise f revs
            (inflate θ)))))))
```

22 And it is still dashed!

Yes, it is.

But we should test it before we go ahead. And we're going to do this a lot with different values of *inflate*, *deflate*, and *update*, so let's make things a little easier for ourselves.

Define a function *try-plane* that takes a function argument *a-gradient-descent*, which can be invoked within the **with-hypers**-expression in frame 129:42.

23 Here is this new dashed definition

```
(define try-plane
  (λ (a-gradient-descent)
    (with-hypers
      ((revs 15000)
       (α 0.001)
       (batch-size 4))
      (a-gradient-descent
        (sampling-obj
          (l2-loss plane) plane-xs plane-ys)
        (list [0.0 0.0] 0.0)))))
```

We use *try-plane* with a specific gradient-descent function, for example

lonely-gradient-descent

24 This definition is very convenient!

Here is the revision chart

▷ (*try-plane lonely-gradient-descent*)

► (**list** [3.98 1.97] 6.16)

It is perfect!

Even though there's a lot of wrapping and unwrapping along the way, it still arrives at the same result as before in frame 129:42.

25 It is a useful function to try the same test repeatedly.

Let's look at another representation, where Θ is identical to **θ**. We refer to this as the *naked* representation.

Here, *p*, which must be deflated, and P, which is inflated, are identical.

Define the *inflate* function.

26 Even though **θ** is identical to Θ, we should stick with the pattern, so *naked-i* maps the identity function over **θ**

```
(define naked-i
  (λ (θ)
    (map (λ (p)
           (let ((P p))
             P))
      θ)))
```

Similarly, *naked-d* takes a P, which must be inflated, and yields a deflated *p* that is identical.

Now define the *deflate* function for this representation.

27 Using the same pattern we have

```
(define naked-d
  (λ (Θ)
    (map (λ (P)
           (let ((p P))
             p))
      Θ)))
```

Exactly!

Knowing that **θ** and Θ are the same, define *naked-u*.

28 **θ** and Θ are the same, so here is *naked-u*

```
(define naked-u
  (λ (Θ gs)
    (map (λ (P g)
           (- P (* α g)))
      Θ
      gs)))
```

Couldn't we have used P_0 instead of P?

No, using P_0 would have assumed that P is accompanied.

29 So, P is not accompanied because *naked-i* merely maps the identity function.

Now define *naked-gradient-descent*.

30 Here it is

```
(define naked-gradient-descent
  (gradient-descent
    naked-i naked-d naked-u))
```

Excellent.

Rewrite the example from frame 24, this time using the naked representation.

31 And here's its revision chart

▷ (*try-plane naked-gradient-descent*)

► (list [3.98 1.97] 6.16)

But the definitions for the lonely and naked representations are still dashed!

They are. We're going to simplify them.

To do that, let's consider something

crazy

Each definition of *inflate* and *deflate*, respectively, looks like this!

```
(define inflate
  (λ (θ)
    (map (λ (p)
           ...)
      θ)))

(define deflate
  (λ (Θ)
    (map (λ (P)
           ...)
      Θ)))
```

And what about *update*?

32 Here it is

```
(define update
  (λ (Θ gs)
    (map (λ (P g)
           ...)
      Θ
      gs)))
```

Why does this matter?

Great question!

And here's what's crazy about the "ates" from frame 20. If we make a consistent change to the dashed *gradient-descent*, we can simplify each of these definitions.

33 How is that possible?

Observe that we pass arguments into each "ate" function and then invoke *map* over them.

34 That is true.

We can use this observation to move the *maps* about so our "ates" can be simplified.

Any thoughts lurking about?

35 Nothing at all.

Let's take *inflate*.

Our current *gradient-descent* invokes *inflate* on $\boldsymbol{\theta}$ like this

(*inflate* $\boldsymbol{\theta}$)

Since the *inflate* functions we have seen so far rely on knowing that $\boldsymbol{\theta}$ is a list and each of them maps some λ-expression over this list, we can rewrite this invocation of inflate temporarily like this

(*map* (λ (*p*) ...) $\boldsymbol{\theta}$)

36 Oh, so regardless of what kind of *inflate* function we encounter, it always starts with invoking *map*.

Correct!

So, we can simplify *inflate* functions by moving the *map* to *gradient-descent*, and letting the *inflate* be simply the λ-expression.

37 Shouldn't that also work for the

deflate

and the

update?

Yes, and here's the crazy answer.

For uses of an "ate" in *gradient-descent*

(*ate* $\boldsymbol{\theta}$) becomes (*map ate* $\boldsymbol{\theta}$)

(*ate* Θ) becomes (*map ate* Θ)

and

(*ate* Θ *gs*) becomes (*map ate* Θ *gs*)

Refine the dashed *gradient-descent* one last time, but this time, the crazy way to get the final *gradient-descent*.

38 Here is the ultim**ate** *gradient-descent*

```
(define gradient-descent                          •
  (λ (inflate deflate update)
    (λ (obj θ)
      (let ((f (λ (Θ)
                 (map update
                   Θ
                   (∇ obj
                     (map deflate Θ))))))
        (map deflate
          (revise f revs
            (map inflate θ)))))))
```

With this final *gradient-descent*, we must remove the *maps* from the definition of each "ate".

Let us start with *lonely-i* in frame 13

```
(define lonely-i
  (λ (θ)
    (map (λ (p)
           (list p))
      θ)))
```

How should we refine this to go with our final *gradient-descent*?

39 Since *gradient-descent* is now responsible for mapping the inflate function over $\boldsymbol{\theta}$, *lonely-i* should be this

```
(define lonely-i
  (λ (p)
    (list p)))
```

And what about *lonely-d* and *lonely-u*?

40 Here they are

```
(define lonely-d
  (λ (P)
    P₀))

(define lonely-u
  (λ (P g)
    (list (− P₀ (* α g)))))
```

The Law of the Crazy "ates"

For any representation, the three "ates" are concerned with only one parameter and its accompaniments, and are not directly concerned with either $\boldsymbol{\theta}$ or Θ.

41

Correct.

Here is the new *lonely-gradient-descent*

```
(define lonely-gradient-descent
  (gradient-descent
    lonely-i lonely-d lonely-u))
```

Where is the revision chart in frame 24?

Here it is

▷ (*try-plane lonely-gradient-descent*)

► (list [3.98 1.97] 6.16)

42

Now we have the same experience with the naked representation. First, refine

naked-i

naked-d

and

naked-u

How are these "ates"?

```
(define naked-i
  (λ (p)
    (let ((P p))
      P)))

(define naked-d
  (λ (P)
    (let ((p P))
      p)))

(define naked-u
  (λ (P g)
    (− P (∗ α g))))
```

Grate!

Now we need the *naked-gradient-descent*

```
(define naked-gradient-descent                ●
  (gradient-descent
    naked-i naked-d naked-u))
```

And where is the revision chart, again?

43 Here it is

▷ (*try-plane naked-gradient-descent*)

► (list [3.98 1.97] 6.16)

Wonderful!

That wraps up this chapter. In the next one, we'll use our new approach with *gradient-descent* to change its behavior for the better!

44 Yes, we must teach it to behave!

Crazy Toys

How about a properly inflated soufflé? We want to deflate it *tout de suite*!

The Nearer Your Destination, the Slower You Become†

†With apologies and thanks, Paul Frederic Simon.

1 Was the soufflé delicious?

We "ate" it and it was gr**ate**!

---

2 Here we learn some new tricks with our new toy, the crazy

gradient-descent

What kinds of tricks?

---

3 We'll learn tricks to make us reach the well-fitted $\boldsymbol{\theta}$ with fewer revisions.

That sounds promising!

Should we begin?

---

4 We are off to the races!

Relay races, to be precise.

Intriguing.

What about relay races?

---

5 Groucho is training a relay team with Chico, Harpo, Gummo, and Zeppo.[†]

[†] Thanks Marx Brothers:
Leonard Joseph "Chico" (1887–1961),
Arthur "Harpo" (1888–1964),
Julius Henry "Groucho" (1890–1977),
Milton "Gummo" (1892–1977),
and Herbert Manfred "Zeppo" (1901–1979).

That's one funny team.

---

6 Indeed.

Chico is many times faster than Harpo, who is many times faster than Gummo, who is many times faster than Zeppo.

They run in that order; each person runs around the track once and passes the baton on to the next.

Zeppo must be a really slow runner.

7

Yes.

For the team to be well-prepared, Groucho must get the slower runners to run faster.

That seems like quite a challenge.

8

Groucho has come up with a clever, perhaps unscrupulous, coaching strategy.

Instead of letting go of the baton when passing it to Harpo, Chico holds on to the baton awhile as Harpo grabs it. This forces Harpo to try to run as fast as Chico for as long as they're both holding on to the baton.

Chico drags Harpo along with him for part of the track, making Harpo's velocity much higher.

Ah!

Harpo absorbs a little bit of Chico's velocity.

9

Correct.

And then Harpo does the same to Gummo.

Gummo absorbs a little bit of Harpo's velocity.

10

And also some from Chico!

Oh yes.

Because Harpo has a little bit of Chico's velocity.

Does Gummo do the same to Zeppo?

11

Yes, he does.

Now the slow runners are all faster because the faster runners that came before have transferred some of their speed to them.

Yes.

Groucho has managed to raise the slower velocities by spreading the velocities across the runners.

They can now complete their race much faster.

12 How does this relate to *gradient-descent*?

Here, again, is the function *naked-u* from frame 142:42

```
(define naked-u
  (λ (P g)
    (− P (∗ α g))))
```

13 Yes.

It's the update part of the naked representation for *gradient-descent*.

Explain how this function updates parameters.

14 This function multiplies the gradient g by the learning rate α, and subtracts the result from the parameter P to yield the next P, so that ultimately we get closer to a well-fitted $\boldsymbol{\theta}$.

Correct.

Recall the loss graph from frame 77:13.

15 Yes, the one that had the two tangents in it.

The very same.

What do we know about each tangent as it approaches the lowest point on the graph?

16 Each tangent gets less steep as it approaches the bottom of the curve.

Indeed.

The slope of the tangent, (i.e., the gradient) gets smaller. In fact, as the curve's bottom is approached, the gradient gets closer and closer to 0.0. Furthermore, at the very bottom of the curve, the gradient is exactly 0.0.

What happens when we multiply a really small gradient with a really small learning rate as we do

$(* \ \alpha \ g)$

in update functions?

17 Oh, we get something even smaller!

So, at each revision closer to the bottom, the amount of change to each parameter gets smaller and smaller, correct?

Yes, it does.

The change that we make to a given parameter at each revision is known as the *velocity* of descent.

So what can we say about the velocity of descent as it approaches the bottom of the curve?

18 The velocity slows down!

Wait a minute! That's exactly like our relay racing team!

And we can speed up the whole process by using Groucho's clever strategy!

19 How do we do that?

Here, once more, is *naked-u* from frame 142:42

```
(define naked-u
  (λ (P g)
    (− P (∗ α g))))
```

What is the velocity in this λ-expression?

20 Since we subtract $(* \ \alpha \ g)$, the change to P, (i.e., the velocity) is

$(- \ (* \ \alpha \ g))$

Correct.

Groucho's strategy implies that we should boost our velocity by adding some fraction μ of the velocity v, of the *previous* revision, to the change we expect to make in the *current* revision.

21 What does this mean for our velocity?

Our new velocity expression then becomes

$$(+\ (*\ \mu\ v)\ (-\ (*\ \alpha\ g)))$$

which is better written

$$(-\ (*\ \mu\ v)\ (*\ \alpha\ g))$$

22 Is μ a hyperparameter?

It is.

We declare it

```
(declare-hyper μ)
```

The hyperparameter μ is between 0.0 and 1.0 and represents the decimal fraction of the previous velocity we want to retain for the next velocity.†

†The recommended scalar for μ is usually about 0.9.

23 Where does v come from?

Here, v represents the velocity of the most recent revision (i.e., the speed of the runner handing off the baton).

24 Is the velocity an accompaniment of its corresponding parameter?

Yes, it is.

What can we say about the shape of v?

25 Since v is the change that is made to its parameter, it should have the same shape as its parameter.

Correct!

Here is *velocity-i*, the *inflate* function

```
(define velocity-i
  (λ (p)
    (list p (zeroes p))))
```

The function *velocity-i* adds an initial accompaniment to the parameter *p*.

26 What is *zeroes*?

The function *zeroes* produces a tensor with the same shape as its argument, but made up entirely of 0.0s.

Here's a same-as chart for it

1. $(\textit{zeroes} \begin{bmatrix} 2.1 & 9.3 & 1.5 \\ 7.2 & 3.3 & 6.6 \end{bmatrix}_{(2\ 3)})$
2. $\begin{bmatrix} 0.0 & 0.0 & 0.0 \\ 0.0 & 0.0 & 0.0 \end{bmatrix}_{(2\ 3)}$

Now explain how the function *velocity-i* works.

27 It produces a zeroed tensor in the shape of *p*.

Why do we let the velocity be a zeroed tensor?

That's because at the first revision, there really hasn't been any change to any parameter[†]. So using a zeroed tensor is a reasonable choice for the initial velocity.

[†]Following from the law on page 142, we can stop thinking about $\boldsymbol{\theta}$ and Θ and focus only on parameters.

28 Okay.

Now define the corresponding deflate function *velocity-d*.

29 This deflate function should result in the parameter, which is at index 0 in the inflated representation

```
(define velocity-d
  (λ (p)
    p_0))
```

Excellent.

We can now define *velocity-u*. It expects an accompanied parameter p where the parameter p_0 is accompanied by its velocity p_1 from the last revision. As with all update functions, the gradient g is its second argument.

Here is a skeleton for *velocity-u*

```
(define velocity-u
  (λ (p g)
    (let ((v [        V        ]))
      (list (+ p_0 v) v))))
```

Find V.

30 We give the name v to the expression V. The body of the **let**-expression is the updated accompanied parameter, which is returned from the function. The accompaniment there is v. Therefore, V must be the velocity, which is the change we must make to p_0.

From frame 22, this velocity is

$$(- \ (* \ \mu \ p_1) \ (* \ \alpha \ g))$$

Correct.

Here is *velocity-u*

```
(define velocity-u
  (λ (p g)
    (let ((v (- (* μ p_1) (* α g))))
      (list (+ p_0 v) v))))
```

Now define *velocity-gradient-descent*.

31 Sure, we provide *velocity-i*, *velocity-d*, and *velocity-u* to *gradient-descent*

```
(define velocity-gradient-descent         ●
  (gradient-descent
    velocity-i velocity-d velocity-u))
```

We now make *try-plane* more general, but still dashed, by adding an additional argument, *a-revs*. This allows us to more easily experiment with different scalars for the *revs* hyperparameter

```
(define try-plane
  (λ (a-gradient-descent a-revs)
    (with-hypers
      ((revs a-revs)
       (α 0.001)
       (batch-size 4))
      (a-gradient-descent
        (sampling-obj
          (l2-loss plane) plane-xs plane-ys)
        (list [0.0 0.0] 0.0)))))
```

Using these modifications, here is the corresponding revision chart that shows how to invoke *a-gradient-descent* for our *plane* example from frame 137:23

```
▷ (with-hypers
    ((μ 0.9))
    (try-plane
      velocity-gradient-descent 5000))
▶ (list [3.98 1.97] 6.16)
```

32 Wow.

We have once again found the same answer but with *revs* being 5000 instead of 15000, by using velocity along with the gradient to help us decide the revisions we make to $\boldsymbol{\theta}$ every time.

Is this form of gradient descent known as *velocity* gradient descent?

Actually, no.

It is known as *momentum* gradient descent†

†Thanks, David Everett Rumelhart (1942–2011), Geoffrey Everest Hinton (1947–), and Ronald James Williams (1944–).

33 That's an odd name.

Why *momentum*?

34

Good question.

That's because we multiply the velocity v by a constant μ. The resulting expression is analogous to the formula of momentum in physics.[†]

[†] $\mathbf{p} = m\mathbf{v}$, where $\mathbf{p}$ is the momentum, m is the mass of an object, and $\mathbf{v}$ is its velocity.

Are there other ways to improve the velocity of descent?

35

Yes, there are, but that's for the next interlude!

Remember to transfer some velocity from this chapter to the interlude.

But what about a snack?

Fast Toys

How about a slice of date-and-pecan pie? It is Groucho's favorite!

Interlude IV
Smooth Operator†

†Thanks, Lily Tomlin (1939–) for Ernestine and Edith Ann; and *Sade*: Sade Adu (1959–), Dave Early (1957–1996), Paul Spencer Dunman (1957–), Stuart Colin Matthewman (1960–), and Andrew Hale (1962–).

Groucho's "date-and-pecan pie"?[†]

[†]Thanks, Rosemary Wilson (1910–1986) and Ruth Pool (1934–).

1 Now we know why it is Groucho's favorite dessert!

Good.

Before we look at other update algorithms, we must understand

smoothing

2 What is smoothing?

Here is a function *smooth*

```
(define smooth                                   ●
  (λ (decay-rate average g)
    (+ (* decay-rate average)
       (* (− 1.0 decay-rate) g))))
```

where *decay-rate* must always be a scalar between 0.0 and 1.0, *average* is a historically-accumulated average[†], and *g* is a gradient. Both *average* and *g* must be tensors of the same shape.

What does *smooth* do?

[†]Shortened to "historical average."

3 Since *decay-rate* is a scalar between 0.0 and 1.0, it seems to be blending two tensors using

decay-rate

and

(− 1.0 *decay-rate*)

as weights.

That's correct.

Let's see an extended example of how it is used over time. Here are seven scalars

50.3 22.7 4.3 2.7 1.8 2.2 0.6

Find

(*smooth* 0.9 0.0 50.3)

4 The result of this *smooth* invocation is the scalar 5.03

1. (*smooth* 0.9 0.0 50.3)
2. (+ (∗ 0.9 0.0) (∗ 0.1 50.3))
3. (+ 0.0 5.03)
4. 5.03

Correct.

Now, how about this?

(*smooth* 0.9 5.03 22.7)

5 We are blending the scalar 5.03 with the next scalar 22.7 in our sequence.

Here is the same-as chart

1. (*smooth* 0.9 5.03 22.7)
2. (+ (∗ 0.9 5.03) (∗ 0.1 22.7))
3. (+ 4.53 2.27)
4. 6.8

That is right.

Let's repeat this one more time.

Find

(*smooth* 0.9 6.8 4.3)

6 Here goes

1. (*smooth* 0.9 6.8 4.3)
2. (+ (∗ 0.9 6.8) (∗ 0.1 4.3))
3. 6.55

Excellent.

Here are the original seven scalars from frame 4

50.3 22.7 4.3 2.7 1.8 2.2 0.6

and the historical averages after they have all been smoothed

5.03 6.8 6.55 6.16 6.07 5.64 5.14†

Compare the *smooth*ed seven scalars to the original seven scalars.

†The underlined scalars are the results of the first three invocations of *smooth*, excluding the starting value of 0.0.

7 The *smooth*ed are much *smooth*er than the original scalars. In other words, the smoothed scalars don't vary as much as the original scalars and the variations between them are much gentler.

Yes, the seven scalars in the *smooth*ed historical averages are much closer to each other than the corresponding seven original scalars are to each other.

Repeatedly invoking *smooth* over these scalars "averages" out variations by blending historical scalars with newer ones.

What's the importance of 0.9 that we pass for *decay-rate*?

8 It means that in order to find the new historical average, we use only 90% of the prior historical average, and every new scalar encountered is diminished to 10% of its value. Thus new scalars that vary wildly from the historical average contribute only a small fraction to the new historical average.

Does *decay-rate* always have to be 0.9?

Oh no, that's just for this example.

In general, the *decay-rate* can be any number between 0.0 and 1.0.

9 Sure.

Now let's consider the first scalar 50.3. The first time we invoke *smooth*, we multiply it by 0.1 and get 5.03.

The next time we invoke *smooth*, this scalar is multiplied by 0.9. This means the contribution of the first scalar to the next *smooth*ed result (rounded to two decimal places) is

$$0.9 \times 0.1 \times 50.3 = 4.53$$

10 Aha!

It contributes less and less to the historical average as newer data are encountered.

Yes, it does.

We refer to *decay-rate* as the *rate of contribution.* The contribution of earlier items decays as more items are incorporated.

Find the formula for the contribution of the scalar 50.3 after n invocations of *smooth*.

11 After the nth invocation of *smooth*, the contribution is

$$0.9^{n-1} \times 0.1 \times 50.3$$

Correct.

In general, this is true of any scalar encountered. The contribution of that scalar decays over time according to this formula.

12 So, *smooth* seems to be a way of incorporating historical information that is less relevant as we move forward.

Yes, but this is also true for tensors of any rank!

Since *smooth* is defined using extended functions, the arguments *average* and g can be tensors with compatible shapes. In most instances, the two have the same shape.

And if so, the smoothed result has the same shape as the arguments.

13 How about an example?

Suppose, after a time, we have a historical average of

[0.8 3.1 2.2]

and now we encounter the following three tensors

[1.0 1.1 3.0]
[13.4 18.2 41.4]
[1.1 0.3 67.3]

How should we blend in these new tensors into our historical average?

14 Using *smooth*, of course!

Should we use 0.9 as the decay-rate?

15

Good idea.

Let's start with the first tensor

```
1. (smooth 0.9 [0.8 3.1 2.2] [1.0 1.1 3.0])
2. (+ (* 0.9 [0.8 3.1 2.2])
      (* 0.1 [1.0 1.1 3.0]))
```

Complete this same-as chart.

Here it is

```
3. (+ [0.72 2.79 1.98] [0.1 0.11 0.3])
4. [0.82 2.9 2.28]
```

16

Correct.

Blending this new historical average

[0.82 2.9 2.28]

with the second tensor[1]

[13.4 18.2 41.4]

we get

```
1. (smooth 0.9
      [0.82 2.9 2.28]
      [13.4 18.2 41.4])
2. (+ (* 0.9 [0.82 2.9 2.28])
      (* 0.1 [13.4 18.2 41.4]))
3. (+ [0.74 2.61 2.05]
      [1.34 1.82 4.14])
4. [2.08 4.43 6.19]
```

Now blend in the third tensor

[1.1 0.3 67.3]

Sure

```
1. (smooth 0.9
      [2.08 4.43 6.19]
      [1.1 0.3 67.3])
2. (+ (* 0.9 [2.08 4.43 6.19])
      (* 0.1 [1.1 0.3 67.3]))
3. (+ [1.87 3.99 5.57]
      [0.11 0.03 6.73])
4. [1.98 4.02 12.3]
```

Very good.

Compare the original three tensors[1]

[1.0 1.1 3.0]
[13.4 18.2 41.4]
[1.1 0.3 67.3]

to the three *smooth*ed tensors[1]

[0.82 2.9 2.28]
[2.08 4.43 6.19]
[1.98 4.02 12.3]

17 It is as if we have smoothed the individual scalars corresponding to the elements of those tensors.

How do we use *smooth* with *gradient-descent*?

That's a topic for the next chapter!

18 All right.

Smooth Toys

smooth 155

To break or not to break?
That is the question.[†]

[†]With apologies to William Shakespeare (1564–1616).

9

Be Adamant

Onwards, then!

The velocity-based update algorithm from frame 149:21 improves the velocity of a revision by borrowing some velocity from the preceding revision.

1 That seems like a useful trick.

It is.

But there are other ways to improve the velocity of a revision. These algorithms work by modifying the fraction of the gradient used at each revision.

2 That's an interesting approach.

We know from frame 148:17 that the gradient approaches 0.0 as we roll down to the bottom of the incline.

What can we say about the velocity of the gradient?

3 Since our α so far has been a constant, we know that it causes the velocity of the gradient descent to slow down in a similar way.

Indeed.

Because α represents the fraction of the gradient we're going to use as our velocity, another approach to addressing this problem is to make this fraction *adaptive*.

4 What does adaptive mean?

Adaptive here means that the fraction is decided based on the gradient and its historical values.

5 Does that mean we revise α at every revision as well?

Good question.

Not directly. Instead, we multiply α with a factor D that reacts to the current gradient and its historical values.

6 How does D behave as our gradient slows down?

The fraction of the gradient we use as our velocity at every revision should reduce more slowly than the rate at which the gradient reduces.

7 This means that D must get larger as the gradient gets smaller, since α itself is constant.

Correct.

We say that D varies *inversely* as the gradient.

8 How do we find this mysterious D?

A simple way to make something vary inversely is to divide 1.0 by it. So, D looks something like

$$\frac{1}{G}$$

Here we refer to G as a *modifier.*

9 And now our task is to find G, which we know must depend on the gradient and its history.

Exactly.

Another thing to remember is that when we multiply α by D, we're doing this

$$\alpha \times D = \alpha \times \frac{1}{G} = \frac{\alpha}{G}$$

10 Oh, so we must divide α by the modifier to change the fraction of the gradient we must use.

Correct.

How can we achieve this?

11 Could we simply say that G is the gradient itself? For example like in this update function where g is the gradient

```
(define naked-u-with-divide
  (λ (P g)
    (- P (* (÷ α g) g))))
```

No, we can't.

If we were to simplify the arithmetic, we would get

$$\frac{\alpha}{g} \times g = \alpha$$

In other words, the effect of g would have been nullified.

12 Oh, right.

Then our velocity of descent would become the constant α and it would not depend upon the gradient, which would not be at all what we've intended.

We need something that takes the history of g into account but is not susceptible to all the variations in g, so that the effect of g is not nullified.

13 It sounds as if we could use our new toy *smooth* here!

Correct!

The solution is to use *smooth* to historically accumulate a modifier that is based on g.

14 Could we see this new update function?

Sure.

We need a representation with an accompaniment based on our smoothed gradients.

Here's a skeleton for *rms-u*[†] that defines a new update algorithm to be used with *gradient-descent*

```
(define rms-u
  (λ (P g)
    (let ((r [      R      ]))
      (let ((α̂‡ (÷ α [    G    ])))
        (list (− P₀ (∗ α̂ g)) r)))))
```

Like other update functions, *rms-u* takes an accompanied parameter and a gradient and revises the accompanied parameter. The accompaniment P_1 is the smoothed value derived from the gradient g.

Here r is the value we determine as the new accompaniment. It is part of the returned accompanied parameter. It also, however, is used inside G.

Find R.

15 R has to be an invocation of *smooth* because it has to be historically averaged.

We'll need a decay rate for it.

[†] *rms* is pronounced "*R-M-S*."

[‡] We use the convention with carets or "hats" over names, for example $\hat{\alpha}$, to denote that it has been derived from another similarly named value (here α), and its intention is the same (here as a learning rate).

For readers who may wish to do so, lexical scope allows for all the hats to be dropped, so to speak.

We will!

It is provided with a hyperparameter

```
(declare-hyper β)                    ●
```

16 Great, so now R looks something like this

(*smooth* β P_1 [S])

because P_1 is the historically averaged value.

Correct.

Now our task is to find S.

17 Isn't S just g?

Not quite.

The gradient g can be negative, and if we get too many consecutive negative gradients, then our historical averages can themselves become negative.

18 Why is becoming negative a problem?

This is a problem because r gets used by G and its being negative can make $\hat{\alpha}$ negative.

When that happens, we end up *ascending* the gradient instead of descending it.

19 Does that mean we would move our $\boldsymbol{\theta}$ in a direction that

increases the loss

instead of in a direction that

decreases the loss?

Yes, that is correct.

So, we should make sure r is always nonnegative.

We recognize this problem from frame 60:14, where we could have negative values but we needed them to be nonnegative.

20 Yes.

We fixed the problem by squaring the value.

Should S be (*sqr* g)?

Correct.

So this is what R looks like

(*smooth* β p_1 (*sqr* g))

Now let's move on to finding G.

21 Why isn't G just r?

Good question.

The problem with squares is that they grow much faster than the scalar that is being squared.

If we were to use r for G, the modified learning rate would increase at a faster rate than the rate at which the gradient reduces.

22 Why is that a problem?

From way back in frame 67:37, we know that this could cause the descent to overshoot the lowest point in the loss curve.

So, how do we modify r so that it tracks the gradient more closely, and not the square of the gradient?

23 Aha!

We can take its square root using the function *sqrt*.

Then, should G be this

(*sqrt* r)?

Yes, that is almost correct.

We need to account for the unlikely possibility that r would be 0.0.

24 Oh, that would cause the division of α to be undefined.

Correct.

This problem, however, is easily solved by adding a tiny constant ϵ known as the *stabilizer*, to (*sqrt* r).

25 What should ϵ be?

We define ϵ

```
(define ϵ 1e−08)
```

Now find G.

26 G must be

(+ (*sqrt* r) ϵ)

What does the final version of *rms-u* look like?

Here it is

```
(define rms-u
  (λ (P g)
    (let ((r (smooth β P_1 (sqr g))))
      (let ((α̂ (÷ α (+ (sqrt r) ϵ))))
        (list (− P_0 (* α̂ g)) r)))))
```

Let's now define *rms-gradient-descent.*

27 We need to first define the corresponding inflate and deflate functions, don't we?

Oops, thanks! Indeed we do.

They look similar to *velocity-i* from frame 150:26 and *velocity-d* from frame 151:29, since we set the initial value of each r accompaniment to a zeroed tensor of the same shape as the parameter.

Define *rms-i* and *rms-d*.

28 Here is *rms-i*. We accompany p with r, a zeroed tensor

```
(define rms-i
  (λ (p)
    (list p (zeroes p))))
```

Similarly, *rms-d* simply extracts the parameter p from the accompanied parameter

```
(define rms-d
  (λ (P)
    P_0))
```

So *now* define

rms-gradient-descent

29 Here it is

```
(define rms-gradient-descent                    ●
  (gradient-descent
    rms-i rms-d rms-u))
```

Could we see an example of its use?

We'll take the same example from frame 152:32. But first, we must determine each hyperparameter.

What should our learning rate be?

30 Since *rms-u* uses a continuously modified learning rate, should we start with a higher learning rate and expect it to be adapted as *rms-gradient-descent* proceeds?

Good guess.

Let's start with

α at 0.01

31 What about *revs*?

In general, *rms-u* tends to reduce *revs* necessary to reach the well-fitted $\boldsymbol{\theta}$. For now, let

revs be 3000

instead of the 5000 from frame 152:32.

32 Okay.

Here's a slightly extended *try-plane*, which now also accepts *an-α*, a starting value for α

```
(define try-plane
  (λ (a-gradient-descent a-revs an-α)
    (with-hypers
      ((revs a-revs)
       (α an-α)
       (batch-size 4))
      (a-gradient-descent
        (sampling-obj
          (l2-loss plane) plane-xs plane-ys)
        (list [0.0 0.0] 0.0)))))
```

How do we invoke this function for our example?

33 We must provide a scalar for β, and then invoke *try-plane*

```
▷ (with-hypers
    ((β 0.9))
    (try-plane
      rms-gradient-descent 3000 0.01))
▶ (list [3.98 1.97] 6.16)
```

We get the well-fitted $\boldsymbol{\theta}$ with 2000 fewer revisions than before!

Yes indeed.

This version of *gradient-descent* has the somewhat cryptic name *RMSProp*.[†]

The term *RMS* stands for *root mean square*, which reflects the fact that we use the *mean* (i.e., the smoothed historical average) of the *squares* and then take its square *root*. The suffix *Prop* is a contraction of the term *back propagation*.

[†]Thanks, Geoffrey Everest Hinton.

34 We have two different algorithms for speeding up the gradient descent, *velocity-u* from frame 151:31 and *rms-u* in frame 27.

Could we do better if we combined them?

An excellent observation!

The last update algorithm, *adam-u*, uses *smooth* for *two* historical averages—one for the gradient and one for its square.

For the gradient, we use the hyperparameter μ from *velocity-u* in frame 152:32 so we benefit from Groucho's clever strategy.

For the square of the gradient, we continue to use β as we did in *rms-u* so that we can modify the learning rate.

35 These hyperparameters are very handy.

Yes, indeed.

Here's *adam-u*†

```
(define adam-u
  (λ (P g)
    (let ((r (smooth β P2 (sqr g))))
      (let ((α̂ (÷ α (+ (sqrt r) ε)))
            (v (smooth μ P1 g)))
        (list (− P0 (* α̂ v)) v r)))))
```

Its parameter has two accompaniments.

Here r and $\hat{\alpha}$ are used identically to *rms-u* in frame 27. The historical average of v, however, is slightly different from frame 151:31.

36 How is it different?

†This algorithm, known as *Adam*, improves gradient descent for stochastic objective functions. Thanks, Diederik Pieter Kingma (1983–) and Jimmy Lei Ba.

For those who might have encountered this update algorithm elsewhere, we have simplified it by dropping the bias correction for v and r.

The first difference is that we use *smooth* for the accumulation. This causes the gradient to be multiplied by (− 1.0 μ). Since μ is typically around 0.9, only a small fraction of the gradient g is used for the next $\boldsymbol{\theta}$. The rest is made up of the historical average of v.

So, the historical average of v is much smoother than in the version from frame 151:31 in *velocity-u*.

37 Oh yes. In *velocity-u* from that frame the gradient g is multiplied by the learning rate, and that is added to v.

Is there another difference?

Yes, there is.

The second difference is that to find our well-fitted parameter P_0, we don't use g directly. Instead we use the historical averages v.

Why is that?

38 It is another way of using the velocity of prior revisions to inform the velocity of the current revision.

Correct.

We must also remember to define an *adam-i* and an *adam-d*.

Each parameter p in $\boldsymbol{\theta}$ is now accompanied by two additional tensors v and r, each with the same shape as p.

Define *adam-i*.

39 Here it is

```
(define adam-i
  (λ (p)
    (let ((v (zeroes p)))
      (let ((r v))
        (list p v r)))))
```

Define *adam-d*.

40 The deflate function again extracts the 0th member from the accompanied parameter, P, to get the next p

```
(define adam-d
  (λ (P)
    P₀))
```

All our deflate functions (except for *naked-d*) so far are the same. Why don't we use the same name for all of them?

A great question.

We could. We're setting up a pattern that leaves room for representations other than *lists* for accompanied parameters.

41 Good idea.

And now define *adam-gradient-descent*.

42 Here it is

```
(define adam-gradient-descent
  (gradient-descent
    adam-i adam-d adam-u))
```

Excellent!

The name of this algorithm, Adam, is short for *adaptive moment estimation.* It is *adaptive* because it uses an adaptive learning rate.[†]

[†]The accompaniment v is known as the gradient's 1st moment and r is its 2nd moment.

43 How about an example of how to invoke *adam-gradient-descent*

Here we learn the same result once again using *try-plane* from frame 152:32 but with fewer revisions

```
▷ (with-hypers
    ((μ 0.85)
     (β 0.9))
    (try-plane
      adam-gradient-descent 1500 0.001))
▶ (list [3.98 1.97] 6.16)
```

44 So now we need only 1500 revisions to get the well-fitted $\boldsymbol{\theta}$. This is far fewer than the 15000 that we started with in the original from frame 129:42.

How did we decide the appropriate scalars for μ and β?

These scalars have been experimentally determined by trying out different combinations to get a lower *revs*.

45 Okay.

We now have different kinds of gradient-descent toys that we can use to learn $\boldsymbol{\theta}$ for various kinds of target functions.

46 So what is next?

The Law of Gradient Descent

The $\boldsymbol{\theta}$ for a target function is learned by using one of the gradient descent functions.

Now we move on to understanding how extended functions work.

But before that, let's take a smoothie break!

[47] Yes, a break is much appreciated.

Faster Toys

How about a chocolate and almond butter smoothie?

Interlude V
Extensio Magnifico!

How was the smoothie?

1 It was real smooth.

We've been assuming that function extension just works for functions like + and ∗.

Unlike *The Berglas Effect,*[†] we reveal our function-extension trick.

[†]Thanks, David Berglas (1926–).

2 Oh, so this interlude is an *extension* of Interlude I?

It is!

We start with a frequently used function on tensors.

This function invokes a given function argument on *each* element of a tensor.

For example, we might want to *add1* to every element of

[3 5 4]

to get

[4 6 5]

3 This seems similar to *map* from frame 81:25.

Yes, the two functions are similar.

The function *tmap* takes a function *f* and a tensor *t* as arguments, and invokes *f* on every element of *t* and assembles the results into a tensor as in this same-as chart

1. (*tmap add1* [3 5 4])
2. [(*add1* 3) (*add1* 5) (*add1* 4)]
3. [4 6 5]

4 It looks as if the *add1* replicated itself and sneaked into the tensor!

This is similar to descending into a tensor from frame 51:19.

It is!

Descending into a tensor is another way of looking at *tmap*. It descends into a tensor to invoke its function argument on each element it finds.

5 But what if we have more than one tensor and we want to invoke a function on elements from each of the tensors?

The function *tmap* is designed to work with multiple tensors, provided the tensors are all of equal length.

For example, here we use two tensors

1. (*tmap* + [3 4 6 1] [1 3 5 5])
2. [(+ 3 1) (+ 4 3) (+ 6 5) (+ 1 5)]
3. [4 7 11 6]

6 Okay.

Now let us see how we can use *tmap* for extending functions.

We start with the extended function *sqrt*. Assume that $sqrt^0$ is the (unextended) primitive function that finds the positive square root of a scalar.

Here is a skeleton of the extended function *sqrt*

```
(define sqrt
  (λ (t)
    (cond
      ((scalar? t) (sqrt⁰ t))
      (else [    A    ]))))
```

When t is a scalar, we find the square root using $sqrt^0$.

What should A be?

7 For the extension behavior, A must descend into the tensor until it finds a scalar and invokes $sqrt^0$ on it.

8 Excellent.

What function do we know that allows us to descend into tensors?

It is *tmap*!

So A must look like

(*tmap* [S] *t*)

---

9 Correct.

Now to find S. This function is invoked on each element of t, and it should produce its square root. If each element of t is a scalar, it should invoke $sqrt^0$ on it, but if each element is a tensor of rank 1 or higher, it must descend into it.

That sounds familiar.

This must mean that S is

sqrt

---

10 Perfect.

In the definition in frame 7, our base test uses *scalar?*. Let's replace it with a different function

of-rank?

which accepts a rank and a tensor and checks if that tensor has the given rank. Here, we'll check for 0

```
(define sqrt
  (λ (t)
    (cond
      ((of-rank? 0 t) (sqrt⁰ t))
      (else (tmap sqrt t)))))
```

This is it, right?

```
(define of-rank?
  (λ (n t)
    (= (rank t) n)))
```

That definition is correct, but here's a more fun one. Let's start with its skeleton

```
(define of-rank?
  (λ (n t)
    (cond
      ((zero? n) [ S ])
      ((scalar? t) [B])
      (else [ R ]))))
```

Find S, B, and R.

11 Let's begin with S, which is true only if S is (*scalar? t*). So, S is

(*scalar? t*)

For B, since the first **cond**-clause test failed, we know that n is greater than 0, so if t is a scalar, then B is

#f

Finally, for R, t has the rank n only if $t|_0$ has the rank $n - 1$. We can verify this recursively. So, R is

(*of-rank?* (*sub1 n*) $t|_0$)

changing both n and t to eventually pass either the first or second base test.

Excellent.

Here is the final *of-rank?*

```
(define of-rank?
  (λ (n t)
    (cond
      ((zero? n) (scalar? t))
      ((scalar? t) #f)
      (else (of-rank? (sub1 n) t|0)))))
```

Using the same tensor t as before in frame 42:44, show a same-as chart for

(*of-rank?* 3 *t*)

12 Here it is

1. (*of-rank?* 3 [[[8] [9]] [[4] [7]]])
2. (*of-rank?* 2 [[8] [9]])
3. (*of-rank?* 1 [8])
4. (*of-rank?* 0 8)
5. #t

Great.

What if 3 were replaced by any other natural number?

13 Then the result would be

#f

Returning to *sqrt*, why is it dashed in frame 10?

As usual, we're going to reconsider it.

This function is specific to square roots, because we invoke $sqrt^0$ only on scalars. Let's refer to this as the

base function

Instead of having a fixed value of the base function of one argument, here $sqrt^0$, we accept it as an additional argument.

14 Does that allow us to extend any base function of one argument?

Yes.

Let's name this generalized function *ext1* because it extends functions of one argument. Here is a skeleton for it

```
(define ext1
  (λ (f)
    (λ (t)
      (cond
        ((of-rank? 0 t) (f t))
        (else (tmap  E  t))))))
```

Invoking *ext1* with a base function *f* results in a function that either invokes *f* on *t* if *t*'s rank is 0, or descends into *t* otherwise.

What is *E*?

15 *E* must also be the function that invokes the base function *f* on scalars, or descends into tensors of higher rank. This must mean *E* is

(*ext1 f*)

Excellent.

Here is a dashed *ext1*

```
(define ext1
  (λ (f)
    (λ (t)
      (cond
        ((of-rank? 0 t) (f t))
        (else (tmap (ext1 f) t))))))
```

Using *ext1*, define *sqrt*.

16 Here it is

```
(define sqrt
  (ext1 sqrt⁰))
```

How about another example?

A good idea.

How can we define the function *zeroes* from frame 150:27 using *ext1*?

17 Oh, we can think of *zeroes* as extending a function that results in 0.0 for every scalar!

Here is how we define *zeroes*

```
(define zeroes
  (ext1 (λ (x) 0.0)))
```

Perfect.

18 But why are the definitions of *ext1*, *sqrt*, and *zeroes* dashed?

This *ext1* so far works on extending functions that operate only on scalars.

Sometimes, however, we need to extend functions like sum^1 in frame 53:24 that only operate on $tensors^1$.

19 Oh, so instead of checking

(of-rank? 0 t)

as we see in *ext1*, we'll have to look for a rank of 1 when extending sum^1.

That is correct.

We refer to this as the

base rank

20 So the base rank for

sum^1

is 1?

Good guess!

What is the base rank for $sqrt^0$?

21 It is 0.

Right.

So when extending a function f, we must also accept its base rank n as an argument.

Here's a skeleton of our updated *ext1*

```
(define ext1
  (λ (f n)
    (λ (t)
      (cond
        ([    N    ] (f t))
        (else (tmap (ext1 f n) t))))))
```

Find N.

22 Here we must check for a rank of n. So, N is

(*of-rank?* n t)

Correct.

Here, then, is the final *ext1*

```
(define ext1
  (λ (f n)
    (λ (t)
      (cond
        ((of-rank? n t) (f t))
        (else (tmap (ext1 f n) t))))))
```

How about *sqrt* and *zeroes* using this function?

23 We must now also provide the base rank for $sqrt^0$ when we invoke *ext1*.

Here *sqrt*'s base rank is 0

```
(define sqrt
  (ext1 sqrt⁰ 0))
```

Similarly, for *zeroes*, the base function also has the base rank 0

```
(define zeroes
  (ext1 (λ (x) 0.0) 0))
```

Perfect.

Now define *sum*, which extends sum^1.

24 We invoke *ext1* with a base rank of 1

```
(define sum
  (ext1 sum¹ 1))
```

Can we see an example where the base rank is 2?

Sure.

Consider the function $flatten^2$ that flattens a $tensor^2$ into a $tensor^1$. It does this by concatenating together each of the nested $tensors^1$.

25 Example, please?

With the notation from pages 113–114

1. ($flatten^2$ $\begin{bmatrix} 1.0 & 0.5 \\ 3.1 & 2.2 \\ 7.3 & 2.1 \end{bmatrix}_{(3\ 2)}$)
2. ($flatten^2$ [[1.0 0.5] [3.1 2.2] [7.3 2.1]])
3. [1.0 0.5 3.1 2.2 7.3 2.1]

26 Is this a function we are going to extend?

We are!

```
(define flatten
  (ext1 flatten² 2))
```

27 Could we see how it works?

Sure.

This is the extended version of *flatten*^{2} that works on tensors of arbitrary rank, but flattens only the innermost tensors^2.

For example

1. (*flatten*
   [[[1.0 0.5] [3.1 2.2] [7.3 2.1]]
   [[2.9 3.5] [0.7 1.5] [2.5 6.4]]])

Complete this same-as chart.

28 Now, we descend into the tensors

2. [(*flatten*
   [[1.0 0.5] [3.1 2.2] [7.3 2.1]])
   (*flatten*
   [[2.9 3.5] [0.7 1.5] [2.5 6.4]])]
3. [(*flatten*^{2}
   [[1.0 0.5] [3.1 2.2] [7.3 2.1]])
   (*flatten*^{2}
   [[2.9 3.5] [0.7 1.5] [2.5 6.4]])]
4. [[1.0 0.5 3.1 2.2 7.3 2.1]
   [2.9 3.5 0.7 1.5 2.5 6.4]]

Correct.

The function *ext1* is useful for extending functions of one argument.

Now let's see how we extend functions of two arguments.

29 So now do we define a function *ext2*?

We do!

Before we do that, however, we need a couple of other comparision functions on ranks.

30 Sort of like
of-rank?
and more interesting?

Yes, indeed!

Sometimes we need to know if the rank of one tensor is higher than another. Here is a function *rank>* that is true if the rank of its first tensor argument is higher than the rank of its second tensor argument.

Here is its quick version

```
(define rank>
  (λ (t u)
    (> (rank t) (rank u))))
```

31 Could we write a recursive version of this as well?

We should!

```
(define rank>
  (λ (t u)
    (cond
      ((scalar? t) #f)
      ((scalar? u) #t)
      (else (rank> t|0 u|0)))))
```

Explain how this function works.

32 If t is a scalar, its rank is 0. Since 0 is not higher than any other rank, then the answer is

#f

On the other hand, if u is a scalar, and we already know that t is not a scalar, then the rank of t is higher than that of u, so the answer is

#t

And finally, if neither are scalars, we recursively compare the ranks of the 0th element of both t and u.

What else do we need?

Now define a function *of-ranks?* that takes arguments n, t, m, and u, where n is the rank we're checking for tensor t, and m is the rank we're checking for tensor u.

33 Here it is

```
(define of-ranks?
  (λ (n t m u)
    (cond
      ((of-rank? n t) (of-rank? m u))
      (else #f))))
```

That was fun!

Great.

Here is an example

1. (*of-ranks?*
   3 [[[8] [9]] [[2] [1]]] 2 [5])
2. (*of-rank?* 2 [5])
3. #f

Explain this same-as chart.

34 Since

(*of-rank?* 3 [[[8] [9]] [[2] [1]]])

is #t, the base test of the **cond** clause succeeds, so we must check if

(*rank* [5]) is 2

which it isn't. Hence we return #f.

Very good.

Now, we're ready to define *ext2*.

It is similar in its basic structure to *ext1*, but because the base function that is being extended has two arguments instead of one, we need *two* base ranks

```
(define ext2                                    ●
  (λ (f n m)
    (λ (t u)
      (cond
        ((of-ranks? n t m u) (f t u))
        (else
         (desc (ext2 f n m) n t m u))))))
```

We make use of two support functions

of-ranks?

and

desc

Since we have two base ranks and two tensor arguments, deciding when we must descend and when we must not requires a little more thought.

35 We know that

of-ranks?

checks whether

t has rank *n*

and

u has rank *m*

This means that in the first clause of the **cond** expression, we check if *t* and *u* have reached their base ranks. If they have, we invoke the base function *f* on them.

Otherwise, it is time to descend into the tensors, and we use *desc* to do that. The first argument to *desc* is very similar to the first argument to *tmap* in *ext1* when it is used to descend into the tensor.

So, *desc* is invoked with

(*ext2 f n m*)

which is similar to

(*ext1 f n*)

which is in the definition of *ext1*.

Correct.

The recursive invocation of *ext2* produces a function that either invokes *f* on the two argument tensors if they each have their respective base rank, or descends into one or both of the tensors. This is the first argument to *desc*.

36 How do we decide which tensor, or tensors, we should descend into?

An excellent question.

To see that, let's look at *desc*

```
(define desc
  (λ (g n t m u)
    (cond
      ((of-rank? n t) (desc-u g t u))
      ((of-rank? m u) (desc-t g t u))
      ((= |t| |u|) (tmap g t u))
      ((rank> t u) (desc-t g t u))
      (else (desc-u g t u)))))
```

Here, *g* is the extended function

(*ext2 f n m*)

because of the way

desc

is invoked from within

ext2

The first couple of clauses address what happens when one of the two tensor arguments has reached its base rank. For example, if we have reached the base rank for *u*, then we need to descend only into *t*, and vice versa.

Define *desc-t*, which descends into *t*, and *desc-u*, which descends into *u*.

37 For *desc-t*, since we are descending into only one tensor, we use *tmap* to invoke *g* over each element of *t* (named *et*) and *u*

```
(define desc-t
  (λ (g t u)
    (tmap (λ (et) (g et u)) t)))
```

For *desc-u*, we similarly use *tmap* to invoke *g* on *t* and each element of *u* (named *eu*)

```
(define desc-u
  (λ (g t u)
    (tmap (λ (eu) (g t eu)) u)))
```

38 Excellent.

Our next clause deals with when t and u have the same number of elements, which we determine using $\nmid t \nmid$ and $\nmid u \nmid$ from frame 33:17. This means we descend into both simultaneously.

What happens if none of these clauses are relevant?

---

39 If the rank of t is higher than the rank of u, then we use *desc-t*, otherwise, we use *desc-u*.

And we decide this by using

rank>

from frame 32!

Could we see an example of how *ext2* is used?

---

40 Sure.

Let $+^{0,0}$ be a function that adds two scalars.

Define an extended version + of this base function.

We must invoke *ext2*, since the base function is a function of two arguments. The base rank for both arguments is 0

```
(define +                                   ●
  (ext2 +^{0,0} 0 0))
```

How about another example?

---

41 Let $*^{0,0}$ be a function that multiplies two scalars.

Define an extended version $*$ of this base function.

As before, we must invoke *ext2*, since the base function is a function of two arguments. The base rank for both arguments here is also 0

```
(define *                                   ●
  (ext2 *^{0,0} 0 0))
```

---

42 Now, *any* function that uses $*$ gets automatically extended. For example, define a function *sqr* that squares its tensor argument t.

Here it is

```
(define sqr                                 ●
  (λ (t)
    (* t t)))
```

---

43 We also have everything we need for defining • from frame 106:26.

Define •.

We can do this by extending $\bullet^{1,1}$ with base ranks of 1 and 1

```
(define •
  (ext2 •^{1,1} 1 1))
```

44 Excellent.

We can use *ext2* in other ways. For example, we can define a function $*^{2,1}$

```
(define *^{2,1}
  (ext2 * 2 1))
```

Explain what this function does.

Here the base function is

$*$

which we defined in frame 41 and

$*$'s definition relies on $*^{0,0}$

Why does it need to be extended?

45 We're using different base ranks. This means that $*^{2,1}$ descends into both its arguments until it has reached a tensor^2 in its first argument, and a tensor^1 in its second argument, and then invokes $*$ only on them. Let's see an example.

Let the tensor^2 p be

[[3 4 5]
 [7 8 9]]

and the tensor^1 t be

[2 4 3]

Now complete this same-as chart, keeping in mind that we are first using $*$, each of whose arguments is at base rank 0

1. (* *p* *t*)
2. (* [[3 4 5] [7 8 9]] [2 4 3])

Here, we first descend into t because it has a higher than 0 rank

3. [(* [3 4 5] [2 4 3])
   (* [7 8 9] [2 4 3])]
4. [[(* 3 2) (* 4 4) (* 5 3)]
   [(* 7 2) (* 8 4) (* 9 3)]]
5. [[($*^{0,0}$ 3 2) ($*^{0,0}$ 4 4) ($*^{0,0}$ 5 3)]
   [($*^{0,0}$ 7 2) ($*^{0,0}$ 8 4) ($*^{0,0}$ 9 3)]]
6. [[6 16 15]
   [14 32 27]]

Indeed.

Here's a same-as chart showing how $*^{2,1}$ behaves on these same two arguments. Because p is at base rank 2 and t is at base rank 1, $*^{2,1}$ invokes $*$ on them

1. $(*^{2,1}\ p\ t)$
2. $(*\ p\ t)$

What happens next?

46 It produces the same result that we see in frame 45.

Correct.

Now let's look at a different pair of tensors, and see how $*$ behaves with them.

Let q be a tensor^2

[[8 1] [7 3] [5 4]]

and let r be another tensor^2

[[6 2] [4 9] [3 8]]

Now complete this same-as chart

1. $(*\ q\ r)$

47 Here, $*$ immediately tackles the two tensors of the same length 3, so it descends into both simultaneously

2. (∗ [[8 1] [7 3] [5 4]]
   [[6 2] [4 9] [3 8]])
3. [[(∗ 8 6) (∗ 1 2)]
   [(∗ 7 4) (∗ 3 9)]
   [(∗ 5 3) (∗ 4 8)]]
4. [[($*^{0,0}$ 8 6) ($*^{0,0}$ 1 2)]
   [($*^{0,0}$ 7 4) ($*^{0,0}$ 3 9)]
   [($*^{0,0}$ 5 3) ($*^{0,0}$ 4 8)]]
5. [[48 2] [28 27] [15 32]]

What happens with $*^{2,1}$?

Let's find out!

48 The invocations of $*^{2,1}$ are at their base ranks of 2 and 1, respectively, so we invoke $*$ on the tensor arguments of $*^{2,1}$

Instead of descending into both tensors simultaneously, it recognizes that q is already at the base rank, and descends into *only* r

1. ($*^{2,1}$ q r)
2. ($*^{2,1}$ [[8 1] [7 3] [5 4]]
[[6 2] [4 9] [3 8]])
3. [($*^{2,1}$ [[8 1] [7 3] [5 4]] [6 2])
($*^{2,1}$ [[8 1] [7 3] [5 4]] [4 9])
($*^{2,1}$ [[8 1] [7 3] [5 4]] [3 8])]

Now finish this same-as chart.

4. [($*^{2,1}$ [[8 1] [7 3] [5 4]] [6 2])
($*^{2,1}$ [[8 1] [7 3] [5 4]] [4 9])
($*^{2,1}$ [[8 1] [7 3] [5 4]] [3 8])]
5. [($*$ [[8 1] [7 3] [5 4]] [6 2])
($*$ [[8 1] [7 3] [5 4]] [4 9])
($*$ [[8 1] [7 3] [5 4]] [3 8])]
6. [[($*$ [8 1] [6 2])
($*$ [7 3] [6 2])
($*$ [5 4] [6 2])]
[($*$ [8 1] [4 9])
($*$ [7 3] [4 9])
($*$ [5 4] [4 9])]
[($*$ [8 1] [3 8])
($*$ [7 3] [3 8])
($*$ [5 4] [3 8])]]
7. [[[($*^{0,0}$ 8 6) ($*^{0,0}$ 1 2)]
[($*^{0,0}$ 7 6) ($*^{0,0}$ 3 2)]
[($*^{0,0}$ 5 6) ($*^{0,0}$ 4 2)]]
[[($*^{0,0}$ 8 4) ($*^{0,0}$ 1 9)]
[($*^{0,0}$ 7 4) ($*^{0,0}$ 3 9)]
[($*^{0,0}$ 5 4) ($*^{0,0}$ 4 9)]]
[[($*^{0,0}$ 8 3) ($*^{0,0}$ 1 8)]
[($*^{0,0}$ 7 3) ($*^{0,0}$ 3 8)]
[($*^{0,0}$ 5 3) ($*^{0,0}$ 4 8)]]]
8. [[[48 2] [42 6] [30 8]]
[[32 9] [28 27] [20 36]]
[[24 8] [21 24] [15 32]]]

Is this different from the result for $*$ in frame 47?

49 Indeed, so we can use the base ranks to change the behavior of extended functions.

Is there a use for that?

There is![†]

But that's for a later chapter.

[†]This may be familiar to some as a precursor to matrix-vector multiplication.

50 Time for a break now.

More Extendy Toys

How about some maple walnut chiffon pie?
Nutty and smooth at the same time!

10 Doing the Neuron Dance†

†With apologies and thanks, *The Pointer Sisters*: June (1953–2006), Ruth (1946–), and Anita (1948–); and also music arrangers Alta Sherral Willis (1947–2019) and Daniel Sembello (1963–2015).

1 Wasn't the maple walnut chiffon pie heavenly?

It was maybe the best slice of pie, ever!

---

2 Onwards, then!

So far, our target functions have been very limited.

How so?

---

3 Functions like *line*, *quad*, and *plane* use only a small number of parameters, and are suitable for only certain kinds of data sets that can be modeled by these simple functions.

Why is that a problem?

---

4 We cannot recognize irises.

Irises? What do irises have to do with anything?

---

5 We'll get to that.

If we have more complex target functions, we could teach them to recognize irises and other things using data sets that consist of appropriately labeled images.

Or, we could teach them to recognize objects, faces, and other interesting features in images. Or, understand speech, or written language, or do many other things that are otherwise difficult for machines to do.

How do we teach them?

---

6 We define these target functions to have a $\boldsymbol{\theta}$ and then we use one of our gradient-descent functions to find the well-fitted $\boldsymbol{\theta}$ that allows us to perform the task we are interested in.

How do we find these larger and more complex target functions?

Like all other functions, we construct them from simpler units.

7 Aha!

That sounds familiar. We always design functions by dividing larger functions up into smaller ones.

Is this similar?

In some ways, yes.

But these smaller functions must also be parameterized, because we still want to use gradient descent optimization to learn the parameters of all of these smaller functions working together.

8 That sounds exciting.

What do these simpler parameterized functions look like?

Let's find out.

Here is a function *rectify*^{0}

```
(define rectify^0                    ●
  (λ (s)
    (cond
      ((< s 0.0) 0.0)
      (else s))))
```

Explain what this function does.

9 The function *rectify*^{0} expects a scalar argument and it results in 0.0 if its argument is negative. Otherwise it is like the identity function.

Correct.

Is *rectify*^{0} a *linear* function?

10 *rectify*^{0} relies on a **cond**-expression, and from frame 101:11, a linear function may use only addition and scaling, but **cond** is different from either of them.

11

Good.

The extended version of *rectify*^{0} is named *rectify*

```
(define rectify
  (ext1 rectify^0 0))
```

Oh, so it works on a tensor, invoking the same behavior on each of its scalars as is familiar from frames 49:11 and 183:23.

So, by extension, is *rectify* also nonlinear?

12

Yes, it is.

Nonlinear functions like *rectify* are referred to as *deciders*.[†] They make a small decision about their arguments and transfer the decision to their result.

[†]Otherwise known as *activation functions*. We use the term *deciders* here to emphasize their intent.

Is a decider one of the simpler functions we use?

13

Yes.

Using a decider as one of the smaller functions in our collection of functions allows us to make tiny decisions involving just a few parameters that assimilate into a final decision such as what kinds of irises we have.

But *rectify* has no parameters.

How can we use it to learn anything?

14

That is a great question!

We combine it with another simple function, but this one is parameterized.

Here's a familiar function. It is similar to *plane* from frame 105:25

```
(define linear^{1,1}
  (λ (t)
    (λ (θ)
      (+ (• θ_0 t) θ_1))))
```

Why does this function have a "1,1" superscript?

The "1,1" superscript reminds us that it expects both $\boldsymbol{\theta}_0$ and t to be tensors^1 and will take on the usual extended function behavior if either of the tensors are of higher rank. And, unlike *rectify*, this function *is* linear.

Explain why.

15 This function uses addition (+) and dot product (•) from frame 106:26, which itself uses only addition and scaling.†

This makes $linear^{1,1}$ a linear function and deserving of its name.

†To make a fine point of this, • in this definition uses one tensor from parameters and one from the argument, which makes the resulting scalar multiplications between a parameter and an argument. Hence we say that • uses scaling. We use addition when all those scalar products are summed. This makes • in this context a linear operation.

Excellent.

Now explain $linear^{1,1}$.

16 The function $linear^{1,1}$ combines its tensor^1 argument t with the parameter $\boldsymbol{\theta}_0$, which is also a tensor^1, into a scalar. It then adds the resultant scalar to $\boldsymbol{\theta}_1$.

Correct.

We compose the non-parameterized, nonlinear decider *rectify* with $linear^{1,1}$ to get this parameterized nonlinear function, $relu^{1,1}$

```
(define relu^{1,1}                    ●
  (λ (t)
    (λ (θ)
      (rectify ((linear^{1,1} t) θ)))))
```

17 That's an odd name, $relu^{1,1}$, isn't it?

The name *relu* is short for *rectifying linear unit.*

Again, the "1,1" superscript is a reminder that we're dealing with tensors^1 for both t and $\boldsymbol{\theta}_0$.

18 Oh, because it combines *rectify* and $linear^{1,1}$.

19

Now it becomes obvious, doesn't it?

Explain the function $relu^{1,1}$.

It *rectifies* the scalar result of $linear^{1,1}$.

20

That is right.

The function $relu^{1,1}$ makes a *weighted decision* about its argument tensor t.

What is a *weighted* decision?

21

Each element of the tensor $\boldsymbol{\theta}_0$ is known as a *weight*. Each weight decides how much the corresponding element in the argument matters in the final decision.

The closer a weight is to 0.0, the less that element in the argument matters.

So, this looks similar to $\boldsymbol{w}$ from frame 22:11.

What about $\boldsymbol{\theta}_1$?

22

Good question.

It is known as a *bias*. It is similar to $\boldsymbol{b}$ also from frame 22:11.

The bias parameter shifts the point at which *rectify* makes its decision to result in 0.0.

How does *bias* do that?

23

If the bias is *positive*, it increases the result produced by •, raising the chances that the result will pass through *rectify* unchanged.

Similarly, if it is *negative*, it decreases the result produced by •, lowering the chances that the result will pass through *rectify* unchanged and therefore more likely to become 0.0.

Ah, so when that result is *rectify*'d, the bias determines whether the final result is 0.0.

Correct.

If the argument were a zeroed tensor, the bias alone would determine if *relu*^{1,1} should result in a 0.0 or not.

24 Could we see an example of *relu*^{1,1} in action?

Here is a same-as chart

with weights

$\boldsymbol{\theta}_0$ being [7.1 4.3 −6.4]

with bias

$\boldsymbol{\theta}_1$ being 0.6

and

with the argument tensor

t being [2.0 1.0 3.0]

```
1. ((relu^1,1 [2.0 1.0 3.0])
    (list [7.1 4.3 −6.4] 0.6))
2. (rectify
     (+
       (• [7.1 4.3 −6.4] [2.0 1.0 3.0])
       0.6))
```

Complete this same-as chart.

25 Here goes

```
3. (rectify
     (+
       (sum
         (* [7.1 4.3 −6.4] [2.0 1.0 3.0]))
       0.6))
4. (rectify
     (+
       (sum [14.2 4.3 −19.2])
       0.6))
5. (rectify
     (+ −0.7 0.6))
6. (rectify −0.1)
7. 0.0
```

Perfect.

Now explain why we get 0.0?

26 We get 0.0 because the linear combination of $\boldsymbol{\theta}_0$, $\boldsymbol{\theta}_1$, and t gives us −0.1, which is less than 0.0.

This is why *rectify* does not pass it through, and instead produces 0.0.

Good.

Functions like *relu*^{1,1} are known as *artificial neurons*. Each neuron has a linear part, like *linear*^{1,1}, and a nonlinear decider like *rectify*.

27 *Neurons* sound like they come from biology.

The Rule of Artificial Neurons

An artificial neuron is a parameterized linear function composed with a nonlinear decider function.

---

28 They do.

The function $relu^{1,1}$ is a simplified model of how real neurons in the brain work.

This is also why our compositionally constructed target functions are known as *neural networks*, or neural nets for short.[†]

[†] Thanks, Warren Sturgis McCulloch (1898–1968) and Walter Harry Pitts, Jr. (1923–1969).

The function $relu^{1,1}$ seems pretty simple.

Can it really help identify irises?

---

29 Great question.

With a sufficiently large number of these units, we can model very complex functions.

That seems very hard to believe.

---

30 It does indeed.

Let's see an illustration of how multiple uses of $relu^{1,1}$s can be combined to do more interesting things.

Exciting!

We start by drawing the graph of $relu^{1,1}$ with $\boldsymbol{\theta}_0$ as [1.0] and $\boldsymbol{\theta}_1$ as −1.0.

For this graph, we assume that for any given x, we find the y by invoking

$((relu^{1,1}\ [x])\ \boldsymbol{\theta})$

As an example, find the result of

y for $x = 0.5$

31 Here it is

1. $((relu^{1,1}$ [0.5]) (**list** [1.0] −1.0))
2. (*rectify*
   (+
     (• [1.0] [0.5])
     −1.0))
3. (*rectify*
   (+
     (*sum*
       (∗ [1.0] [0.5]))
     −1.0))
4. (*rectify* −0.5)
5. 0.0

This gives us a point (0.5, 0.0) on the graph.

Correct.

Here is the graph

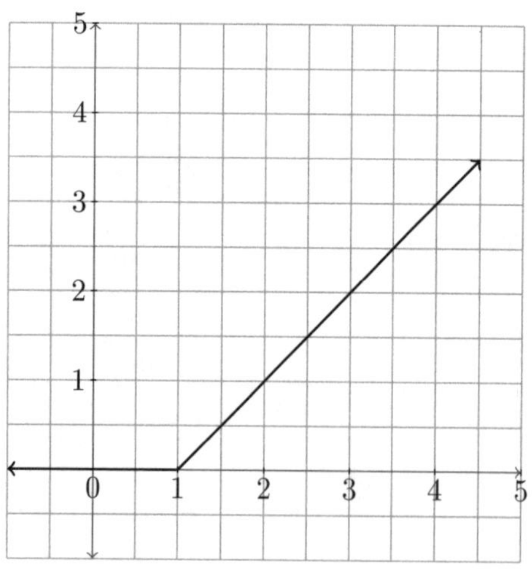

32 That looks like a line with slope 1.0 that is cut off below the x-axis.

Yes.

It has a sharp bend at the point it hits the x-axis.

Explain why this is so.

33 This is because *rectify* does not let any y less than 0.0 pass through.

Excellent.

Let's assume that $\boldsymbol{\theta}_0$ is a tensor^1 with exactly one element, and let's name that element p. In other words, $\boldsymbol{\theta}_0$ is

$[p]$

Similar to *line*, p determines the slope of the slanted portion of the graph, and $\boldsymbol{\theta}_1$ is where the line cuts the y-axis (or would cut it if *rectify* didn't stop it).

Find the point where the graph of $\mathit{relu}^{1,1}$ meets the x-axis and has a bend in it.

34 The equation of the line is

$y = px + \boldsymbol{\theta}_1$

At the point it crosses the x-axis, y is 0.0. Solving for x

$$\begin{aligned} 0.0 &= px + \boldsymbol{\theta}_1 \\ -px &= \boldsymbol{\theta}_1 \\ x &= -\frac{\boldsymbol{\theta}_1}{p} \end{aligned}$$

That's right.

In this equation, when p is positive, x and $\boldsymbol{\theta}_1$ move in opposite directions because of the negative sign

When $\boldsymbol{\theta}_1$ is increased, x decreases

and

when $\boldsymbol{\theta}_1$ is decreased, x increases

35 Does this mean that the graph would shift to the right when $\boldsymbol{\theta}_1$ is decreased, and it would shift to the left when $\boldsymbol{\theta}_1$ is increased?

Here's what it looks like when $\boldsymbol{\theta}_1$ increases from -1.0 to $+0.5$

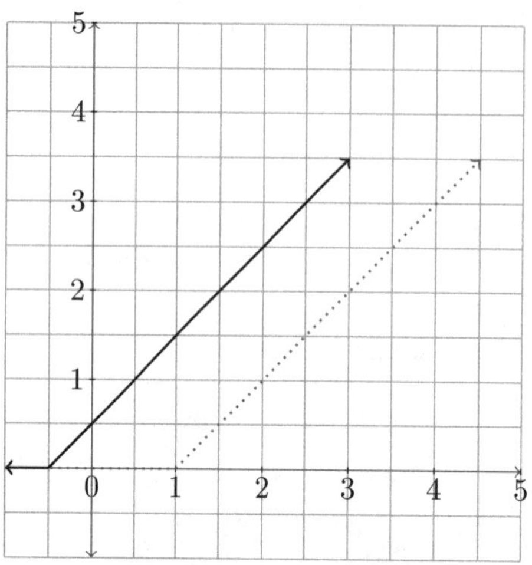

Here, the shifted graph (i.e., when $\boldsymbol{\theta}_1$ is $+0.5$) is solid. The graph has shifted to the left as we have increased $\boldsymbol{\theta}_1$.

Draw the graph when we reduce $\boldsymbol{\theta}_1$ instead from -1.0 to -1.5.

36 The dark line now moves to the right while the dotted line stays the same

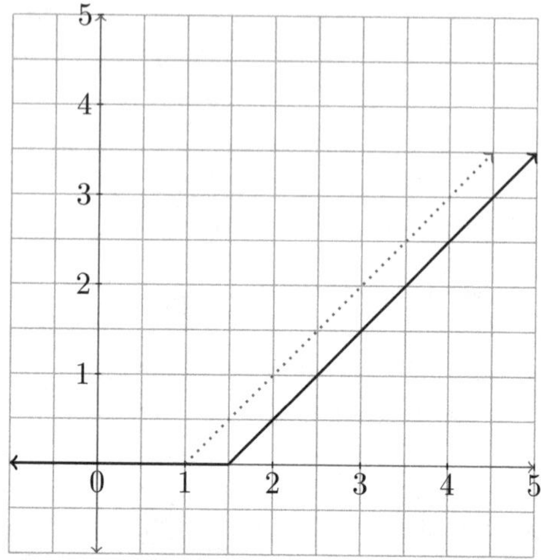

But, how does this allow us to build *interesting* functions?

Patience! It *is* a virtue, after all.

Explain this function *half-strip*

```
(define half-strip
  (λ (x θ)
    (− ((relu^{1,1} [x]) (list θ_0 θ_1))
       ((relu^{1,1} [x]) (list θ_0 θ_2)))))
```

37 For a given x, this function determines $relu^{1,1}$ results, once for $\boldsymbol{\theta}_0$ and $\boldsymbol{\theta}_1$ and then once for $\boldsymbol{\theta}_0$ and $\boldsymbol{\theta}_2$. Finally, it subtracts the second result from the first.

Yes, that is correct.

Let's look at the graph for a *half-strip* where $\boldsymbol{\theta}_0$ is as before (i.e., [1.0]) and

$\boldsymbol{\theta}_1$ is -1.0

Let's take

$\boldsymbol{\theta}_2$ to be -1.5

Here, the two $relu^{1,1}$s are the same as in the graph in frame 36

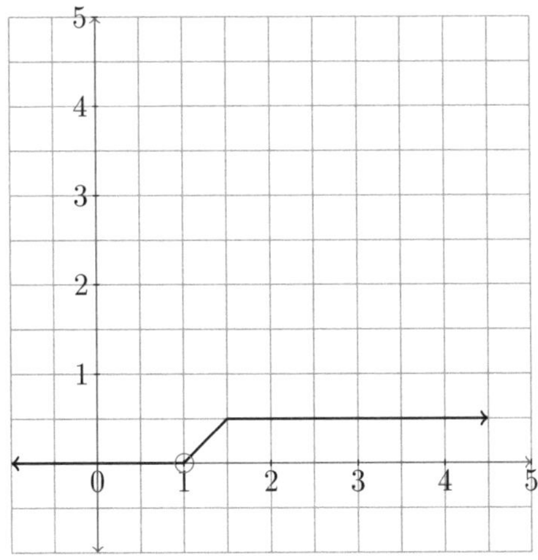

Why does this graph look this way?

38 For all x less than 1.0, both $relu^{1,1}$s are 0.0, so the dark line lies on the x-axis. Between $x = 1.0$ and $x = 1.5$, the first $relu^{1,1}$ starts to become positive, but the second $relu^{1,1}$ is still 0.0.

This causes their difference to rise until $x = 1.5$, but then both $relu^{1,1}$s start rising at the same rate, so the difference between them stays the same, at 0.5.

Why is it named as a *half-strip*? And, what is that orange circle at one end of it?

The space between the x-axis and the dark line looks like a *strip* that begins where the line meets the x-axis. We refer to this as the *left* end of the strip. We highlight ends with orange circles.

39 This strip seems to have only one end.

Indeed.

Since the strip has only one end (and not two), it is named a *half*-strip.

40 So can we get a function *full-strip* that has both ends of the strip?

Yes, we can, by subtracting two half-strips.

Here's another graph which shows two *half-strips* with different values for $\boldsymbol{\theta}_1$ and $\boldsymbol{\theta}_2$. Let's choose $\boldsymbol{\theta}_1$ to be −3.0 and $\boldsymbol{\theta}_2$ to be −3.5

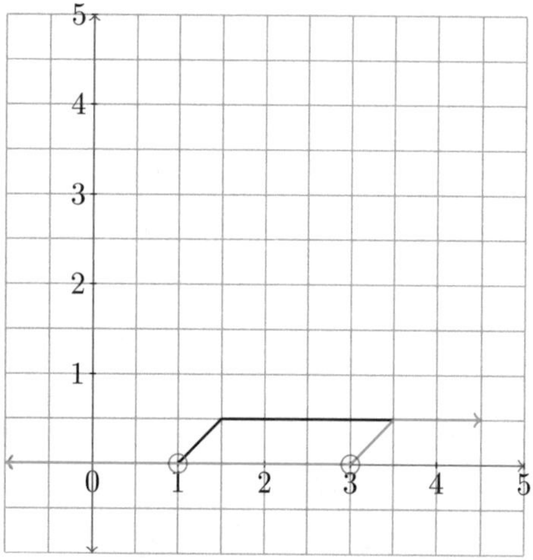

The dark half-strip here is the first half-strip in frame 38, and the turquoise one is the second half-strip.

41 Okay.

The second half-strip shifted to the right here because p in frame 34 is a positive number, lower values of $\boldsymbol{\theta}_1$, −3.0, and $\boldsymbol{\theta}_2$, −3.5, in the turqoise half-strip cause it to lie to the right of the dark half-strip that has values of −1 and −1.5.

Correct.

We now combine two half-strips to define a full strip

```
(define full-strip
  (λ (x θ)
    (− (half-strip x (list θ0 θ1 θ2))
       (half-strip x (list θ3 θ4 θ5)))))
```

42 It seems as if we are subtracting the second half-strip from the first.

Could we see what the graph looks like?

Sure.

Let's take our parameters from the two half-strips in frame 41.

We invoke *full-strip* with $\boldsymbol{\theta}_0$ and $\boldsymbol{\theta}_3$ both being $[1.0]$. We let $\boldsymbol{\theta}_1$ be -1.0 and $\boldsymbol{\theta}_2$ be -1.5. And finally, we let $\boldsymbol{\theta}_4$ be -3.0 and $\boldsymbol{\theta}_5$ be -3.5.

Here's the graph for it

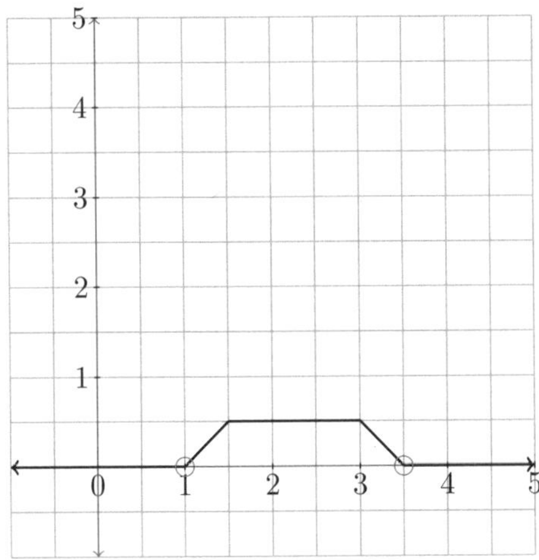

Why does this graph look this way?

43 Our two half-strips have a y-value of 0.0 for all x-values less than 1.0.

Between $x = 1.0$ and $x = 1.5$, the first half-strip rises to 0.5, but the second one is still 0.0. So the dark line, which represents the difference, rises to 0.5 as well and stays at 0.5 until $x = 3.0$.

At $x = 3.0$, the value of the second half-strip starts to rise towards 0.5 so the difference starts to fall until $x = 3.5$ at which point it becomes 0.0 again and stays that way for every remaining value of x.

Why do we have 6 different parameters for *full-strip*?

Good observation.

This allows us to have different slopes at the two ends of the strip, and it allows us to control how wide and tall we would like our strip to be.

44 Why is this named a *full-strip*?

45

This is a *full-strip* because the space between the dark line and the x-axis now has a left end (at $x = 1.0$) and also a right end (at $x = 3.5$) where the dark line meets the x-axis for a second time.

By appropriately manipulating $\boldsymbol{\theta}_0$, $\boldsymbol{\theta}_3$, $\boldsymbol{\theta}_1$, $\boldsymbol{\theta}_4$, $\boldsymbol{\theta}_2$, and $\boldsymbol{\theta}_5$, we get strips of any size and any slopes at the two ends.

What good are these full-strips and half-strips?

46

Full and half strips can be combined using addition and subtraction.

For example

```
(+ (full-strip x
       (list [1.0] –1.0 –1.5
                [1.0] –3.0 –3.5))
    (half-strip x
       (list [1.0] –1.0 –1.5)))
```

Adding the full and half strips together has given us a nonlinear function.

Could we see its graph?

47

Here is its graph

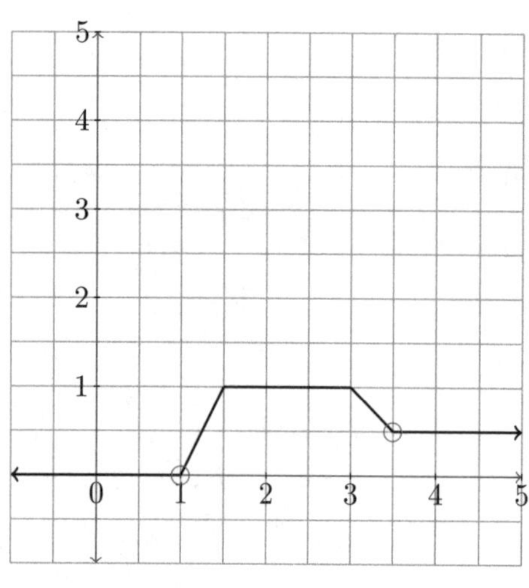

We have two orange circles here for the ends of the strips, and a more interesting graph.

Yes.

Just how interesting a function we can come up with is usually estimated by the number of parameters available for us to update and the number of invocations of $relu^{1,1}$ we rely on.

How many parameters and $relu^{1,1}$ invocations do we have here?

48 The function *half-strip* needs 3 parameters and has 2 $relu^{1,1}$ invocations.

The function *full-strip* needs 6 parameters and has 4 $relu^{1,1}$ invocations.

So, the function in frame 46 has 9 parameters and 6 $relu^{1,1}$ invocations.

Since $relu^{1,1}$ is an artificial neuron, this is an example of how to combine simple artificial neurons to get a more complex function.

49 How can we get even more interesting functions using neurons?

To get yet more interesting functions, we break them down into full and half strips[†] and combine them using addition and subtraction.

Here's a very interesting function broken up into strips (shown with dotted turquoise lines)

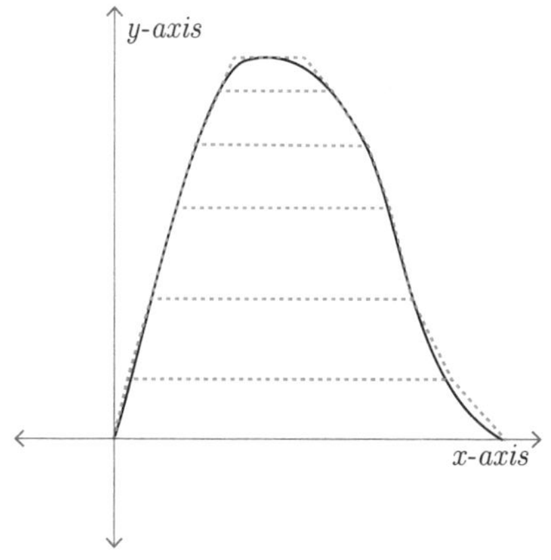

†Thanks, Henri Léon Lebesgue (1875–1941).

50 Can the strips in this graph be constructed using *full-strip* and then added together?

Yes, they can.

We say that these strips together *approximate* the original graph.

51 What does approximate here mean?

The edges of the strips are straight lines, but the graph of the function itself may not follow those straight lines exactly. For example, see the top strip in the graph in frame 50.

This means our strips get us close to the graph, but there are always going to be differences when the graph is curved.†

This is why we say that the strips approximate the function.‡

52 Okay.

†The strips give us what is known as a piecewise-linear approximation.

‡We can increase the number of strips by decreasing the height of each of the strips, and this allows us to get arbitrarily close to the actual curve of the function.

While ours has been merely a simple demonstration with only tensors[1] whose length is always 1, the general principles have been proven for a tensor[1] of any length, and for many different kinds of deciders. The results are known as the theorems of *universal approximation.*†

53 Wow. This way of constructing target functions with strips seems quite burdensome.

†Thanks, Halbert Lynn White Jr. (1950–2012), George Cybenko (1952–), Maxwell Stinchcombe (1957–), and Kurt Hornik (1963–).

The idea of using strips is to illustrate only that artificial neurons can be used as building blocks for very complex functions. We don't use it in practice.

54 How do we build neural networks in practice?

We build them in a more elegant fashion so that they are easier to design and build.

But that can wait until the next chapter.

55 Excellent.

What's for dessert?

Neural Toys

A *medovik* (медовик) is required.
All eleven layers of it!

11
In Love with the Shape of Relu†

†With apologies and thanks to Ed Sheeran (1991–).

How was the *medovik*?[†]

[†]Thanks, 20th Century Cafe (2013–2021) and especially Michelle Polzine.

1 Gooey and yummy.

The *medovik* is appropriate because now we're going to learn about layers.

2 What kinds of layers?

Chapter 10 is about individual neurons.

Here, we put individual neurons together into *layers* in order to build bigger neural networks.

3 What are layers?

We can think of a layer as a group of neurons (like $relu^{1,1}$) that all operate on the same tensor.

More technically, a layer is made up of a *layer function* and a $\boldsymbol{\theta}$ that contains parameters for the layer function.

4 What is a layer function?

A layer function is a function of the form

```
(λ (t)
  (λ (θ)
    ... tensor producing body ...))
```

5 That looks like a target function.

It is, and all layer functions can be target functions.

The tensor argument t to the layer function is known as the *input* to the layer.

6 The layer function also needs a $\boldsymbol{\theta}$ before it can produce a tensor.

Correct.

We provide the *layer function* with an input *and* a $\boldsymbol{\theta}$, and the results of each of its neurons are gathered into a tensor, which is the result produced by the layer function.

7 Is this result the *output* of the layer?

But of course!

8 It's time for an example, isn't it?

It definitely is.

Let's begin with an example of a

layer

that has, say,

4 neurons

As we have just stated above, this layer takes in a tensor and results in a tensor. For now, let's imagine that it takes a tensor^1 t of length 7.

9 The only kind of neuron we know of right now is

$relu^{1,1}$

That is correct.

This layer function then invokes each of those 4 $relu^{1,1}$s on t, this length 7 tensor^1.

10 Won't it also need to send some weights (from frame 199:21) and biases (from frame 199:22) in a $\boldsymbol{\theta}$ for these invocations?

A very good observation.

Let's suppose that we have 4 weights, which are tensors^1

$w|_0$, $w|_1$, $w|_2$, and $w|_3$

11 And what about the biases?

Let's refer to the biases for each of those 4 $relu^{1,1}$s as

$b|_0$, $b|_1$, $b|_2$, and $b|_3$

12 Okay.

What is the shape of each of these weights?

$w|_0$, $w|_1$, $w|_2$, and $w|_3$

13 Since we're sending them to $relu^{1,1}$, they should each have the same shape as t, which is

(**list** 7)

With that information, what can we say about the shape of w?

14 We can say that w has the shape

(**list** 4 7)!

And how about the shape of b?

15 Since the biases to any $relu^{1,1}$ must be a scalar, b is a tensor of shape

(**list** 4)

Excellent.

Now w and b become the first two members of the $\boldsymbol{\theta}$ with which we'll invoke the $relu^{1,1}$s.

What do each of those 4 $relu^{1,1}$s produce?

16 They produce 4 scalars.

Should we put these 4 scalars into a tensor^1?

Very perceptive.

17 That seems a little clumsy.

Here's a way to write this layer function

```
(λ (t)
  (λ (θ)
    (let ((w θ_0) (b θ_1))
      [((relu^{1,1} t) (list w|_0 b|_0))
       ((relu^{1,1} t) (list w|_1 b|_1))
       ((relu^{1,1} t) (list w|_2 b|_2))
       ((relu^{1,1} t) (list w|_3 b|_3))])))
```

Here we invoke $relu^{1,1}$ 4 times, with t as the input tensor and we build 4 separate $\boldsymbol{\theta}$s from the elements of w and b.

It is, and we'll clean it up shortly.

What is important is that each $relu^{1,1}$ produces a scalar, which means that the result of this layer is a tensor^1 of shape

(list 4)

18 So this layer function accepts an input t of shape

(list 7)

and a $\boldsymbol{\theta}$

with weights of shape

(list 4 7)

and biases of shape

(list 4)

to produce a result of shape

(list 4)

Can we generalize this?

Indeed, we can.

Layers with this structure are known as *dense* layers.†

†Also known as *fully-connected* layers.

19 There seems to be a special relationship between the shapes of the tensors in this layer.

There is!

In general, the layer function of a dense layer with m neurons takes one argument t which is a tensor^1 of shape

(list n)

It then accepts a suitable $\boldsymbol{\theta}$

with weights of shape

(list m n)

and biases of shape

(list m)

and invokes each of those m neurons on t, to produce

m

scalars, which form a tensor^1.

We say that the *width* of this layer is m.

20 In our example, m is 4 and n is 7.

Since a dense layer of width m produces a tensor of the shape

(list m)

in our example, the tensor will have the shape

(list 4)

There ought to be a law for this!

The Law of Dense Layers

(Initial Version)

A dense layer function invokes m neurons on an n element input tensor^1 and produces an m element output tensor^1.

As frame 17 points out, the expression for the result tensor is somewhat clumsy.

21 Is there a clearer way to write it?

There is!

The function $*^{2,1}$ in frame 192:48 is a good place to start. It is a function of two arguments. The first is a tensor^2 and the second is a tensor^1.

22 It multiplies each tensor^1 element of its first argument with its second argument, a tensor^1.

So, in our example layer function in frame 17, could we use $*^{2,1}$ and achieve the same result instead of using 4 separate invocations of $relu^{1,1}$?

An insightful observation.

Since w is a tensor^2, it becomes the first argument to $*^{2,1}$, and the input tensor t becomes the second argument.

If w has the shape

(list m n)

and t has the shape

(list n)

the result of the invocation

($*^{2,1}$ w t)

also has the shape

(list m n)

23 But $relu^{1,1}$ does more than just the multiplication.

Don't we need more?

The Law of Dense Layers

(Final Version)

A dense layer function invokes m neurons on an n-element input tensor^1 that produces an m-element output tensor^1 in a single invocation of $*^{2,1}$.

24 This definition is the same as $\bullet$, except that it uses $*^{2,1}$ instead of $*$.

We do!

The function $relu^{1,1}$ uses $\bullet$ and *rectify* in order to produce its final scalar result. In order to reproduce the same behavior as m $relu^{1,1}$s, we also need to write $\bullet^{2,1}$ that uses $*^{2,1}$ to produce m scalars

```
(define •^{2,1}                                  ●
  (λ (w t)
    (sum
      (*^{2,1} w t))))†
```

†Some may recognize this as *matrix-vector multiplication.*

25 In frame 23, ($*^{2,1}$ w t) produces a result of shape (**list** m n). Then *sum* is invoked on this result.

The function *sum* reduces each of the m nested tensors^1 to a single scalar, which results in a tensor^1 of shape (**list** m).

So the result of a $\bullet^{2,1}$ between a tensor^2 of shape

(**list** m n)

and a tensor^1 of shape

(**list** n)

must be a tensor^1 of shape

(**list** m)

That is correct.

If

w's shape is (**list** m n)

and

t's shape is (**list** n)

derive the shape of ($\bullet^{2,1}$ w t).

26 Yes, that is correct.

Show a same-as chart for

($\bullet^{2,1}$ *w t*)

where *w* is

$$\begin{bmatrix} 2.0 & 1.0 & 3.1 \\ 3.7 & 4.0 & 6.1 \end{bmatrix}_{(2\ 3)}$$

and where *t* is

[1.3 0.4 3.3]†

Here is the start of a same-as chart

1. ($\bullet^{2,1}$ *w t*)

Complete it very carefully.

†In this example and some of the following ones, m is smaller than n. In general, however, m and n are independent and are not constrained by each other.

Since we use extended operators, we must descend into tensors until their base ranks are met

2. ($\bullet^{2,1}$ $\begin{bmatrix} 2.0 & 1.0 & 3.1 \\ 3.7 & 4.0 & 6.1 \end{bmatrix}_{(2\ 3)}$ [1.3 0.4 3.3])
3. (*sum* ($*^{2,1}$ [[2.0 1.0 3.1] [3.7 4.0 6.1]] [1.3 0.4 3.3]))
4. (*sum* [($*$ [2.0 1.0 3.1] [1.3 0.4 3.3]) ($*$ [3.7 4.0 6.1] [1.3 0.4 3.3])])
5. (*sum* [[2.6 0.4 10.23] [4.81 1.6 20.13]])
6. [(*sum* [2.6 0.4 10.23]) (*sum* [4.81 1.6 20.13])]
7. [(sum^1 [2.6 0.4 10.23]) (sum^1 [4.81 1.6 20.13])]
8. [13.23 26.54]

27 Great.

Here is *linear*, which is similar to $linear^{1,1}$ from frame 197:14, except that it uses $\bullet^{2,1}$ instead of $\bullet$

```
(define linear                              ●
  (λ (t)
    (λ (θ)
      (+ (•^{2,1} θ_0 t) θ_1))))
```

Okay.

What should the shape of $\boldsymbol{\theta}_1$ be?

28 Let's now assume that

t

has the shape

(list n)

and

$\boldsymbol{\theta}_0$

has the shape

(list m n)

As in frame 25, the shape of

$(\bullet^{2,1}\ \boldsymbol{\theta}_0\ t)$

is

(list m)

Since $\boldsymbol{\theta}_1$ is the bias to be added to the outputs of $\bullet^{2,1}$, and because we want each neuron to have its own bias, it must also have the shape

(list m)

---

29 What does this tell us about the shape of

((*linear* t) $\boldsymbol{\theta}$)

Its shape is

(list m)

which means it is a

tensor^1

of the same length as the number of neurons in the layer.

---

30 Exactly!

We now define the layer function *relu*, which is similar to *relu*^{1,1} from frame 198:17, except that it uses *linear* instead of *linear*^{1,1}

```
(define relu
  (λ (t)
    (λ (θ)
      (rectify ((linear t) θ)))))
```

How would we use this with our example from frame 9?

We would invoke it with a

t

that has the shape

(list 7)

and a

$\boldsymbol{\theta}$

made up of

(list w b)

where

w

has the shape

(list 4 7)

and

b

has the shape

(list 4)

What is the shape of the output tensor[1]?

31 Since we have *relu* as the layer function, the number of neurons is determined by how our $\boldsymbol{\theta}$ is shaped.

Since *rectify* does not affect the shape of

(*linear* t)

it has the same shape, which is a tensor[1] of the same length as the number of neurons in the layer.

In this example, it is

(list 4)

Absolutely right.

A layer of m neurons with an input of length n should be provided a $\boldsymbol{\theta}$ where $\boldsymbol{\theta}_0$ has the shape

(list m n)

and $\boldsymbol{\theta}_1$ has the shape

(list m)

What is the shape of the output tensor of this layer?

32 It is the same as the number of neurons in the layer

(list m)

Very good.

We use this relationship between the shapes of t, $\boldsymbol{\theta}_0$, and $\boldsymbol{\theta}_1$ of *relu* to design our networks.

33 Could we see another example of these shapes?

Sure.

Suppose we have an input tensor[1] of shape

(list 4)

and we want to pass it to a layer of 3 neurons so that we get a tensor of shape

(list 3)

what should the shape of $\boldsymbol{\theta}_0$ be?

34 Based on frame 32, n is 4, m is 3, so the shape of $\boldsymbol{\theta}_0$ should be

(list 3 4)

And what should the shape of $\boldsymbol{\theta}_1$ be?

35 It should be the same as

(list m)

which here is

(list 3)

The list of shapes of the tensor[2] and tensor[1] parameters necessary for a layer is known as the *shape list* of the *layer*.

What is the shape list for our example layer above?

36 It is

```
(list
  (list 3 4)
  (list 3))
```

And, in general, for a dense layer of m neurons and an input length of n?

37 It is

```
(list
  (list m n)
  (list m))
```

Perfect.

Let's start, as hinted in frame 3, putting together simple networks using our only known layer function *relu*.

38 Will we see more layer functions?

There are more coming up, but for now we restrict ourselves to *relu*.

Here is a simple *network function*

```
(define 1-relu
  (λ (t)
    (λ (θ)
      ((relu t) θ))))†
```

Here we have 1 layer, since there is only one invocation of the layer function *relu*.

†Feel free to skip this framenote.
This *1-relu*'s body in two η-reductions simplifies to

relu

Thanks, Alonzo Church.

39 What is a network function?

A network function assembles layer functions together so that the output of one layer becomes the input to the next layer.

40 But that also looks like a target function?

It does.

41 If they are so similar, why do we have different names for them?

Their ultimate purposes are different.

Network functions are intended to be target functions for a gradient descent optimization process where a $\boldsymbol{\theta}$ will be learned.

Layer functions, on the other hand, are used to build network functions.

42 So *1-relu* is a 1-layer network function, built using the layer function *relu*.

Can we see network functions with more than one layer?

Here is a skeleton of a 2-layer network function

```
(define 2-relu
  (λ (t)
    (λ (θ)
      ((relu
         ((relu t) θ))
       R ))))
```

43 How is this a 2-layer network function?

The result tensor of the first, inner invocation of *relu* is passed on to the second, outer invocation of *relu*.

44 Ah, so the output of the first layer, becomes the input to the second layer.

Aren't we supposed to find R?

In a minute.

Let us understand the skeleton a little more. Each of those

relus

requires

two tensor parameters in $\boldsymbol{\theta}$

How many tensor parameters should $\boldsymbol{\theta}$ have?

45 Because we have two layers in this network function, and we need two tensor parameters for each layer. The $\boldsymbol{\theta}$ then must have four tensor parameters.

Correct.

The first two parameters, $\boldsymbol{\theta}_0$ and $\boldsymbol{\theta}_1$, are meant for the first layer (i.e., the inner *relu*).

This inner *relu* can simply access them directly from $\boldsymbol{\theta}$.†

Does it matter that when the first layer function is invoked with $\boldsymbol{\theta}$, it has 4 members in it?

†A slightly more persnickety version of this would be to construct a new list from $\boldsymbol{\theta}_0$ and $\boldsymbol{\theta}_1$ and pass that to the innermost *relu* instead. Here, however, we use the simpler alternative.

46 In frame 27, we see that *relu* contains a *linear* where only $\boldsymbol{\theta}_0$ and $\boldsymbol{\theta}_1$ are used.

So, it doesn't matter that the $\boldsymbol{\theta}$ for the first layer has more than *two* members in it because the remaining members are not used by that layer function.

Good.

The last two parameters, $\boldsymbol{\theta}_2$ and $\boldsymbol{\theta}_3$, are arguments to the outer *relu*.

Now find R.

47 R must be the $\boldsymbol{\theta}$ argument of the outer *relu*, which must be a list consisting of $\boldsymbol{\theta}_2$ and $\boldsymbol{\theta}_3$. So is this

(list $\boldsymbol{\theta}_2$ $\boldsymbol{\theta}_3$)?

Correct.

But there's another function that can be used here and is more general.

48 What function is that?

It is a function that gives us the rest of the list starting at the ith member of a non-empty list l, where i is positive.

We write it†

$l_{i\downarrow}$

†Thanks, Kenneth Eugene Iverson (1920–2004).

49 An example?

For example

1. (**list** 2 4 8 9 6 3 7)$_{4\downarrow}$
2. (**list** 6 3 7)

50 Ah!

This example gives us the rest of the list starting at index 4.

So instead of

(**list** $\boldsymbol{\theta}_2$ $\boldsymbol{\theta}_3$)

we can use

$\boldsymbol{\theta}_{2\downarrow}$

Perfect.

Here's *2-relu*

```
(define 2-relu
  (λ (t)
    (λ (θ)
      ((relu
          ((relu t) θ))
        θ2↓))))
```

We use $\boldsymbol{\theta}_{2\downarrow}$ to get the rest of $\boldsymbol{\theta}$ starting at index 2. Now let's define a 3-layer network function, *3-relu*.

51 Can we use *2-relu* to define *3-relu*?

Yes we can![†]

Define a function *3-relu* which is a 3-layer network function, with three *relus*. And do it using *2-relu*.

[†]Thanks, Keith Chapman (1959–) for the creation of *Bob the Builder* (1997–).

52 How about this?

```
(define 3-relu
  (λ (t)
    (λ (θ)
      ((2-relu
          ((relu t) θ))
        θ2↓))))
```

Very good.

We first invoke *relu* on the input t, and let it use up the first two members of $\boldsymbol{\theta}$. This is the output of the first layer.

So, $\boldsymbol{\theta}$ must have two tensor parameters for each of those

relus

Now explain the rest of it.

53 We pass the output of the first layer to *2-relu*, which is a 2-layer network function, and provide it with all but the first two members of $\boldsymbol{\theta}$.

Can we generalize these functions for any given natural number k of layers?

Yes, indeed!

But we'll get there in a couple of steps. Let us begin with a simple recursive function that can do this

```
(define k-relu
  (λ (k t θ)
    (cond
      ((zero? k) t)
      (else (k-relu (sub1 k)
              ((relu t) θ)
              θ2↓)))))
```

We start with a tensor t and run it through k invocations of *relu*, at each invocation using up two members of $\boldsymbol{\theta}$ to produce a final output tensor.

54 It is defined so that at least one of the expression's values shrinks. Here k shrinks because of (*sub1 k*) and $\boldsymbol{\theta}$ shrinks because of $\boldsymbol{\theta}_{2\downarrow}$.

But this isn't quite correct, is it?

It is not!

The problem is that network functions, as in *1-relu*, *2-relu*, and *3-relu* above, must take their arguments t and $\boldsymbol{\theta}$ *one at a time.* So *k-relu* needs nested λ-expressions. And, the **else**-clause would have to include more parentheses.

55 Could we do this slowly?

Yes, indeed.

In the dashed version above, there are three arguments. In the next dashed version, we take the first argument and separate it out into a λ of its own

```
(define k-relu
  (λ (k)
    (λ (t θ)
      (cond
        ((zero? k) t)
        (else ((k-relu (sub1 k))
               ((relu t) θ)
               θ2↓))))))
```

The only implication of this is that when we invoke *k-relu*, we must first provide the argument for *k*, and then provide the other two

((*relu* *t*) $\boldsymbol{\theta}$)

and

$\boldsymbol{\theta}_{2\downarrow}$

56 In other words, instead of invoking

(*k-relu* (*sub1* *k*) ((*relu* *t*) $\boldsymbol{\theta}$) $\boldsymbol{\theta}_{2\downarrow}$)

we invoke

((*k-relu* (*sub1* *k*)) ((*relu* *t*) $\boldsymbol{\theta}$) $\boldsymbol{\theta}_{2\downarrow}$)

And we can repeat that for

(λ (*t* $\boldsymbol{\theta}$) ...)

as well.

Correct.

Here is the final *k-relu*

```
(define k-relu
  (λ (k)
    (λ (t)
      (λ (θ)
        (cond
          ((zero? k) t)
          (else (((k-relu (sub1 k))
                  ((relu t) θ)
                  θ2↓))))))))†
```

57 This definition seems quite complex.

†Each step from frame 54 is known as "Currying." Thanks, Moses Schönfinkel and Haskell Brooks Curry.

Let's analyze it case-by-case.

When k is 0, we have no layers. So the result is the input, t.

When k is positive, we find the result of the first layer

((*relu* t) $\boldsymbol{\theta}$)

invoking *relu* on the input t, and then taking that result, and invoking it on $\boldsymbol{\theta}$. This uses up the first two members of $\boldsymbol{\theta}$.

What happens next?

58 The expression (*k-relu* (*sub1* k)) gives us a neural network consisting of $k - 1$ layers. We invoke this slightly smaller network on the result of the first layer

((*relu* t) $\boldsymbol{\theta}$)

and provide it the remaining members of

$\boldsymbol{\theta}$

Could we see an example?

Here is an example where k is 4, with t and $\boldsymbol{\theta}$ as the remaining arguments

1. (((*k-relu* 4) t) $\boldsymbol{\theta}$)
2. (((*k-relu* (*sub1* 4))
   ((*relu* t) $\boldsymbol{\theta}$))
   $\boldsymbol{\theta}_{2\downarrow}$)
3. (((*k-relu* 3)
   ((*relu* t) $\boldsymbol{\theta}$))
   $\boldsymbol{\theta}_{2\downarrow}$)
4. (((*k-relu* 2)
   ((*relu*
   ((*relu* t) $\boldsymbol{\theta}$))
   $\boldsymbol{\theta}_{2\downarrow}$))
   $\boldsymbol{\theta}_{2\downarrow 2\downarrow}$)
5. (((*k-relu* 1)
   ((*relu*
   ((*relu*
   ((*relu* t) $\boldsymbol{\theta}$))
   $\boldsymbol{\theta}_{2\downarrow}$))
   $\boldsymbol{\theta}_{2\downarrow 2\downarrow}$))
   $\boldsymbol{\theta}_{2\downarrow 2\downarrow 2\downarrow}$)

Complete the rest of this same-as chart.

59 Here it is

6. (((*k-relu* 0)
   ((*relu*
   ((*relu*
   ((*relu*
   ((*relu* t) $\boldsymbol{\theta}$))
   $\boldsymbol{\theta}_{2\downarrow}$))
   $\boldsymbol{\theta}_{2\downarrow 2\downarrow}$))
   $\boldsymbol{\theta}_{2\downarrow 2\downarrow 2\downarrow}$))
   $\boldsymbol{\theta}_{2\downarrow 2\downarrow 2\downarrow 2\downarrow}$)
7. ((*relu*
   ((*relu*
   ((*relu*
   ((*relu* t) $\boldsymbol{\theta}$))
   $\boldsymbol{\theta}_{2\downarrow}$))
   $\boldsymbol{\theta}_{2\downarrow 2\downarrow}$))
   $\boldsymbol{\theta}_{2\downarrow 2\downarrow 2\downarrow}$)

So (*k-relu* 4) gives us 4 invocations of *relu*!

60 Great.

Now let us look more carefully at a $\boldsymbol{\theta}$ that goes with a network function created using *k-relu*.

What should $\boldsymbol{\theta}$ look like for any given k?

In the definition of *k-relu*, we see that every recursive invocation of *k-relu* is accompanied by a $\boldsymbol{\theta}_{2\downarrow}$, which peels off 2 tensor parameters from $\boldsymbol{\theta}$.

Since this happens k times for k layers, the length of $\boldsymbol{\theta}$ is *2k*.

---

61 In this $\boldsymbol{\theta}$, which members are weights and which ones are biases?

From the definition of *relu*, we know that its $\boldsymbol{\theta}_0$ is a weight, and its $\boldsymbol{\theta}_1$ is a bias.

This means that in a $\boldsymbol{\theta}$ for k layers, every member at an even index[†] is a weight tensor, and every member at an odd index is a bias tensor.

[†]Since lists are indexed starting at 0, we consider 0 to be even.

---

62 For the ith layer, at which index would we find its weight tensor?

We would find it at *2i*.

---

63 And the bias tensor?

We would find it at *2i* + 1.

---

64 Excellent.

So, if the width of the ith layer of the neural network is

m

and the length of its input is

n

What are the shapes of the tensors at

2i

and

2i+1

The tensor at *2i* is the weight tensor and it has the shape

(**list** m n)

The tensor at *2i+1* is the bias tensor and it has the shape

(**list** m)

Great.

It's time for a slightly bigger example. Let's take a 3-layer network where the input is a tensor[1] of shape

(**list** 32)

and the width of

the first dense layer is 64

the second dense layer is 45

the third dense layer is 26

What is the network function for this network?

65 It is

(*k-relu* 3)

And, what is the length of

$\boldsymbol{\theta}$?

66 It is twice the number of layers

6

Correct.

The first layer is 64 neurons wide, with the input of shape

(**list** 32)

So, $\boldsymbol{\theta}_0$ must be of shape

(**list** 64 32)

and the shape of $\boldsymbol{\theta}_1$ must be

(**list** 64)

What about the second layer?

67 The second layer receives its input from the first layer, so its input has the shape

(**list** 64)

The width of this layer is 45 so $\boldsymbol{\theta}_2$ must have the shape

(**list** 45 64)

and the shape of $\boldsymbol{\theta}_3$ must be

(**list** 45)

The third layer receives its input from the second layer, so its input has the shape

(**list** 45)

68 What are $\boldsymbol{\theta}_4$ and $\boldsymbol{\theta}_5$?

The width of this layer is

26

so

$\boldsymbol{\theta}_4$

must have the shape

(list 26 45)

What about $\boldsymbol{\theta}_5$?

69 The shape of

$\boldsymbol{\theta}_5$

comes directly from the width of the layer

(list 26)

Correct.

If we combine all these shapes into a single list, we get a *shape list* for the *network*.

What is the shape list for this network?

70 It is

```
(list
  (list 64 32)
  (list 64)

  (list 45 64)
  (list 45)

  (list 26 45)
  (list 26))
```

Excellent.

Together (*k-relu* 3) and this list of shapes fully describe our example neural network.

71 How do we go from this description of a neural network to a fully working one?

Step-by-step!

We'll learn the next step in the next chapter.

72 Ooh ... time for another snack!

Shapey Toys

How about a triple berry trifle?
With some whipped cream, of course!

12 Rock Around the Block†

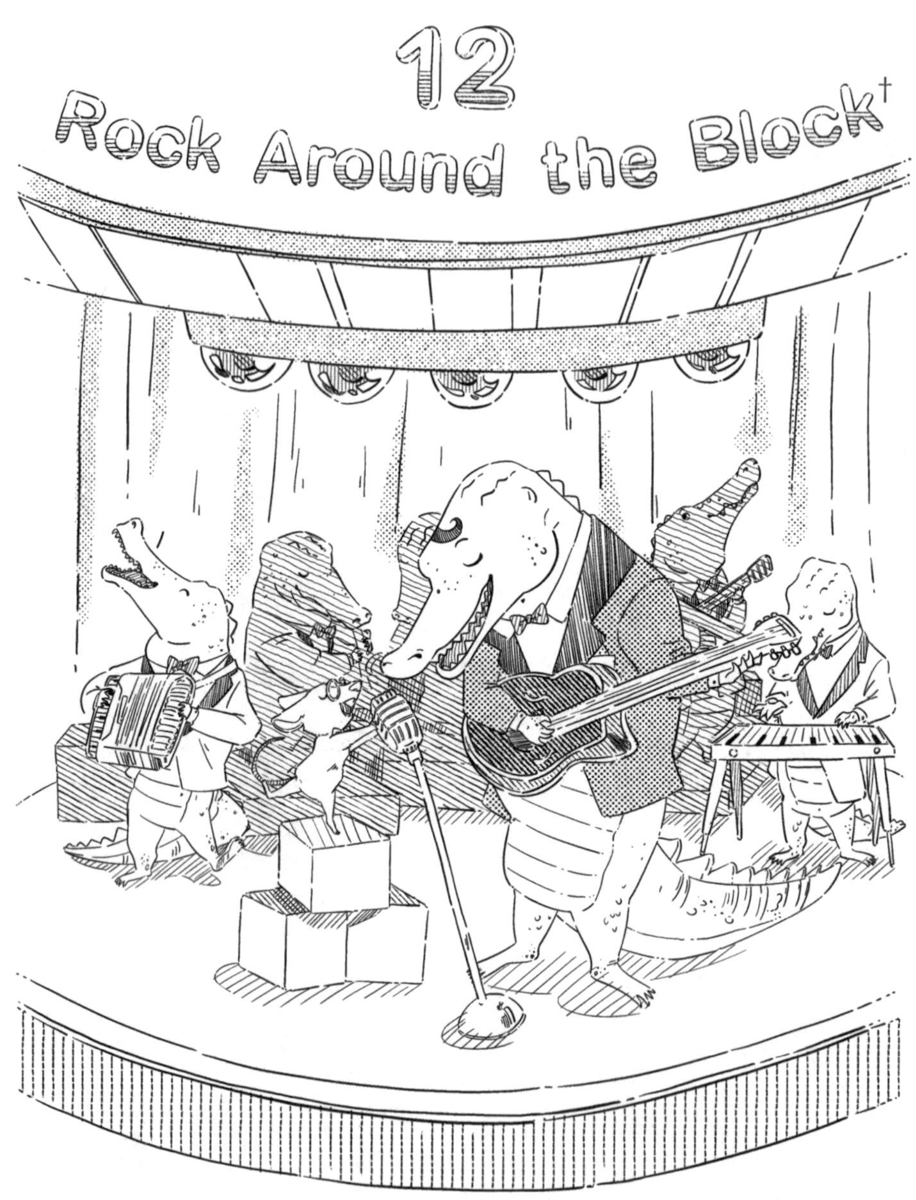

†With apologies and thanks to William John Clifton Haley (1925–1981), Bill Haley and His Comets of the 1954 recording for Decca records, Marshall Edward Lytle (1923–2013), Francis Eugene Beecher (1921–2014), William Famous Williamson (1925–1996), John Andrew Grande (1930–2006), William Gussak (1920–1994), Donato Joseph Cedrone (1920–1954), Joseph D'Ambrosio (1934–2021), Producer Milton Gabler (1911–2001), and song writers Max Charles Freedman (1893–1962) and James Edward Myers (1919–2001).

Refreshed?

1 The triple berry trifle hit the spot.

Let's go back to our 3-layer network from frame 232:65 where the input is a tensor[1] of shape

(**list** 32)

and the width of

the first dense layer is 64

the second dense layer is 45

the third dense layer is 26

2 Yes, where our network function is

(*k-relu* 3)

And what about its shape list?

3 Interesting.

It is in frame 233:70

```
(list
  (list 64 32)
  (list 64)
  (list 45 64)
  (list 45)
  (list 26 45)
  (list 26))
```

Correct.

Here, we have constructed our network function separately from its shape list and we built the shape list by considering only the widths of each layer.

4 Is there a problem with doing things that way?

While this separation is sometimes useful, it is more convenient when defining large and complex networks, to

> define the layer functions and shapes *together* for each layer

and then

> *stack the layers* to combine them into a single network function and a single list of shapes

5 Hmm, that sounds a little abstract.

Let's make it real, then.

We begin by introducing *blocks*.[†]

[†] A *block* is short for *network building block*.

6 What is a *block*?

A block associates a layer function with its shape list.

7 Could we see an example?

Certainly!

Here is a block for the first layer in our example network

```
(define layer1
  (block relu
    (list
      (list 64 32)
      (list 64))))
```

Now we invoke the function *block* on two arguments.

Explain these two arguments.

8 The first argument is the layer function *relu* and the second argument is the shape list for 64 neurons, and an input tensor^1 of length 32 with shapes in frame 232:67.

Should we define the second layer similarly?

We should.

Show a block for the second layer, *layer2* from that frame, with 45 neurons in it.

9 The shapes for the second layer are also in frame 232:67. Here is how we define the block *layer2*

```
(define layer2
  (block relu
    (list
      (list 45 64)
      (list 45))))
```

And what about the third layer?

10 It is defined like this

```
(define layer3
  (block relu
    (list
      (list 26 45)
      (list 26))))
```

But we still haven't seen what *block* does!

An excellent point.

Here's how we define *block*

```
(define block
  (λ (fn shape-lst)
    (list fn shape-lst)))
```

We refer to

fn

here as the

block function

and the

shape-lst

here as the

block list

11 So it just puts them together in a list?

Simple, isn't it?

Define *block-fn*, which takes a block and returns its function, and *block-ls*, which takes a block and returns its shape list.

12 Here they are

```
(define block-fn
  (λ (ba)
    ba_0))

(define block-ls
  (λ (ba)
    ba_1))
```

Now let's see the real magic in these blocks.

As frame 233:71 shows, a neural network is fully described by a network function and a shape list.

13 Oh, that means a neural network can also be a block!

So stacking blocks together also produces another block.

Let's define the neural network in the example from frame 232:65

```
(define 3-layer-network
  (stack-blocks
    (list
      layer1
      layer2
      layer3)))
```

14 What is *stack-blocks*?

Here, *stack-blocks* is a function that takes a list of blocks and produces a new block whose function

> is a combination of the individual block functions

and whose shape list

> is made up by joining the individual block lists

15 That needs some breaking down, doesn't it?

Let's break that down a little by way of our example, then.

We want our network to first invoke the *relu* from *layer1* on the input tensor^1 of length 32 using the first two parameters of $\boldsymbol{\theta}$ whose shapes are given by the shape list of *layer1*.

What happens to the output of that invocation?

16 The output of the invocation of that *relu* will be a tensor^1 of length 64.

We invoke the *relu* from *layer2* on it, using the next two parameters of $\boldsymbol{\theta}$ whose shapes are given by the shape list of *layer2*.

Then we do the same thing with the output of this invocation but for *layer3*.

Precisely.

So, in the network, the three *relu*s from each of the layer blocks are *composed* together and this *composite* function consumes 6 parameters from a given $\boldsymbol{\theta}$.

What about the shapes of these 6 parameters?

17 The shapes of these 6 parameters are given by joining together the shape lists of each of the three layer blocks.

The first two from *layer1*, the third and fourth from *layer2*, and the fifth and sixth from *layer3*.

Can we now define *stack-blocks*?

Yes, but in little pieces.

Here's a function *block-compose*. It expects two block functions f and g as its first two arguments. Its third argument, j is the number of parameters from $\boldsymbol{\theta}$ that f will consume

```
(define block-compose
  (λ (f g j)
    (λ (t)
      (λ (θ)
        ((g
           ((f t) θ))
         θ_j↓)))))
```

Explain what this function does.

18 It returns a block function that expects a tensor t followed by $\boldsymbol{\theta}$, and then first invokes f on t and then $\boldsymbol{\theta}$.

The result of this invocation is sent as an argument to the invocation of g, along with a $\boldsymbol{\theta}$ from which the first j parameters have been removed, because those j parameters are intended for f.

Could we see an example of how this function works?

Sure.

Let us compose two *relu*s together. We know that a *relu* expects two parameters, so *j* will be 2

```
1. (block-compose relu relu 2)
2. (λ (t)
     (λ (θ)
       ((relu
          ((relu t) θ))
        θ2↓)))
```

19 This is the same function as *2-relu*, isn't it?

It is!

We could also define *2-relu* this way

```
(define 2-relu
  (block-compose relu relu 2))
```

20 This doesn't seem like enough to define *stack-blocks*.

No, it isn't.

We must also find a method to join the two block lists.

21 There must be a function for that.

There is, and it is called *append*. Here is how it works

```
1. (append (list 3 6 1) (list 7 2))
2. (list 3 6 1 7 2)
```

22 How does it behave on the block lists of *layer1* and *layer2*?

Let us find out

1.
```
(append
  (list
    (list 64 32)
    (list 64))
  (list
    (list 45 64)
    (list 45)))
```

Finish this same-as chart.

23 Here it is

2.
```
(list
  (list 64 32)
  (list 64)
  (list 45 64)
  (list 45))
```

So *append* preserves the shapes, but joins the lists of shapes in the order of the arguments.

Correct.

We can use *block-compose* in frame 18 and *append* in frame 22 to define a function *stack2* that stacks two blocks *ba* and *bb*. Here is its skeleton

```
(define stack2
  (λ (ba bb)
    (block
      (block-compose
        (block-fn ba)
        (block-fn bb)
        [    B    ])
      (append
        [    C    ]
        [    D    ]))))
```

Find *B*, *C* and *D*.

24 *B* is the third argument to *block-compose* so it must be the number of parameters consumed by the block function

(*block-fn ba*)

which is

|(*block-ls ba*)|

C and *D* are shape lists that must be appended to get the final shape list for the block. Therefore

C is (*block-ls ba*)

and

D is (*block-ls bb*)

Great.

Here is *stack2*

```
(define stack2
  (λ (ba bb)
    (block
      (block-compose
        (block-fn ba)
        (block-fn bb)
        |(block-ls ba)|)
      (append
        (block-ls ba)
        (block-ls bb)))))
```

25 Are we now ready to define *stack-blocks*?

We are!

The function *stack-blocks* takes one argument *bls*, which is a list of blocks that we must stack

```
(define stack-blocks
  (λ (bls)
    (stacked-blocks bls_1↓ bls_0)))

(define stacked-blocks
  (λ (rbls ba)
    (cond
      ((null? rbls) ba)
      (else
        (stacked-blocks rbls_1↓
          [      A      ])))))
```

Here, the predicate *null?* checks whether a list has any members. The stacking is done by *stacked-blocks* whose first argument is a list of blocks, and whose second argument is a block that starts off the stacking.

26 It seems that these definitions follow the law of simple accumulator passing.

We're invoking *stacked-blocks* with the second argument as the first block in *bls*, and the first argument as the remaining blocks in *bls*.

We must find A, mustn't we?

We must!

The function *stacked-blocks* accepts two arguments, the first being a

list of blocks *rbls*

and the second

a block *ba*

onto which the blocks from *rbls* will be stacked.

The second argument *ba* can be thought of as an accumulator that holds a partially-combined block.

Now find A.

27 Here, if *rbls* is empty, then we don't need to do any further stacking and, we return the partially-combined block *ba*.

Otherwise, we must combine the accumulator block

ba

with the first block

$rbls_0$

and use it as the new value of the accumulator as we traverse down the rest of the blocks using *stacked-blocks*.

So, A is

($stack2\ ba\ rbls_0$)

Excellent.

Here's the complete definition

```
(define stack-blocks                                  ●
  (λ (bls)
    (stacked-blocks bls_1↓ bls_0)))

(define stacked-blocks
  (λ (rbls ba)
    (cond
      ((null? rbls) ba)
      (else
        (stacked-blocks rbls_1↓
          (stack2 ba rbls_0))))))
```

28 How about an example of how it works?

Sure.

```
1. (stack-blocks
     (list
       layer1
       layer2
       layer3))
2. (stacked-blocks
     (list
       layer2
       layer3)
     layer1)
3. (stacked-blocks
     (list
       layer3)
     (stack2 layer1 layer2))
4. (stacked-blocks
     (list)
     (stack2
       (stack2 layer1 layer2)
       layer3))
5. (stack2
     (stack2
       (block relu
         (list
           (list 64 32)
           (list 64)))
       (block relu
         (list
           (list 45 64)
           (list 45))))
     layer3)
```

Now finish this same-as chart.

29 Here we go

```
6. (stack2
     (block (λ (t)
              (λ (θ)
                ((relu
                   ((relu t) θ))
                 θ2↓)))
       (list
         (list 64 32)
         (list 64)
         (list 45 64)
         (list 45)))
     (block relu
       (list
         (list 26 45)
         (list 26))))
7. (block (λ (t)
            (λ (θ)
              ((relu
                 ((relu
                    ((relu t) θ))
                  θ2↓))
               θ4↓)))
     (list
       (list 64 32)
       (list 64)
       (list 45 64)
       (list 45)
       (list 26 45)
       (list 26)))
```

The Law of Blocks

Blocks can be stacked to form bigger blocks and complete networks.

Excellent.

We can also define functions that produce specific kinds of blocks. Here's a useful one

```
(define dense-block                    ●
  (λ (n m)
    (block relu
      (list
        (list m n)
        (list m)))))
```

Here n is the length of the input tensor and m is the number of neurons. Explain what *dense-block* does.

30 It produces a dense layer block with *relu* as the block function and the corresponding dense layer shape list for m neurons working on a tensor[1] of length n.

Great.

Using *dense-block*, rewrite our definitions of *layer1*, *layer2*, and *layer3*.

31 Here they are

```
(define layer1
  (dense-block 32 64))

(define layer2
  (dense-block 64 45))

(define layer3
  (dense-block 45 26))
```

Once we have a network defined like this, and we have a data set, we can find a well-fitted $\boldsymbol{\theta}$ for the network function such that the members of $\boldsymbol{\theta}$ have exactly the shapes dictated by the shape list of the network.

But we'll learn how to do that in the next chapter.

[32] What's our next dessert?

Blocky Toys

How about a stack of crêpes suzette? Flambéed!

This space reserved for caramel stains

13
An Eye for an Iris

How was that stack of crêpes suzette?[†]

[†]Thanks, Henri Charpentier (1880–1961) and thanks, Julia Child (1912–2004) for popularizing.

1 Orangey!

Up and away, then!

Here we introduce Uncle Edgar. He loves growing irises.

2 First apples and now irises!

Uncle Edgar has 150 iris plants in his garden from 3 different species

Iris Setosa

Iris Versicolor

Iris Virginica

He has 50 plants of each species.

3 That's a lot of plants!

Uncle Edgar is obsessed with data about his irises.

4 What kind of data?

He takes a flower from each plant, and measures

the width and length of the *sepals*

the width and length of the *petals*

and he records the species of the plant from which the flower has grown.[†]

Uncle Edgar believes that these four scalars are enough to correctly classify an iris according to its species.

[†]Thanks, Edgar Shannon Anderson (1897–1969) for the original iris data set.

5 What's a sepal?

A sepal is one of the divisions of the *calyx*. The calyx connects the flower to its stem.

6 What does Uncle Edgar's data set look like?

Here is an entry in Uncle Edgar's data set

Petal Length: 5.1 cm.

Petal Width: 3.5 cm.

Sepal Length: 1.4 cm.

Sepal Width: 0.2 cm.

Species: *Setosa*

7 Those four numbers can be put into a tensor[1] of length 4.

Correct.

We rewrite this entry in our iris data set as

x: [5.1 3.5 1.4 0.2]

y: *Setosa*

8 But y is not a tensor here!

That is correct.

We cannot use this data set directly with our functions yet. We must *encode* a set of discrete species as a tensor.

9 How can we do that?

Since we have 3 species, we use a tensor[1] of length 3, assigning an index to each species.[†]

So, for example, we say that

index 0 corresponds to *Setosa*

index 1 corresponds to *Versicolor*

index 2 corresponds to *Virginica*

10 How would we encode, say, *Versicolor*?

[†]These indices are generally assigned arbitrarily, but we choose to assign them alphabetically.

Since the index of *Versicolor* is 1, we make the element of the tensor at index 1 be 1.0 and the elements at the other two indices be 0.0. The resulting tensor would look like

[0.0 1.0 0.0]

What would the tensors for *Setosa* and *Virginica* be?

11 The index for *Setosa* is 0; the tensor would look like

[1.0 0.0 0.0]

The index for *Virginica* is 2; the tensor would look like

[0.0 0.0 1.0]

Correct.

This way of assigning outputs is an encoding known as

one-hot[†]

It is a common way of assigning input tensors to *classes*. Here we have three classes, one for each species.

[†]Thanks, Leopold Kronecker (1823–1891).

12 Why do we use 1.0?

Why not some other scalar like 328.9?

A very good question.

It has to do with *degrees of belief*.

13 What is a degree of belief?

It is the confidence we have about a certain statement.

Suppose we know for certain that we have an iris of the species *Versicolor*. Then we say with 100% confidence that the iris belongs to that class

$$100\% = 100/100 = 1.0$$

14 Oh, so that is why we say that the different indices representing each species should be 1.0, since it represents a 100% confidence.

Correct.

At the same time, if an iris belongs to one species, we have 0% confidence that the iris belongs to either of the other species.

15 That is why the scalars at indices other than the one for a given species are 0.0.

So the output tensor reflects our confidence that a certain iris belongs to a particular species.

Yes, that is exactly the interpretation of our output tensor.

So what should Uncle Edgar's entry in frame 8 look like as tensors?

16 Since this entry corresponds to *Setosa*, and our index for that is 0, so the entry looks like

x: [5.1 3.5 1.4 0.2]

y: [1.0 0.0 0.0]

Excellent.

We rewrite all the remaining points, so that our iris data set consists entirely of tensors.

How can we define a function to automatically classify a new iris if we know only its measurements?

17 Should we use the toys we have in our toy chest?

Yes, we should!

We must find a target function whose $\boldsymbol{\theta}$ can be learned using gradient descent on Uncle Edgar's data set.

18 Great.

How do we get started?

We begin by designing a network made from dense layers like in chapter 12.

19 Exciting!

Our first decision is how many layers we want, and how wide to make each layer.

20 How do we decide that?

Let's start with the output layer, which is the last layer in our network.

We know that each y in our data is a one-hot encoding of size 3, so, in order to compare a predicted y with an actual y, each predicted y must also be a tensor[1] of shape

(list 3)

Based on what we know of dense layers, how wide should the output layer be?

21 It should have a width of 3.

Correct.

The network we're building assigns each input x a class y by producing a *one-hot-like* tensor.

22 What is a one-hot-like tensor?

It is like a one-hot tensor, but here the degrees of belief for the individual classes may be any number between 0.0 and 1.0. We refer to this encoding as

one-hot-like

23 Does this mean that our degree of belief for a given class is neither 0% nor 100%?

That is exactly what it means.

24 How do we then decide what class that tensor represents?

In a one-hot-like encoding, the class with the highest degree of belief is the one we deem to be predicted. For example, a predicted y could be something like

[0.2 0.7 0.1]

What class does this represent?

25 Here the highest degree of belief is at

index 1

which stands for the class

Versicolor

We need more layers in our network, don't we?

For Uncle Edgar's data set, we add just one more layer.

26 Is it still a deep network?

Yes, indeed!

Let's make the width of this layer 6.

27 Why 6? Why not 8 or 2?

In general, the layers closer to the input are wider than the layers closer to the output.

28 Why is that?

The layers closer to the input are responsible for learning some of the more primitive characteristics of the data set, and the layers closer to the output learn more advanced characteristics based on the output produced by the earlier layers.

Here we pick the width 6 because it is reasonably larger than 3. The actual choice of the widths is done somewhat empirically.

29 Does that mean we establish it through experiments?

That is correct.

The design of the network and the choices of scalars for the hyperparameters are often determined by experimenting on the whole data set, or smaller subsets of it, although the statistics of the data set can help with some design decisions.

30 Okay.

---

31 Back to our problem of irises.

Yes.

We have now established a design for our deep neural network.

It has two layers, the first one being 6 neurons wide and the second one being 3 neurons wide.

---

32 Using *dense-block* from frame 247:30, define this network.

Here it is

```
(define iris-network
  (stack-blocks
    (list
      (dense-block 4 6)
      (dense-block 6 3))))
```

What next?

---

33 Now we *train* the network.

What does training the network mean?

---

34 Training is the process of learning a well-fitted $\boldsymbol{\theta}$ for the network function using a data set.

So to train *iris-network*, we must find a well-fitted $\boldsymbol{\theta}$ for its network function using Uncle Edgar's data set.

---

35 We must, but there is one more thing we need first.

We need an initial estimate of $\boldsymbol{\theta}$ to start the process.

Why can't we use zeros as we did before?

---

36 We do use zeros for all the bias parameters in a $\boldsymbol{\theta}$.

Okay. That means that all the tensors^1 in our $\boldsymbol{\theta}$ are initialized with 0.0.

What about the weights, which are the tensors^2 in our $\boldsymbol{\theta}$?

The story is different for the weights, because it leads to a big problem.

When all the scalars in a tensor^2 are the same (in this case 0.0), all the tensor^1 elements of that tensor^2 are also identical.

What does that mean for the result of $*^{2,1}$ that is part of *relu*?

37 All the tensors^1 in the output of the $*^{2,1}$ will be identical, and consequently, the result produced by *relu* will contain identical scalars.

Correct.

So rather than each neuron making a different small decision about its input, all the neurons in the layer end up learning to make the same decision over and over again.

38 So it seems as if we need to have non-identical scalars in the tensors^2 in $\boldsymbol{\theta}$.

The best thing to do for a network made up of *relu*s is to initialize the weights in $\boldsymbol{\theta}$ with random scalars.

39 How does having randomly initialized weights help?

Since randomly initializing weights generally ensures that each weight has a different value most of the time, every neuron in the network will behave differently.

40 So each neuron will learn to make different decisions.

Correct.

It makes the network more effective at what we're trying to make it do. This is known as *breaking the symmetry* between neurons.

41 Okay, let's go with that then.

We can't as yet.

We encounter a second problem when we use random weights in networks with lots of layers.

42 What problem is that?

Imagine a single scalar in an input tensor. As it makes its way through each layer, it is multiplied by a weight scalar, and added to a sum, and when there are many layers, each of those layers indirectly multiplies that input scalar.

43 So in the output of the network, the effect of a scalar in the input is felt through the multiplication of a number of weights.

That is correct.

What would happen if all those weights were large numbers?

44 Ah, the outputs could become very large due to the presence of so many large weights.

What does it mean for our network?

It means the numbers are too large to give us meaningful results, and will often give rise to numerical errors in the program. We refer to this as

exploding

45 What if we made those weights really tiny fractions?

Conversely, if those weights are tiny fractions, multiplying them together with a scalar in the input is likely to yield a number that is really close to zero. We call this

vanishing

46 Oh, that's not really good either, is it?

A related problem with having weights too large or too small is that the gradients that we calculate for them when using gradient descent can also become very large or very small. This is known as the *exploding* or *vanishing* gradient problem.

Together these problems make it difficult to train the network.

47 So, we need our weights to be

random

not too large

not too small

That's a tall order!

Actually, it isn't.

Let us begin by addressing the first requirement. Here is a function

random-tensor

that takes three arguments

c a central value

v a variance

s a shape

48 Does this function produce a tensor of shape s with random scalars?

It does!

The arguments c and v control the nature of these randomly generated scalars.

49 How do they do that?

The central value argument c dictates that the average of all the random numbers in the tensor should be as close to c as possible.

In other words, the random numbers are sprinkled somewhat evenly around the value of c.

50 Okay.

What does *variance* mean?

51 The variance argument v determines how far away from c a given random number is likely to be.

For example, a smaller value of v will mean that most of the random numbers are closely clustered around c whereas a larger value of v will mean that some random numbers are more likely to be farther away from c.

How does all this help in initializing our network?

---

52 In order to avoid the instability and vanishing problems, we should always initialize our weights to a central value of

0.0

What about the variance?

---

53 Without getting into the mathematical proof of it, the best value for *variance* is given by

$$\frac{2}{n}$$

where n is the length of the input of the layer.[†]

[†]This result is specific to networks that use *rectify* and is known as *He initialization* (see Epilogue).

So each layer has a different variance based on the length of its input.

That's a curious formula.

---

54 Yes, that formula makes sure that in deep networks, the weights stay in a very tight cluster around 0.0 so that when a scalar from the input tensor is multiplied with weights in each layer, the result neither explodes nor vanishes.

Okay.

So we must now use the shape list of *iris-network* and apply these initialization rules to it.

The Rule of Layer Initialization

(Initial Version)

The bias tensor[1] of a layer is initialized to contain only 0.0
The weight tensor[2] of a layer is initialized to random scalars
with a central value of 0.0
and a variance of $2/n$
where n is the length of the input to the layer.

Yes, and we can bake that into a function.

Here is a function *init-θ* that accepts a single argument *shapes*, which is a shape list corresponding to a ***θ***

```
(define init-θ
  (λ (shapes)
    (map init-shape shapes)))
```

Its task is to produce a randomly initialized ***θ*** based on the shapes found in the shape list.

55 It maps the function *init-shape* over each shape in *shapes*.

This means that *init-shape* must generate the tensor we need from its argument shape.

Correct.

When that shape is of the form

(**list** *m*)

we know that it corresponds to a bias tensor. This means we have to construct a tensor with 0.0's in that shape.

56 Is there a function for that?

57

There is!

It is called *zero-tensor* and it takes a *shape* as its argument and produces a tensor with that shape, but every scalar in that tensor is 0.0.

For example

```
1. (zero-tensor (list 5))
2. [0.0 0.0 0.0 0.0 0.0]
```

Seems like exactly what the doctor ordered.

What if our shape corresponds to a weight tensor?

58

In the case of dense layers, the shape corresponding to a weight tensor is of the form

(**list** *m n*)

where *m* is the number of neurons in the layer and *n* is the length of the input of the layer.

How should we initialize a tensor with this shape?

As per our rule, it must be randomly initialized with a central value of 0.0 and a variance as given in frame 53.

59

Correct.

Here's a skeleton for *init-shape*

```
(define init-shape
  (λ (s)
    (cond
      ((= |s| 1) (zero-tensor s))
      ((= |s| 2)
       (random-tensor 0.0 [ V ] s)))))
```

Find *V*.

V is the variance of the weights, which is 2 divided by the length of input. In the case of the shape of weight tensors, this is given by the second member of the shape

s_1

Therefore, *V* is

($\div$ 2 s_1)

60

Here is *init-shape*

```
(define init-shape
  (λ (s)
    (cond
      ((= |s| 1) (zero-tensor s))
      ((= |s| 2)
       (random-tensor 0.0 (÷ 2 s_1) s)))))
```

Are we now ready to train our neural network?

61

Yes, we are!

Let's pick a data set to train it with.

Are we going to pick Uncle Edgar's data set of 150 plants?

62

Yes, but we won't use all of them.

We'll save some of those points for testing our network.

Why haven't we done this for our previous data sets?

63

Great question.

Our previous data sets have been used to illustrate only the process of gradient descent and how to improve it.

In practice, once a $\boldsymbol{\theta}$ has been learned, we must test it on points not seen before in order to assess the performance of the network.

How many points should we set aside from the data set?

64

We'll reserve 10%, or 15 points, of the data set, with 5 picked randomly from each of the three classes. We'll refer to this as our *test set.*

Is that enough?

On larger data sets, the general guideline is to use 20% of the data set for testing. Since our data set here is quite small, we limit the test set to 10%.

65 Okay.

We'll refer to the *xs* and *ys* for this test set as

(*iris-test-xs*, *iris-test-ys*)

The remaining 135 points form the *training set*. Let's refer to the *xs* and *ys* for this as

(*iris-train-xs*, *iris-train-ys*)

66 Those names sound reasonable.

Should we train our network now?

Yes, we should!

What is the target function we need?

67 It is the network function of *iris-network* which is

(*block-fn iris-network*)

Great.

Let us give it a name

```
(define iris-classifier
  (block-fn iris-nctwork))
```

68 Should we also name the shape list?

That's a good idea!

```
(define iris-θ-shapes
  (block-ls iris-network))
```

69 Now could we please train the network?

Here's the skeleton for finding $\boldsymbol{\theta}$ using stochastic gradient descent with *naked-gradient-descent* and *sampling-obj*

```
(define iris-θ
  (with-hypers
    ((revs 2000)
     (α 0.0002)
     (batch-size 8))
    (naked-gradient-descent
      (sampling-obj
         [          L          ]
         iris-train-xs iris-train-ys)
      [           I            ])))
```

Find *L* and *I*.

70 *L* is an expectant function. It is the invocation of *l2-loss* on a target function, which here is *iris-classfier*. So, *L* is

(*l2-loss iris-classifier*)

I must be an initial $\boldsymbol{\theta}$, initialized with random values but with the shapes given by *iris-$\boldsymbol{\theta}$-shapes*. We find it using

(*init-$\boldsymbol{\theta}$ iris-$\boldsymbol{\theta}$-shapes*)

Good answer.

Here's how we train our network to obtain *iris-$\boldsymbol{\theta}$*, which is the well-fitted $\boldsymbol{\theta}$ for our training set

```
(define iris-θ
  (with-hypers
    ((revs 2000)
     (α 0.0002)
     (batch-size 8))
    (naked-gradient-descent
      (sampling-obj
        (l2-loss iris-classifier)
        iris-train-xs iris-train-ys)
      (init-θ iris-θ-shapes))))
```

The function *iris-classifier*, together with *iris-$\boldsymbol{\theta}$*, form a *model.*

71 What is a model?

A model is an approximation of an *idealized* function represented by the data set. This idealized function yields, for every x in the xs of the data set, the corresponding y from ys, but also produces a y for any given x, even if it is not in xs.

72 Why is this function idealized?

We refer to it as idealized because we assume its existence, but the evidence we have of this is only the data set itself. In other words, we don't have a

(λ (*x*) … *some y* …)

that defines this function.

For our irises, we define *iris-model*

```
(define iris-model
  (λ (t)
    ((iris-classifier t) iris-θ)))
```

Explain how this function behaves.

73 This function first invokes *iris-classifier* with the input tensor t and then *iris-*$\boldsymbol{\theta}$. Its result is the output tensor produced by *iris-classifier*.

We can generalize *iris-model* into a function *model* that constructs a model out of its two arguments, a target function and a $\boldsymbol{\theta}$

```
(define model                    ●
  (λ (target θ)
    (λ (t)
      ((target t) θ))))
```

Explain how this function works.

74 It accepts a *target* and a $\boldsymbol{\theta}$ and results in a function that expects an argument, and invokes *target* on that argument and the given $\boldsymbol{\theta}$.

In other words, it produces a model derived from *target* and $\boldsymbol{\theta}$.

Excellent.

Now define *iris-model* using *model*.

75 Here it is

```
(define iris-model
  (model iris-classifier iris-θ))
```

Perfect.

If our model is trained properly, it should produce results as close to the idealized function as possible.

For example, if *iris-model* is given a new set of measurements that are not present in the training set, it still correctly classifies most of the time.

76 How do we know that the $\boldsymbol{\theta}$ in this model is well fitted?

That is an excellent question, but we'll discover the answer to that in the next interlude!

77 Oh, and we need a snack, too, don't we?

Classy Toys

How about an exquisite mille-feuille?
Layers upon layers of deliciousness!

Interlude VI
How the Model Trains†

†Thanks, Sir Henry Joseph Wood (1869–1944).

---

1 The mille-feuille was wonderful.

The layers were delightful!

---

2 In this interlude, we learn how to determine if a given model is good enough.

So then we can determine if

iris-model

is good enough.

---

3 Correct.

So, let's quantify what "good enough" means.

That would be helpful.

---

4 For a given input, classifiers produce a one-hot-like encoding, as in frame 255:23. This output tensor[1] encodes a class that the input belongs to.

Yes.

The index with the highest degree of belief gives us the class.

---

5 To determine if *iris-model* is good enough, we run *iris-model* on the *xs* of a test data set.

In frame 265:66, we have saved a few points in the form of *iris-test-xs* and *iris-test-ys* for testing. Here's where they come into play.

Write an expression for how we can invoke *iris-model* on this test set.

We can invoke *iris-model* directly on *iris-test-xs*

(*iris-model iris-test-xs*)

Perfect.

Let's name the result of this expression *iris-pred-ys*. Then, we compare the classes represented by *iris-pred-ys* with the known classes represented by *iris-test-ys* from Uncle Edgar's Iris's data set.

We say that the model is accurate for those inputs where the two classes are the same.

6 What about when the classes are not the same?

Those are known as *classification errors*.

The ratio of the number of accurate classifications to the total number of test inputs we have is known as the *accuracy* of the model.

7 Ah, so we can measure the accuracy of *iris-model* to decide if *iris-*$\boldsymbol{\theta}$ is good enough.

Correct.

8 What's a good accuracy score? Is it 1.0 (i.e., the model is accurate on all the test inputs)?

That usually depends upon the problem we're dealing with, but when problems are sufficiently complex, no model is accurate on all inputs. Not even *homo sapiens*.

For this problem, we'll consider 0.9 to be a good enough accuracy score.

9 So if 9 out of 10 inputs are correctly classified, we'll consider *iris-*$\boldsymbol{\theta}$ to be good enough.

Yes, that's right.

This way of judging models is quite general, and we can use it for other classifiers as well.

10 Aha!

Does that mean we can define functions to measure the accuracy of classifiers in general?

It does.

11 Exciting.

And we can use those functions to determine if any given model is good enough for the problem we are dealing with.

Can we start defining these functions?

Absolutely.

Here is a function *argmax*^{1} that finds the index in a tensor^1 with the highest degree of belief. It accepts a one-hot-like tensor^1 and determines the index of its highest scalar. For example

(*argmax*^{1} [0.1 0.3 0.6])

Write a same-as chart for this expression.

12 The highest value in this tensor^1 is 0.6, which is at index 2

1. (*argmax*^{1} [0.1 0.3 0.6])
2. 2

How do we define this function?

Here is the start of *argmax*^{1}

```
(define argmax^1
  (λ (t)
    (let ((i (sub1 |t|)))
      (argmaxed t i i))))
```

13 It invokes a helper function *argmaxed* with a simple accumulator passing of arguments.

How is *argmaxed* defined?

14

Here's a skeleton for *argmaxed*. It takes a tensor^1 t, a count-down index i, and a, which holds the index of the highest element seen in the tensor^1 so far

```
(define argmaxed
  (λ (t i a)
    (let ((â (next-a t i a)))
      (cond
        ((zero? i) â)
        (else
          [          M          ])))))
```

Define *next-a*, which is used to find $\hat{a}$, the next a.

We must find whether a must change to i or stay the same. If i, has a higher scalar at it in t than the one at it in a, then we use i as the next a. Otherwise, we leave a alone

```
(define next-a
  (λ (t i a)
    (cond
      ((> t|i t|a) i)
      (else a))))
```

15

Perfect.

Now find M.

When the count-down index is greater than 0, we continue with the next lower index, but now using $\hat{a}$ as the new a. So M is

```
(argmaxed t (sub1 i) â)
```

16

Excellent.

Here is the completed *argmaxed*

```
(define argmaxed
  (λ (t i a)
    (let ((â (next-a t i a)))
      (cond
        ((zero? i) â)
        (else
          (argmaxed t (sub1 i) â))))))
```

Does this satisfy the law on page 43?

Indeed it does.

Since *next-a* and *argmax*^{1} are not recursive, we can ignore them when determining if *argmaxed* follows the law of simple accumulator passing. The invocation within *argmaxed* is not wrapped, so we need to look at only the formals of *argmaxed*

t does not change

i changes towards passing a base test

and

a accumulates a result

How do we use *argmax*^{1}?

17

When we have two one-hot-like tensors^1, say t and u, that represent the same class, what can we say about

$(argmax^1\ t)$

and

$(argmax^1\ u)$

We would expect them to be equal. In other words

$(= (argmax^1\ t)\ (argmax^1\ u))$

would be true.

18

Correct.

We can use this property to begin counting the number of tests that succeed.

Here's a function

class=^{1}

that expects

two one-hot-like tensors^1

and

checks if they represent the same class

```
(define class=¹
  (λ (t u)
    (cond
      ((= (argmax¹ t) (argmax¹ u)) 1.0)
      (else 0.0))))
```

Explain what this function does.

It returns 1.0 if the two tensors^1 represent the same class, and returns 0.0 otherwise.

What is the purpose of such a function?

19

We'll see shortly.

Let us extend this function

```
(define class=
  (ext2 class=¹ 1 1))
```

Ah, so we can compare *iris-pred-ys* with *iris-test-ys* with a single invocation of *class=*

(*class= iris-pred-ys iris-test-ys*)

But this just gives us a tensor^1 of 1.0's and 0.0's.

And that is exactly what we want, because then we can *sum* this tensor[1] to count the number of inputs where *iris-model* is accurate

```
(sum
  (class= iris-pred-ys iris-test-ys))
```

How do we find the accuracy from this?

20 We must divide it by the number of test inputs

```
(÷ (sum
     (class= iris-pred-ys iris-test-ys))
   †iris-test-xs†)
```

Excellent.

We can generalize this into an accuracy checker for any given model, a test *xs* and a test *ys*

```
(define accuracy
  (λ (a-model xs ys)
    (÷ [           C           ]
       [ D ])))
```

Find *C* and *D*.

21 We can find the predicted *ys*

```
(a-model xs)
```

and compare it with *ys*

```
(class= (a-model xs) ys)
```

and then *sum* the result to get *C*

```
(sum (class= (a-model xs) ys))
```

D is the number of inputs, which is

```
†xs†
```

Perfect.

Here is the completed *accuracy*

```
(define accuracy                              ●
  (λ (a-model xs ys)
    (÷ (sum (class= (a-model xs) ys))
       †xs†)))
```

How can we use this function to measure the accuracy of *iris-model*?

22 We can invoke the accuracy function

```
▷ (accuracy
    iris-model
    iris-test-xs iris-test-ys)
▶ 1.0
```

Wow. Does that mean our model is 100% accurate?

It does happen to be 100% accurate on our small test set of 15 points. This is not so unusual because our data set is simple.

In larger, real-world data sets, accuracies rarely reach such high levels.

23 How have we arrived at those hyperparameter scalars that were chosen to train *iris-classifier*?

Those hyperparameter scalars are derived empirically, but there is a more systematic way to determine them.

24 That's exciting!

What is the way?

When trying to determine these scalars empirically, we try different combinations for them.

If we know the sequence of scalars that we want to test for each hyperparameter, we can systematically "loop" through each of those scalars for each hyperparameter until we get a satisfactory $\boldsymbol{\theta}$.

25 Do we use *accuracy* to determine if a $\boldsymbol{\theta}$ is satisfactory?

Yes.

We can do that if our target function is a classifier. There are other tests for other kinds of target functions.

This way of testing different combinations for the best one is known as

grid search

26 Do we need something to help us perform a grid search?

We do!

Here's how we do grid searches

```
(grid-search
  accurate-enough-iris-θ?
  ((revs 500 1000 2000 4000)
   (α 0.0001 0.0002 0.0005)
   (batch-size 4 8 16))
  (naked-gradient-descent
    (sampling-obj
      (l2-loss iris-classifier)
      iris-train-xs iris-train-ys)
    (init-θ iris-θ-shapes)))
```

27 This is similar to **with-hypers**, but it seems as if there could be more than one scalar for each

hyperparameter

Indeed.

These are the sequences containing *at least* one scalar (and typically more) that **grid-search** tries for each

hyperparameter

28 How are these sequences used in **grid-search**?

In this example, **grid-search** first starts with

revs is 500

α is 0.0001

and

batch-size is 4

It then finds a ***θ*** using the body

```
(naked-gradient-descent
  (sampling-obj
    (l2-loss iris-classifier)
    iris-train-xs iris-train-ys)
  (init-θ iris-θ-shapes))
```

29 This body is similar to what we would use with **with-hypers**.

Correct.

Once it has this $\boldsymbol{\theta}$, it tests it with the function *accurate-enough-iris-$\boldsymbol{\theta}$?*, which yields #t if this $\boldsymbol{\theta}$ is accurate enough.

30 How is *accurate-enough-iris-$\boldsymbol{\theta}$?* defined?

Here we define *accurate-enough-iris-$\boldsymbol{\theta}$?* that checks whether the accuracy of a given $\boldsymbol{\theta}$ when used with *iris-classifier* and the test set

(*iris-test-xs*, *iris-test-ys*)

is high enough

```
(define accurate-enough-iris-θ?
  (λ (θ)
    (≥ (accuracy
          (model iris-classifier θ)
          iris-test-xs iris-test-ys)
       0.9)))
```

31 This function yields #t if the accuracy is greater than or equal to 0.9.

What happens when a $\boldsymbol{\theta}$ is not accurate enough?

A great question.

If *accurate-enough-iris-$\boldsymbol{\theta}$?* for a $\boldsymbol{\theta}$ is #t, then **grid-search** yields that $\boldsymbol{\theta}$.

If however, *accurate-enough-iris-$\boldsymbol{\theta}$?* for a $\boldsymbol{\theta}$ is #f, then **grid-search** tries another combination.

Then, it keeps the scalars for *revs* and α the same as before, but it goes on to the next scalar for *batch-size*, which is 8.

32 So the new combination to try

revs would be 500

α would be 0.0001

and

batch-size would be 8

33

Excellent.

After it reaches the final scalar in the *batch-size* sequence and the $\boldsymbol{\theta}$ is still not accurate enough, it starts *batch-size* again at the beginning of the sequence, i.e., at 4.

For α, however, it continues with the next scalar in the sequence 0.0002, and then tries *all* the scalars of *batch-size* again.

And when it runs out of α and *batch-size* scalars?

34

It does the same thing: starts with α and *batch-size* back at the beginning, but chooses *revs*'s next scalar, and it continues to test whether the $\boldsymbol{\theta}$ from the body is good enough.

What happens if we don't find any $\boldsymbol{\theta}$ that is good enough and we run out of scalars for *revs* as well?

35

Then **grid-search** itself gives us #f.

This means that the grid search failed.

36

Correct.

When that happens, we have to try different sequences of scalars for hyperparameters in the **grid-search**, or possibly try a different target function (e.g. a network with a different number of layers or different layer widths) to use as a classifier. Or, in some situations, we might have to settle for lower accuracy.

Okay.

Here is the general form of **grid-search**

```
(grid-search good-enough?
  ((hyperparameter scalar scalar ...)
   ...)
  body)
```

where *body* produces a $\boldsymbol{\theta}$, *good-enough?* tests whether that $\boldsymbol{\theta}$ is good enough, and the *scalar* sequences define all the different combinations that we would like to try for each

hyperparameter

37 This **grid-search** is a systematic way to determine hyperparameter scalars.

It is!

For now, another snack!

38 Something delicious again?

Training Toys

How about some Belgian waffles? Swimming in maple syrup!

Interlude VII Are Your Signals Crossed?

The Belgian waffles[†] also taste delicious dripping in strawberries and whipped cream.

[†] Thanks, Maurice Remi Pierre Vermersch (1914-2021).

1 A tasty delight!

Let's learn about *signals.*

2 What are signals?

They are best learned through an example.

A pair of loquacious learners, Alice and Bob, are close friends and even closer neighbors, but they are forbidden from using their phones at night.

3 So what do these loquacious learners do?

They decide to use flashlights[†] to communicate.

[†] Thanks, David Misell (1846–1948).

4 How do they do that?

They use the International Morse Code.[†]

[†] Thanks, Alfred Lewis Vail (1807–1859), thanks, Samuel Finley Breese Morse (1791–1872) and thanks, Friedrich Clemens Gerke (1801–1888).

5 You mean the one with dots and dashes?

Exactly!

A dot (.) is a short flash and a dash (–) is a long flash. Each letter of the English alphabet is encoded as a series of dots and dashes separated from each other by a short space.

For example, the letter A is

.–

6 What about the letter B?

The letter B has the code

–...

7 So the letters can be of different lengths?

Yes.

The International Morse Code has many different symbols, but here we restrict our attention to exactly 26 symbols: one for each letter of the alphabet.

8 Does that mean we can transmit any message using only dots and dashes for each letter?

Indeed!

That way, Alice and Bob can talk all night using their flashlights.

Alice and Bob decide to build a machine to decode these flashlight messages.

9 They have to make one machine for Alice and another one for Bob!

Yes, they do.

The machine uses an *optical sensor* on the window to detect flashes of light from the other learner's flashlight.

10 What's an optical sensor?

An optical sensor converts light that falls on it to an electrical output.

The machine then measures the *voltage* of that electrical output.

11 What's voltage?

It is a measure of the strength of the electrical output of the optical sensor.

When there is no light falling on the sensor, the voltage is

0.0 volts†

When light from a flashlight falls on the sensor, the voltage is

proportional to the light's strength

For this example, we'll take the sensor's voltage to be between

0.0 (when the flashlight is off)

and

1.0 (when the flashlight is on)

†Thanks, Alessandro Volta (1745–1827).

12 How does the optical sensor behave when it is receiving a message?

Let's assume Bob is sending

•▬

which is the letter A.

Initially, Bob's flashlight is dark. It is turned on for a short period for the dot (•) and then turned off for a short period. Then it is turned back on for a longer period for the dash (▬) and finally it is turned off.

13 How does the output of the optical sensor change over these events?

Initially, when the flashlight is dark, Alice's optical sensor has an output of 0.0 volts. Then, when it is turned on for the dot, the output of the optical sensor rises to 1.0 volts and it stays at 1.0 volts as long as the flashlight is on.

When Bob turns off the flashlight after the dot, the output of the optical sensor drops to 0.0 again for a short while.

Then, when Bob turns on the flashlight again for the dash, the output of the optical sensor rises again to 1.0 volts, and stays there for a longer period, since the dash requires more time, and then drops back to 0.0 volts.

14 Is there a visual way to understand these events?

There is.

Let's assume that Bob is able to send one letter in the duration of a second.[†] Then, we can draw a graph of the voltage on Alice's optical sensor with respect to time over exactly one second.

Here's the graph of the letter A. We refer to it as a *signal graph*

• —

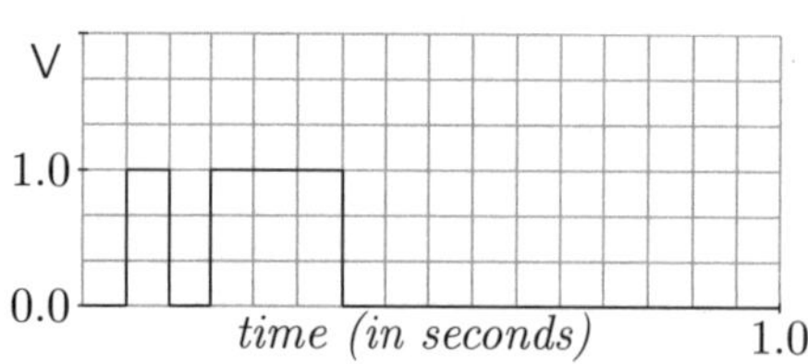

Here V is the abbreviation for *volts*.

[†]This may be very fast, but we assume Bob is lightning fast.

15 Oh, this graph shows how the voltage goes up and goes down for each dot and dash.

That is correct.

16 Could we see another example?

Sure.

Here is the letter Y

-·--

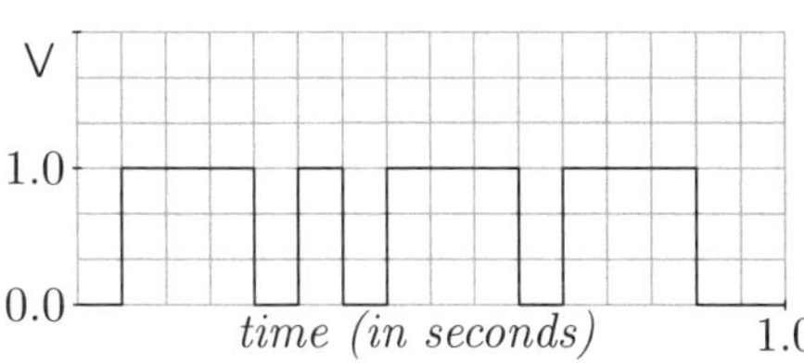

17 So this graph shows how the voltage coming out of the optical sensor varies over one second.

Correct.

A *signal* is the variation of a physical quantity (here, its *voltage*) over time.

18 So the output of the optical sensor is a signal?

It is an example of what is known as an *analog* signal.†

†This is also known as a *continuous* signal.

19 What is Alice going to do with this analog signal?

Since Alice wants to use neural networks to decode these signals, they must be converted to tensors^1.

Alice uses an *analog-to-digital converter* to convert these electrical signals to tensors^1.†

†For those familiar with signal processing, we have skipped some details in the description of converting analog signals to tensors since we are primarily concerned with the tensors themselves.

20 What do these tensors look like?

Let's first make some simplifying assumptions.

In frame 15, Bob sends flashes at 1 letter per second. We can break up Bob's stream of flashes at 1 second intervals, so that each interval contains one letter.

21 So a message containing 10 letters takes 10 seconds?

Correct.

We break up a 1-second period into 16 segments and then assign a scalar to each of those 16 segments, to obtain a tensor[1] corresponding to a single letter in the message.

22 What scalars are assigned to each tensor element?

We use the voltage of the signal in the middle of the *i*th segment as the *i*th scalar in the tensor[1].

23 Could we see this on the graph?

Of course.

Here again is the letter Y

–·––

In this graph, we use an orange circle to mark the scalar picked for each segment

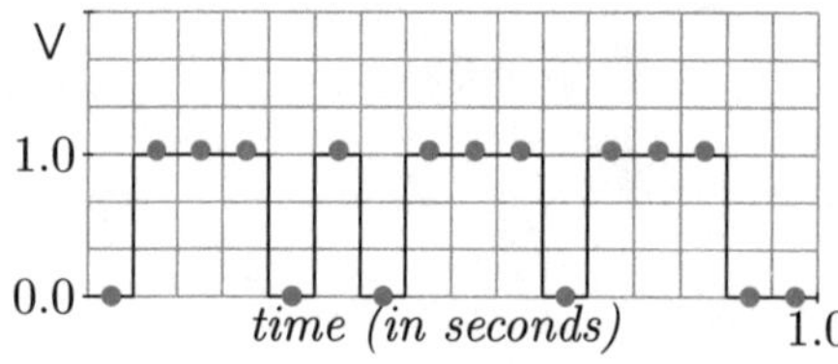

24 Each of those *orange* dots represents a scalar element in the tensor[1].

25

Here is the whole tensor[1]

[0.0 1.0 1.0 1.0 0.0 1.0 0.0 1.0 1.0 1.0 0.0 1.0 1.0 1.0 0.0 0.0]

Quick! How many 1.0's and 0.0's are here, and where?

Ooh! That's a ton of 1.0's and 0.0's!

26

There are, indeed!

Thankfully, we can abbreviate signals like these. We use ellipses to make our signals easier to read. Here's how we abbreviate the signal above

$[0.0\ 1.0\ \overset{2}{\ldots}\ 0.0\ 1.0\ 0.0\ 1.0\ \overset{2}{\ldots}\ 0.0\ 1.0\ \overset{2}{\ldots}\ 0.0\ 0.0]$

The signal here has 16 segments, as before, but contiguous repeated values are denoted by ellipses. The segments represented by the ellipsis get their values from the segment just before the ellipsis, and the count above the ellipsis represents how many more consecutive segments we have with that same value.[†]

[†] We adopt the convention that an abbreviated tensor never ends in an ellipsis. We see this in the example above which ends in 0.0 instead of an ellipsis.

Very convenient.

Could we see some more examples?

27

Sure.

Let's play with this abbreviation a little. Consider this signal where there are

4 off, 4 on, 4 off, and 4 on

$[0.0 \overset{3}{\ldots} 1.0 \overset{3}{\ldots} 0.0 \overset{3}{\ldots} 1.0 \overset{2}{\ldots} 1.0]$

Design two similar signals where in the first signal, there are

3 off, 3 on, 3 off, 3 on, 3 off, and 1 on

and in the second signal, there are

5 off, 5 on, 5 off, and 1 on

Here they are

$[0.0 \overset{2}{\ldots} 1.0 \overset{2}{\ldots} 0.0 \overset{2}{\ldots} 1.0 \overset{2}{\ldots} 0.0 \overset{2}{\ldots} 1.0]$

and

$[0.0 \overset{4}{\ldots} 1.0 \overset{4}{\ldots} 0.0 \overset{4}{\ldots} 1.0]$

28

The digital signals we have so far are tensors^1 where we have a *scalar* at each time segment.†

We refer to these as

signals^1

†We refer to *time segments* simply as *segments.*

Oh, so we use the same superscript as we do for tensors.

29

Correct.

We refer to these as

1-dimensional signals^1

What does 1-dimensional mean?

30

It means that the signal consists of values that vary along only one axis, or *dimension.* And that dimension is *time.*

Okay.

31

So, when we refer to a signal^1, it stands for a 1-dimensional signal represented by a tensor^1.

Are there signals^2?

An excellent question!

Yes, a signal^2 is a 1-dimensional signal that contains a tensor^1 in each segment. So, it is actually a tensor^2.

32 Could we see an example of a signal^2?

Sure.

Here is a signal^1 s

$[0.0 \overset{2}{\dots} 1.0\ 0.0 \overset{10}{\dots} 0.0]$

Here is another signal^1 t

$[1.0\ 0.0 \overset{13}{\dots} 1.0]$

33 Do we derive a signal^2 from these two signals^1?

We "zip" a signal^2 from these two signals s and t by picking one scalar each from s and t in lock-step and putting them into a tensor^1. The resulting signal^2 has 16 segments, each with a 2-element tensor^1.

34 An example, please.

Sure.

The scalar at index 0 of s is

0.0

The scalar at index 0 of t is

1.0

So the resulting tensor^1 at index 0 of the signal^2 is

[0.0 1.0]

Find the tensor^1 at index 1 of the signal^2.

35 Sounds reasonable.

The scalar at index 1 of s is

0.0

The scalar at index 1 of t is

0.0

So the resulting tensor^1 at index 1 of the signal^2 is

[0.0 0.0]

Excellent.

We repeat this for all the segments to get this signal^2

$$\begin{bmatrix} 0.0 & 1.0 \\ 0.0 & 0.0 \\ 0.0 & 0.0 \\ 1.0 & 0.0 \\ 0.0 & 0.0 \\ & \vdots_{10} & \\ 0.0 & 1.0 \end{bmatrix}_{(16\ 2)}$$

36 What if we need to zip more than two signals?

A great question.

In general, when we zip d signals, each of shape

(**list** n)

we get a signal^2 of shape[†]

(**list** n d)

Here, d is referred to as the

depth of the signal^2

[†]This zipping of signals^1 into a signal^2 may be familiar to some as being analogous to *transposing* a matrix.

37 The depth of the signal^2 is the number of signals^1 that are used to construct it.

How about an example?

The Law of Zipped Signals

A signal^2 is formed by zipping signals^1, and the signal^2 as well as its constituent signals^1 all have the same number of segments.

Sure.

Let's take the two signals s and t in frame 33 and zip them along with the signal u

$$\begin{bmatrix}0.0 & 1.0 & 0.0 & \overset{11}{\cdots} & 1.0 & 0.0\end{bmatrix}$$

Here is what it looks like

$$\begin{bmatrix}0.0 & 1.0 & 0.0\\ 0.0 & 0.0 & 1.0\\ 0.0 & 0.0 & 0.0\\ 1.0 & 0.0 & 0.0\\ 0.0 & 0.0 & 0.0\\ & \vdots^{9} & \\ 0.0 & 0.0 & 1.0\\ 0.0 & 1.0 & 0.0\end{bmatrix}_{(16\ 3)}$$

What is the depth of the signal^2 here?

38 It is 3, since we have built this signal^2 from 3 signals^1.

Perfect!

In the signals we have seen so far, the signal begins at 0.0 and changes to 1.0 in the following segment. We refer to the first time we see this change in the signal as its *start*.

Now we relax this assumption to make things more interesting. We'll assume that the start of the signal can occur anywhere in the tensor, as long as the complete signal is present within the 16-segment tensor.

39 Could we see an example?

Sure.

Here again, is the signal graph of the letter A, but with a later start

·–

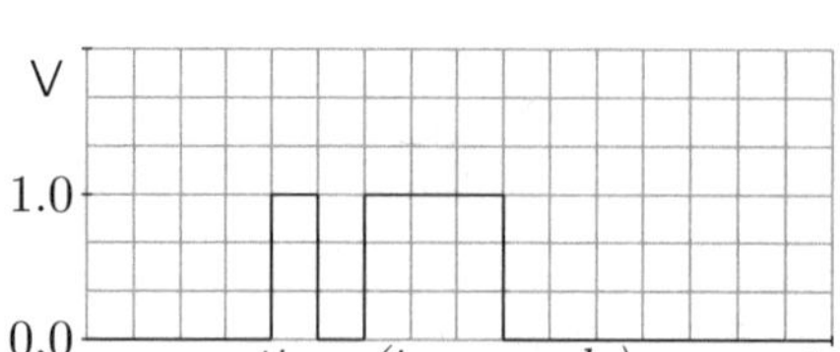

What is the tensor corresponding to this?

40 It is

$$[0.0 \overset{3}{\ldots} 1.0\ 0.0\ 1.0 \overset{2}{\ldots} 0.0 \overset{5}{\ldots} 0.0]$$

Excellent.

This shifting the "start" of the signal is known as *translation.*

41 So should our locquacious learners build their machines to take translation into account?

Yes, they absolutely should!

Now let's learn about *noise.*

42 What is *noise*?

The signal graphs that we have seen so far are *ideal.* In reality, physical signals are never so well-behaved. They have random variations.

43 Could we see how these signal graphs look?

---

44 As an example, the signal graph for A would more likely resemble this

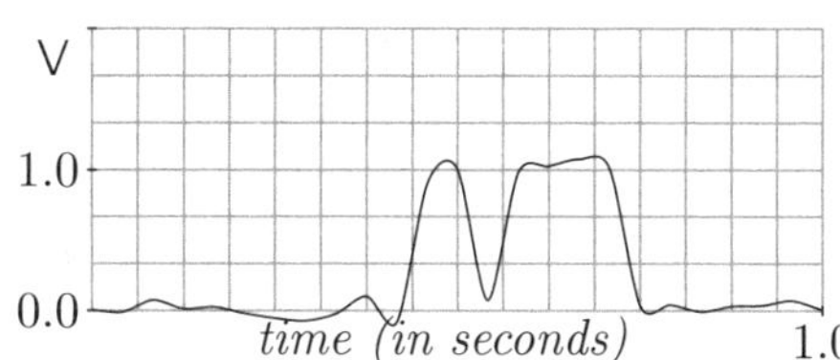

But, because of randomness, the variations would be different each time the signal is sent or received.

Oh, so the elements in the signal are rarely, if ever, exactly 0.0 or 1.0.

---

45 Correct.

For example, our signal[1] for the letter Y would probably resemble this

[0.05 1.2 0.96 −0.03 1.1 0.09 1.0 0.9 −0.02 1.1 1.2 0.2 −0.01 −0.04 0.1 0.08]

That signal[1] definitely looks noisy!

How are we to use these signals?

---

46 Our loquacious learners' receivers can decode messages by running these signals through a neural network.

And this neural network must decode these signals even in the presence of noise and translation.

That's exciting.

Are we going to learn how to write such a neural network?

---

47 We are, but that is for later!

Can't wait to get started!

Zippy Toys

zipping signals 292

How about a profiterole?
With some crunchy choux!

14 It's Really Not That Convoluted

Wasn't the profiterole beyond belief?	1	Yes, and it was crunchy!
Here we learn about a new kind of layer.	2	Is this layer going to help Alice and Bob decode flashlight messages?
Indeed. To decode their messages, we need to now learn about *correlation* between two 1-dimensional signals.	3	What is correlation?
Correlation is a way to detect the occurrence of a pattern anywhere within a signal.	4	Why do we need to detect patterns within a signal?
Detecting patterns within a signal helps us to determine which letter that signal represents. We detect a pattern by *scanning* the signal from beginning to end and measuring the similarity between a portion of the source signal and the pattern.	5	What is scanning?
Scanning is the process of examining every segment of the signal starting at its beginning and going to its end, one segment at a time.	6	Could we see an example?

Sure.

Here is s, a signal[1] of 16 segments that contains a single dot (.) and happens to encode the letter E, but translated by 3 segments

$[0.0 \overset{2}{\dots} 1.0\ 0.0 \overset{10}{\dots} 0.0]$

This is the source for this example. For now, we're going to consider only ideal signals, but the same principles work for noisy signals.

7 Could we also see its graph?

Here is the letter E

▪

Here is its graph

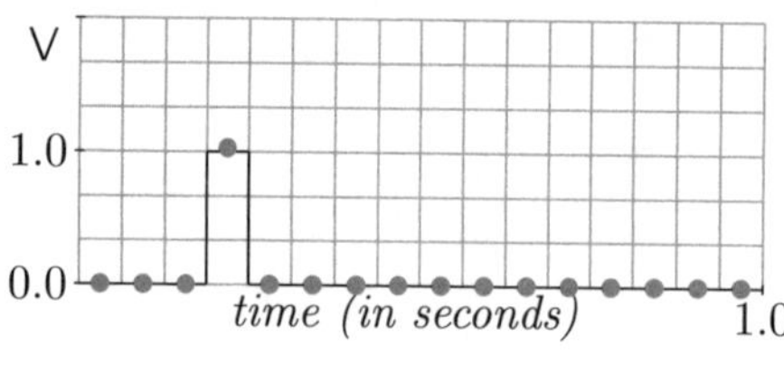

What is its abbreviated signal[1]?

8 Here it is, again

$[0.0 \overset{2}{\dots} 1.0\ 0.0 \overset{10}{\dots} 0.0]$

Here's another signal[1], but it is much shorter than s

$[0.0\ 1.0\ 0.0]$

9 This signal[1] seems very similar to the interesting part of s, the longer signal[1].

This signal[1] is a *pattern* that we use to match against the source. We refer to this shorter signal[1] as a filter[1].†

†Filters are also known as *kernels*.

10 This filter has length 3.

All filters are shorter than the source, but are they all of length 3?

They don't have to be. We usually pick them to be a small *odd* number. We use small numbers because small patterns are easier to match. More complex patterns are matched by using many small filters.

11 How do we match this filter?

This is where correlation comes in.

We first align the filter and the source at index 0 of the source

[0.0 1.0 0.0]
[0.0 0.0 0.0 1.0 0.0 $\overset{10}{\dots}$ 0.0]

12 The filter here aligns with the first three elements of the source.

The three elements in the source where the filter and the source overlap determine a tensor^1 for example

[0.0 0.0 0.0]

We refer to this as the

overlap at *position* 0

13 The overlap determines the elements from the source that overlap with the filter when it is aligned with the source at position 0.

Correct.

Now, let's take the dot product (•) of the filter with this overlap[†]

1. (• [0.0 1.0 0.0] [0.0 0.0 0.0])
2. (*sum*
   (∗ [0.0 1.0 0.0] [0.0 0.0 0.0]))
3. (*sum*
   [0.0 0.0 0.0])
4. 0.0

[†]As a convention here, the first argument to • is *always* the filter.

14 But, what does that mean?

This dot product provides a *scalar* measure of how similar the overlap is to the filter.

15 Is it important that this be a scalar?

Yes.

Scalars provide a simple measure of how good a match is.

16 What does the measure of 0.0 mean?

It means that the filter is not similar to the overlap at all.

17 What should we do now?

Now we slide the filter one element to the right, to overlap position 1

    [0.0 1.0 0.0]
[0.0 0.0 0.0 1.0 0.0 $\overset{10}{\ldots}$ 0.0]

What is the overlap now?

18 It is

[0.0 0.0 1.0]

Correct.

What should we do next?

19 We must find the dot product between the overlap and the filter

1. (• [0.0 1.0 0.0] [0.0 0.0 1.0])
2. (*sum*
   (∗ [0.0 1.0 0.0] [0.0 0.0 1.0]))
3. (*sum*
   [0.0 0.0 0.0])
4. 0.0

The dot product is 0.0 again.

Correct.

There is no match at overlap position 0 or overlap position 1.

20 So should we slide the filter another position to the right?

---

21 Exactly.

We slide to the new overlap position 2

```
        [0.0 1.0 0.0]
[0.0 0.0 0.0 1.0 0.0 .¹⁰. 0.0]
```

What is the dot product now?

We can find out

```
1. (• [0.0 1.0 0.0] [0.0 1.0 0.0])
2. (sum
     (* [0.0 1.0 0.0] [0.0 1.0 0.0]))
3. (sum
     [0.0 1.0 0.0])
4. 1.0
```

It is 1.0 this time!

---

22 That is correct.

We have a positive (i.e., not a 0.0) value here. This suggests that there is a match between the source and the filter at overlap position 2.

What about the remaining overlap positions?

---

23 All the remaining overlap positions up to 13 give us 0.0.

Why do we stop at overlap position 13?

---

24 That is because beyond position 13, the last element of the filter would extend beyond the last element of the source.

What do we do next?

---

25 We collect the scalars from the dot products at each overlap position from 0 to 13 into a 14 segment signal^1

```
[0.0 0.0 1.0 0.0 .⁹. 0.0]
```

This signal^1 is the result of *correlation* between the source *s* and the filter.

So, correlation determines the dot product of the filter and the overlap at each of the positions from 0 to 13, and builds a signal^1 from these dot products!

Correct.

In general, if our source has n segments, and the filter has m segments, the correlation has the length

$$n - m + 1$$

26 So that is why the signal in frame 25 has

$$16 - 3 + 1 = 14$$

elements.

Precisely.

The result of the correlation function has "peaks" where the filter resembles, i.e., correlates with, the source.

27 Like the 1.0 at overlap position 2 in frame 21?

Yes.

The way we have so far defined our overlap positions from 0 to $n - m + 1$ is inconvenient for two reasons. The first is that a shorter correlation result implies that some information has been lost.

In order to prevent this loss of information, it would be good to have the source signal and the result signal be the same length.

28 What is the second reason?

The second reason is that partial matches between the source and the filter at the boundaries of the source cannot be detected.

29 Why can't they be detected?

That is because we started our overlap positions at 0, and we end when the last element of the filter aligns with the last element of the source.

30 Could we see an example?

Sure.

As an example, if our source, say t, is this

$$[1.0\ 0.0\ \overset{12}{\ldots}\ 0.0\ 1.0]$$

then here is its graph

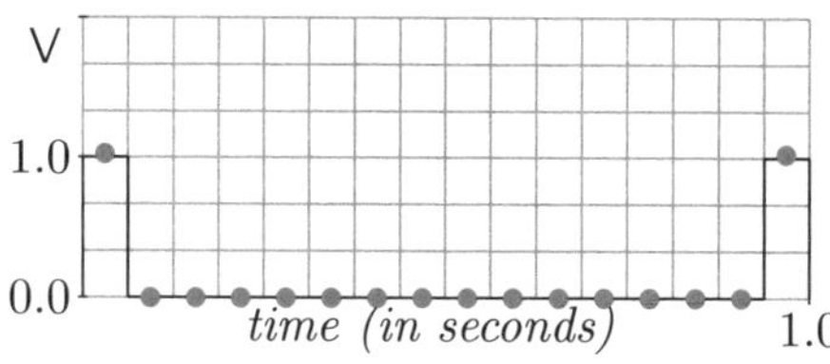

31 Oh, then our overlaps miss the partial matches between the source and filter at the beginning of the source and at the end of the source.

Right.

To fix both of these problems, we begin by overlapping at the position −1

$$\begin{array}{l}[0.0\ 1.0\ 0.0]\\ \quad\ [1.0\ 0.0\ \overset{12}{\ldots}\ 0.0\ 1.0]\end{array}$$

32 But there is no element at index −1 in any tensor!

A good observation!

For this, we pretend that the source is “padded” with enough 0.0s on both sides

$$\begin{array}{l}[0.0\ 1.0\ 0.0]\\ \ 0.0[1.0\ 0.0\ \overset{12}{\ldots}\ 0.0\ 1.0]0.0\end{array}$$

33 This allows us to consider an overlap at position −1 of the source.

Why both sides?

So that we also consider an overlap position 14 where the filter extends beyond the last element of the source

$$\begin{array}{r}[0.0\ 1.0\ 0.0]\quad\\ 0.0[1.0\ 0.0\ \overset{12}{\ldots}\ 0.0\ 1.0]0.0\end{array}$$

34 By adding these two overlap positions −1 and 14 to the 14 other overlap positions we already have, we get a total of 16 overlap positions.

This means the result of correlation is a signal whose length is the same as its source.

35 Could we see an example of how padding works?

Sure.

Let's find the correlation between the filter

[0.0 1.0 0.0]

and the source

[1.0 0.0 $\overset{12}{\dots}$ 0.0 1.0]

What does the overlap look like at position −1?

36 It should include a padded 0.0 at the beginning so that the middle element of the filter is aligned with the 0th element of the source

[0.0 1.0 0.0]

Let's now take the dot product with the filter and the overlap

1. (• [0.0 1.0 0.0] [0.0 1.0 0.0])
2. (*sum*
   (∗ [0.0 1.0 0.0] [0.0 1.0 0.0]))
3. (*sum*
   [0.0 1.0 0.0])
4. 1.0

What would the dot product become at overlap position 14?

37 Here it is

1. (• [0.0 1.0 0.0] [0.0 1.0 0.0])
2. (*sum*
   (∗ [0.0 1.0 0.0] [0.0 1.0 0.0]))
3. (*sum*
   [0.0 1.0 0.0])
4. 1.0

What about the rest of the overlap positions?

They are all 0.0, giving us the correlation

[1.0 0.0 $\overset{13}{\dots}$ 1.0]

We refer to this as the *result* signal.

38 Why do we refer to it as a signal?

We refer to it as a signal because it now can be a source for more filters, allowing us to *cascade* correlations on a series of different filters.

39 What does it mean to cascade correlations?

It means that we perform correlations in a sequence such that the result of one correlation operation is provided as input to the next correlation operation using a different filter.

40 Why is this important?

The Law of Correlation

(Single Filter Version)

The *correlation* of a filter of length m with
a source signal[1] of length n,
where m is odd (given by $2p + 1$),
is a signal[1] of length n obtained by *sliding* the filter from
overlap position $-p$ to overlap position $n - p - 1$,
where *each segment of the result* signal[1] is obtained by
taking the *dot product* of
the *filter* and the
overlap in the source
at *each overlap position.*

This is useful in detecting complex patterns, i.e., patterns built from other patterns as in frame 11.

41 Ah! That definitely would be useful.

But, our result looks the same as our source.

This is because of the filter we have chosen. It has the unique property that it copies *features* that it finds in the source to the output of the correlation.[†] This, in general, is not true. Other filters can be more selective in identifying other features, leading to different looking result signals.

[†] This filter is also known as the Kronecker delta. Named after Leopold Kronecker.

42 What are features?

Features are specific kinds of patterns that we look for in the source.

For example, a transition from a lower value (closer to 0.0) in one segment to a higher value (closer to 1.0) in the next is a "rising edge" feature. Similarly we could have a "falling edge" feature.

43 Do different features require different filters?

Yes, they do.

44 For decoding our loquacious learners' messages, do we have to define these different features and their corresponding filters?

Yes, but rather than *define* the filters ourselves, we use neural networks to *learn* the filters for us.

45 Does that mean filters are part of the $\boldsymbol{\theta}$ for a neural network that uses correlation?

The Rule of Filters

Filters are tensor parameters in a $\boldsymbol{\theta}$.

Exactly.

We consider filters to be parameters† to a *correlation layer* (i.e., a layer of neurons that uses the correlation operation) in the network, and we learn these filters by training the network on a data set where the *xs* are signals^1.‡

†These parameters are also known as *filter weights*.
‡For now. Later, we shall see how *xs* is transformed.

46 Just as with our loquacious learners' signals^1.

But what about the *ys*?

The *ys* are the corresponding letters encoded in a one-hot-like fashion from frame 253:12.

For example, the one-hot tensor^1 for the letter B is

$$[0.0\ 1.0\ 0.0\ \overset{22}{\cdots}\ 0.0]$$

We refer to the two tensors in this data set as

morse-xs

and

morse-ys

So our neural network classifies each signal^1 in a message into one of 26 classes, one corresponding to each of the 26 letters in our alphabet.

47 Does that mean this neural network uses correlation functions to learn the different filters necessary to identify each letter?

Correct.

But we need to evolve our correlation function a little before we can use it in layered neural networks.

48 Why do we need to do that?

49 In a typical neural network classifier, we're simultaneously trying to detect multiple features in a single source.

Is there a way to do that in a single invocation as we did with $*^{2,1}$ from frame 218:22?

50 Yes, there is.

To do that, we need an analogous operation that correlates against multiple filters in a single function invocation.

So, how do we handle that?

51 Let's imagine we have b different filters. Each of these filters is a signal^1 and they are all of length m.

What can we say about these b different filters?

Together, these b filters can be formed into a tensor^2 of shape

(list b m)

52 Yes, indeed.

We refer to this tensor^2 as a *filter bank* (or just *bank*).

How do we correlate a source with a whole bank of filters?

53 We take each filter in the bank and correlate it with the single source of length n, thus giving us b different results, where each result is a tensor^1 of the same length as the source.

Does that mean the output can be packaged into a tensor^2 of shape (list b n)?

54 That is tempting, but then our result would not be a signal^1, as we expect at the output of a correlation step. Nor would it be a signal^2 because it wouldn't have the same number of segments as the source signal, which is n. It would instead have b signals^1 in it.

Is this a problem?

Yes, it is.

It prevents us from cascading the result of this correlation into another correlation layer of the network.

55 Oh, that means it gets in the way of detecting more complex features (patterns built from other patterns) as hinted at in frame 41.

So how do we make the output of our correlation on a filter bank look like a signal^2?

We zip those b results, one from each of the b filters in the bank, into a signal^2 of

$(\textsf{list}\ n\ b)$

56 How about an example?

Let us again take a bank of two filters

$$\big[[0.0\ 2.0\ 1.0]\ [1.0\ 2.0\ -1.0]\big]_{(2\ 3)}$$

and the source signal

$$[0.0 \overset{2}{\ldots} 1.0\ 0.0 \overset{10}{\ldots} 0.0]$$

What is the correlation of each of the filters in this bank with the source signal?

57 Correlating the source signal with the bank's first filter

$$[0.0\ 2.0\ 1.0]$$

we get

$$[0.0\ 0.0\ 1.0\ 2.0\ 0.0 \overset{10}{\ldots} 0.0]$$

and correlating the source signal with the bank's second filter

$$[1.0\ 2.0\ -1.0]$$

we get

$$[0.0\ 0.0\ -1.0\ 2.0\ 1.0\ 0.0 \overset{9}{\ldots} 0.0]$$

We now zip, as in frame 292:37, both of those signals into a signal[2]

$$\begin{bmatrix} 0.0 & 0.0 \\ 0.0 & 0.0 \\ 1.0 & -1.0 \\ 2.0 & 2.0 \\ 0.0 & 1.0 \\ 0.0 & 0.0 \\ & \vdots^{9} \\ 0.0 & 0.0 \end{bmatrix}_{(16\ 2)}$$

58 Okay.

But if we want to cascade correlations using signals[2], shouldn't correlation work on signals[2] as well?

An excellent question.

Let's see how correlation works on signals[2].

Say our signals[2] have n segments (in our examples, n is 16), each being a tensor[1] of length d.

59 So it is a signal[2] of length n and depth d.

In order to correlate with signals[2] our filters must themselves be signals[2], hence now called filters[2], and they must have the same depth as the source.

What should the depth of our filters be?

60 They must also be of depth d.

Correct.

Also, like before, we have a bank of b filters[2], where each filter[2] has m segments.

The correlations produce a result signal[2] of depth b.

61 So in this general form, the source, the filter, and the result are all signals[2].

They are, indeed.

Let us summarize the shapes of our signals. The source has the shape

(list n d)

and we have a bank of b filters of shape

(list b m d)

where m is the width of each filter.

62 Could we see an example?

Yes.

Here is the signal^2 from frame 292:36 made by zipping

the signal^1 s from frame 291:33

with

the signal^1 t also from frame 291:33

Let's name this signal^2 st

$$\begin{bmatrix} 0.0 & 1.0 \\ 0.0 & 0.0 \\ 0.0 & 0.0 \\ 1.0 & 0.0 \\ 0.0 & 0.0 \\ \vdots_{10} & \\ 0.0 & 1.0 \end{bmatrix}_{(16\ 2)}$$

What are n and d for st?

63 For st, n is 16 and d is 2.

Since the depth of our source is 2, the depth of our filters should also be 2. Here is a bank of 4 filters^2

```
[[[0.0 0.0] [0.0 1.0] [0.0 0.0]]
 [[0.0 0.0] [1.0 0.0] [0.0 0.0]]
 [[0.0 1.0] [1.0 0.0] [0.0 0.0]]
 [[0.0 0.0] [1.0 0.0] [1.0 0.0]]]
```

What are b, m, and d here?

64 Since we have 4 filters^2, b is 4. Each filter^2 has 3 segments, so m is 3, and the depth d is 2 like before.

Very good.

Let's start with our bank's first filter^2

[[0.0 0.0] [0.0 1.0] [0.0 0.0]]

at overlap position -1.

65 If we start at overlap position -1, how do we pad a signal^2?

We assume that the padded elements are shaped like the other elements, and filled with 0.0s. We pad *st* like this

$$\begin{matrix}[0.0\ \ 0.0] \\ \begin{bmatrix}0.0 & 1.0\\ 0.0 & 0.0\\ 0.0 & 0.0\\ 1.0 & 0.0\\ 0.0 & 0.0\\ & \vdots_{10} & \\ 0.0 & 1.0\end{bmatrix}_{(16\ 2)} \\ [0.0\ \ 0.0]\end{matrix}$$

66 So, instead of using the scalar 0.0 at overlap position -1, we pad the source with a tensor^1 made up of 0.0s.

What is the overlap at position -1?

67 It is

[[0.0 0.0] [0.0 1.0] [0.0 0.0]]

Correct.

Now we take the dot product of the filter and the overlap

1. (• [[0.0 0.0] [0.0 1.0] [0.0 0.0]]
   [[0.0 0.0] [0.0 1.0] [0.0 0.0]])
2. [(• [0.0 0.0] [0.0 0.0])
   (• [0.0 1.0] [0.0 1.0])
   (• [0.0 0.0] [0.0 0.0])]
3. [0.0 1.0 0.0]

What can we say about the result?

68 Our result is a tensor[1] with 3 elements in it, which is the same as the width of our filters.

Oh, but that means the result is not a scalar as we claim it should be in frame 16.

Correct.

How do we turn this tensor[1] into a scalar?

69 From the law on page 54, we know that *sum* reduces the rank of a tensor (of rank 1 or higher) by 1.

Excellent.

When correlating signals[2], we additionally sum the result of the dot product at each overlap position

1. (*sum*
   (• [[0.0 0.0] [0.0 1.0] [0.0 0.0]]
   [[0.0 0.0] [0.0 1.0] [0.0 0.0]]))
2. (*sum*
   [0.0 1.0 0.0])
3. 1.0

70 Now we have a scalar!

The rest of the correlation of this filter is similar. We slide the filter one position down and repeat until we reach overlap position 14, where we pretend the source is padded with

$$[0.0\ 0.0]$$

This ultimately gives us the result signal

$$\begin{bmatrix}1.0 & 0.0 & \overset{13}{\cdots} & 1.0\end{bmatrix}$$

of shape

(**list** 16)

71 We have to repeat this correlation for all the remaining filters, don't we?

Yes, we must.

This gives us a total of 4 result signals[1]

$$\begin{bmatrix}\underline{1.0} & 0.0 & 0.0 & 0.0 & 0.0 & \overset{10}{\cdots} & 1.0\end{bmatrix}$$
$$\begin{bmatrix}\underline{0.0} & 0.0 & 0.0 & 1.0 & 0.0 & \overset{10}{\cdots} & 0.0\end{bmatrix}$$
$$\begin{bmatrix}\underline{0.0} & 1.0 & 0.0 & 1.0 & 0.0 & \overset{10}{\cdots} & 0.0\end{bmatrix}$$
$$\begin{bmatrix}\underline{0.0} & 0.0 & 1.0 & 1.0 & 0.0 & \overset{10}{\cdots} & 0.0\end{bmatrix}$$

Find the final signal[2].

72 To get a signal[2] from these 4 signals[1], we zip them together to get

$$\begin{bmatrix}\underline{1.0} & \underline{0.0} & \underline{0.0} & \underline{0.0}\\ 0.0 & 0.0 & 1.0 & 0.0\\ 0.0 & 0.0 & 0.0 & 1.0\\ 0.0 & 1.0 & 1.0 & 1.0\\ 0.0 & 0.0 & 0.0 & 0.0\\ & \vdots_{10} & & \\ 1.0 & 0.0 & 0.0 & 0.0\end{bmatrix}_{(16\ 4)}$$

Now we have a way of accepting a signal[2] and producing a signal[2], and cascading this signal[2] within a layered neural network!

73 So is this our final version of the correlation function?

It is!

In a neural network, what we learn are the filters (i.e., the filters are parameters inside $\boldsymbol{\theta}$.) The neural network learns to recognize patterns in the input that can then be classified when the filter bank associated with each correlation layer is trained.

In our example, our loquacious learners use correlation to classify each signal as the corresponding letter.

74 In our example so far

n is 16

m is 3

and

b is the number of filters in the bank

But, what is d?

A good question.

In a layered neural network, d is the depth of the signal produced by the previous layer. We'll see exactly how correlation works within a neural network later.

75 Does correlation have a name we can use in our functions?

The Law of Correlation

(Filter Bank Version)

The *correlation* of a filter bank of shape (**list** b m d) with a source signal^2 of shape (**list** n d) is a signal^2 of shape (**list** n b) resulting from zipping the b signals^1 resulting from correlating the b filters^2 in the bank with the source.

Yes!

We name it

correlate

It is an extended function similar to $\bullet^{2,1}$ from frame 219:24.

In the next chapter, we'll learn how to use *correlate*.

76 Whew! That was a dizzy ride.

Maybe a light snack this time?

Slidy Toys

How about a piece of funnel cake?
Funnel cakes *are* convoluted!

15 ...But It Is Correlated!

1 Are we satiated from the funnel cake?

It was sweet and hearty, and hardly light!

---

2 Now that we have correlation, let's use it inside neural networks!

We have to make a layer function out of it as we did with $\bullet^{2,1}$, don't we?

---

3 Yes, we do!

Is correlation a *linear* function like in frame 101:11?

An interesting question.

It is primarily lots of dot products, so it certainly feels as if it should be linear.

Is it?

---

4 It is!

While we won't go into the whole proof here, correlation can be fully described by linear functions. We think of it as an enthusiastic $\bullet$ between tensors.

Here's a function *corr* that combines a tensor t with two tensors, $\boldsymbol{\theta}_0$ and $\boldsymbol{\theta}_1$ from $\boldsymbol{\theta}$

```
(define corr                                   ●
  (λ (t)
    (λ (θ)
      (+ (correlate θ₀ t) θ₁))))
```

So $\boldsymbol{\theta}_0$ is a filter bank, since we expect t to be a signal^2.

What is $\boldsymbol{\theta}_1$?

---

5 $\boldsymbol{\theta}_1$ is known as the bias parameter, which is a tensor^1 that contains one scalar for each filter in the bank.

Why do we need the bias parameter in *corr*?

---

6 Just as in *linear* from frame 199:22, the bias parameter controls the point at which a subsequent invocation of *rectify* makes its decision to result in 0.0.

Do we combine *corr* and *rectify* similarly to how we combined *linear* and *rectify* to get the function *relu* in frame 198:17?

7

Yes, exactly!

We are now ready to define a correlation unit *recu*[†] like *relu* that we use for dense layers.

[†]This function is also known as *conv*, or *conv1D*, in other neural network systems. Here, however, we use the name *recu* to emphasize its similarity with *relu*.

What is *recu* short for?

8

Great question.

It stands for *rectifying correlational unit*

```
(define recu                                  ●
  (λ (t)
    (λ (θ)
      (rectify ((corr t) θ)))))
```

It is indeed a small variation on *relu*.

Do we use *recu* as we use *relu*?

9

Almost.

The primary difference lies in the shapes of the parameters in the corresponding $\boldsymbol{\theta}$. For *recu*, $\boldsymbol{\theta}_0$ must be a filter bank, which is a tensor^3, whereas $\boldsymbol{\theta}_0$ for *relu* is a tensor^2.

Define the shape list for *recu* where

  b is the number of filters

  m is the width of each filter

and

  d is the depth of the incoming signal

The shape list of a *recu* consists of one shape for the filter bank and one shape for the bias tensor.

The filter bank has the shape

```
(list b m d)
```

and the bias tensor has the shape

```
(list b)
```

So the shape list would be

```
(list
  (list b m d)
  (list b))
```

Let's look at the shapes of the inputs and outputs to a *recu*.

If the shape of the input signal[2] t is

(list n d)

where $\boldsymbol{\theta}_0$ has the shape

(list b m d)

and where $\boldsymbol{\theta}_1$ has the shape

(list b)

What is the shape of the output of the *recu* layer?

10 Since *rectify* does not change the shape of its argument, the shape of the output is the same as the shape of

((*corr* t) $\boldsymbol{\theta}$)

which is the shape of

(+ (*correlate* $\boldsymbol{\theta}_0$ t) $\boldsymbol{\theta}_1$)

The shape of the result of + is driven by the shape of

(*correlate* $\boldsymbol{\theta}_0$ t)

which, from the Law of Correlation on page 317 is

(list n b)

Perfect.

Now define *recu-block*, which defines a single *recu* layer, given b, m, and d as arguments.

11 Okay

```
(define recu-block
  (λ (b m d)
    (block recu
      (list
        (list b m d)
        (list b)))))
```

Great.

Networks that use correlation have a special name. They are known as *Convolutional Neural Networks* or CNNs.†

†Thanks, David H. Hubel (1926–2013), Torsten Wiesel (1924–), and Kunihiko Fukushima (1936–).

12 Why aren't they named *Correlational* neural networks?

Convolution is a function that is like correlation, except the filters are mirrored (i.e., reversed) before invoking the correlation. CNNs were first characterized using this function.

Since filters are learned during training of the network, it does not matter if we mirror them or not—they are learned in the appropriate direction. So we can avoid the mirroring, leaving just the correlation.

13 So, even though the network is named a convolutional neural network, we restrict ourselves to correlations.

The good thing is we can *still* abbreviate them as CNNs.

Is it time to define our CNN?

Let's jump right into it.

Just as we did for *iris-network* in frame 255:21, let us start with the output side of things.

What does our network need to produce as an output?

14 It needs to produce a one-hot-like vector of length 26. This means our output layer must produce a tensor^1 of shape

```
(list 26)
```

Correct.

Let us use that as a design guideline, and propose that our output *recu* layer should have 26 filters, one for each letter we want to detect.

15 That sounds like a great idea.

But that doesn't sound quite right. From frame 10, we know that this *recu* layer will produce a signal^2 of shape

```
(list 16 26)
```

An excellent observation.

We must now convert this signal^2 to a tensor^1.

16 How can we do that?

Let's consider an example.

Suppose that our input signal represents the letter Q. Assuming our network is trained well, one of the 26 filters in that *recu* layer will produce a strong output (i.e, a peak) in some segment, while other filters will have a very weak output.

For example, one of the segments will have a tensor[1] of length 26 that might look like this

[0.1 0.0 0.2 0.0 0.1 0.0 0.1 0.0
0.2 0.0 0.1 0.0 0.1 0.0 0.2 0.0
0.8 0.0 0.1 0.0 0.2 0.0 0.1 0.0
0.1 0.0]

17 We can see a peak of 0.8 at the position corresponding to Q.

What about the other segments?

They will likely have tensors[1] that don't have peaks that stand out.

For example

[0.2 0.1 0.2 0.0 0.1 0.0 0.1 0.0
0.0 0.0 0.1 0.0 0.1 0.1 0.0 0.0
0.0 0.0 0.0 0.1 0.1 0.0 0.0 0.0
0.2 0.0]

18 So how do we generate a tensor[1] out of this signal[2]?

We add all these segments together.

Adding them together will produce a tensor[1] where we'll still have a peak at Q's position.

19 That's an easy solution.

How do we add them?

Let's define sum^2, which adds all the tensors[1] in a tensor[2] together

```
(define sum^2
  (λ (t)
    (summed^2 t (sub1 ⌈t⌉) 0.0)))

(define summed^2
  (λ (t i a)
    (cond
      ((zero? i) (+ t|_0 a))
      (else
       (summed^2 t (sub1 i) (+ t|_i a))))))
```

20 This looks exactly like sum^1.

It is, in fact, identical.

Except, that in the expression

$t|_0$

the result is a tensor[1], not a scalar.

Because + is an extended operator, $summed^2$ accumulates a tensor[1], which becomes the result of sum^2.

21 So could we just do this?

```
(define sum^2 sum^1)   ●
```

Awesome, isn't it?

Now we extend this function

```
(define sum-cols
  (ext1 sum^2 2))
```

22 It is *magnifico*!

We can use this at our output to convert a signal[2] into a tensor[1].

Almost.

We convert the sum to an *average* first, by dividing it with the number of segments. This is known as *global average pooling.*

23 Why do we need to do this?

With *sum-cols* alone, the sum of small partial matches could end up exceeding the actual peak, leading to poor network performance.

24 Okay.

Should we extract the number of segments in t like this

$(shape\ t)_0$?

There is one more factor to consider.

Since *sum-cols* is extended, it may receive a batch of signals², making the rank of t greater than 2. So, we must extract the shape of the nested signals² like this

$(shape\ t)_{(\text{-}\ (rank\ t)\ 2)\downarrow}$

25 Oh, and then its first member is the number of segments in the signal

$(shape\ t)_{(\text{-}\ (rank\ t)\ 2)\downarrow 0}$

So if t has the shape (**list** 8 16 4), we get

1. $(\textbf{list}\ 8\ 16\ 4)_{(\text{-}\ 3\ 2)\downarrow 0}$
2. $(\textbf{list}\ 8\ 16\ 4)_{1\downarrow 0}$
3. $(\textbf{list}\ 16\ 4)_0$
4. 16

Correct, so here is the layer function *signal-avg*

```
(define signal-avg
  (λ (t)
    (λ (θ)
      (÷ (sum-cols t)
         (shape t)(- (rank t) 2)↓0))))
```

What would the shape list of this layer look like?

26 Since it does not use any parameters from $\boldsymbol{\theta}$, its shape list is

(**list**)

Excellent.

Now define a block for this layer.

27 Here it is.

```
(define signal-avg-block
  (block signal-avg
    (list)))
```

Will this be the output layer in our network?

Yes, it will.

Let's start building the other layers, which will all be *recu* layers.

28 How many such layers would we need?

Let's go with 8 layers.

29 Did we find that empirically as well?

We did, but there's method to our madness.

We expect the earlier layers in the network to detect patterns that are simple. For example, these could be features like rising edges and falling edges of the signal.

30 How many layers should we dedicate to that?

Let's give those simple patterns two layers.

The next two layers would match groups of these features into features like dots, dashes and spaces.

31 This is what we mean by more complex features in frame 307:41.

Exactly.

The following four layers then detect various groups of those features.

32 So will the filters for these layers learn to detect combinations of dots and dashes?

It is hard to say exactly what patterns the filters will learn, since that happens in training.

The idea of a hierarchy of features helps with the initial design, which we then refine through experimentation.

33 Okay.

The design of our network in frame 30 is described two layers at a time.

We can conveniently define a block of two layers, and use this block over and over again.

Here is the skeleton for *fcn-block*

```
(define fcn-block
  (λ (b m d)
    (stack-blocks
      (recu-block b m d)
      (recu-block b m B))))
```

This function defines a block of two *recu* layers, each of which has b filters, the width m, and the first layer accepts a signal[2] of depth d.

Find B.

34 The output of the first recu layer will be a signal of depth b. Since the output of the first *recu* layer becomes the input to the next *recu* layer, B becomes

b

because the third argument to *recu-block* is the depth of its input signal.

Why is this block called *fcn-block*?

Here, *fcn* stands for *fully convolutional network*, because the layers we use are only *recu* with the exception of the output *signal-avg* layer and there are no dense layers.

Here is the completed definition of *fcn-block*

```
(define fcn-block
  (λ (b m d)
    (stack-blocks
      (recu-block b m d)
      (recu-block b m b))))
```

35 So many names ...

Could we please define our network now?

Here it is

```
(define morse-fcn
  (stack-blocks
    (list
      (fcn-block 4 3 1)
      (fcn-block 8 3 4)
      (fcn-block 16 3 8)
      (fcn-block 26 3 16)
      signal-avg-block)))
```

36 How did we arrive at those arguments to the 4 invocations of *fcn-block*?

For our filters, we choose a width of 3, which is sufficient for our network.

The last invocation of *fcn-block* requires 26 filters, as in frame 15.

The first invocation is given 4 filters, to match 4 different features in the input signal. It produces an output signal of depth 4.

37 So that is why the next block has the *d* argument as 4.

Correct.

And we can see that in every other call to *fcn-block*, the depth of the signal is equal to the number of filters in the previous block.

We use 8 and 16 filters, respectively, for the other two blocks to allow for a sufficient capacity to match the requisite patterns of features matched by earlier blocks.

38 And how are we going to train this network?

We have to start by initializing a $\boldsymbol{\theta}$ for it.

39 We can use *init-*$\boldsymbol{\theta}$!

We should, but it doesn't yet know how to handle filter banks with shapes of length 3.

40 So should we update *init-shape*?

We should. Here's *init-shape* from frame 264:60.

```
(define init-shape
  (λ (s)
    (cond
      ((= |s| 1) (zero-tensor s))
      ((= |s| 2)
       (random-tensor 0.0 (÷ 2 s_1) s)))))
```

41 It does not have a **cond**-clause for shapes of length 3.

Let's add it

```
(define init-shape
  (λ (s)
    (cond
      ((= |s| 1) (zero-tensor s))
      ((= |s| 2)
       (random-tensor 0.0 (÷ 2 s_1) s))
      ((= |s| 3)
       (random-tensor 0.0
         (÷ 2 [   A   ]) s))))))
```

42 Aren't we supposed to find A?

Soon, but we've yet to determine a rule for initializing filter banks.

According to the Rule of Layer Initialization on page 262, the variance argument to *random-tensor* is given by the formula

$$\frac{2}{n}$$

43 Yes, n is the length of the input tensor[1] of that layer.

44

It is.

The real intent behind it, though, is that n is the number of scalars from the input that are multiplied by weights in the layer to produce a single scalar. This is known as

fan-in

Dense layers are built using $*^{2,1}$ and *sum*, so the fan-in is the length of the input tensor^1.

How is it different for *recu* layers?

45

We use *correlate* for *recu* layers.

In order to produce a single scalar in the output, *correlate* uses only

$m \times d$

scalars, because the overlap with any given filter is m segments long, and we sum the dot products at each of those segments in the overlap. Each of those dot products uses d scalars from the input.

Ah, so for a filter bank, the fan-in is always

$(* \; m \; d)$

46

Correct.

If s describes the shape of a filter bank, how do we find m and d?

The shape of a filter bank is

(**list** $b \; m \; d$)

so m is

s_1

and d is

s_2

47

Perfect.

Now find A.

A is the fan-in for a *recu* layer which is

$(* \; s_1 \; s_2)$

Excellent.

48 And now we train the network?

This is the completed definition of *init-shape*

```
(define init-shape
  (λ (s)
    (cond
      ((= |s| 1) (zero-tensor s))
      ((= |s| 2)
       (random-tensor 0.0 (÷ 2 s₁) s))
      ((= |s| 3)
       (random-tensor 0.0
         (÷ 2 (* s₁ s₂)) s)))))
```

Sometimes it helps the training process if the data set is transformed so that it makes the design of our network easier. We call this *preprocessing*.

49 What transformations do we need for our data set?

First, our data set in frame 309:47 introduces *morse-xs* as a signal^1. As later frames show us, *correlate*, and hence *recu* layers work with signals^2. So, we must transform *morse-xs* into a signal^2 by wrapping each scalar in an element of *morse-xs* into a tensor^1.

So, for example, here is a signal^1

```
[−0.26  0.02 −0.17 0.0
 −0.02 −0.10  0.03 0.0
 −0.16  1.16 −0.13 0.97
  1.01  0.93 −0.18 0.13]
```

Show the transformation of this signal^1 into a signal^2.

50 Here it is

```
[[−0.26] [ 0.02] [−0.17] [0.0]
 [−0.02] [−0.10] [ 0.03] [0.0]
 [−0.16] [ 1.16] [−0.13] [0.97]
 [ 1.01] [ 0.93] [−0.18] [0.13]]
```

Excellent.

Now for another transformation. The signal data we have varies between a low of approximately 0.0 to a high of approximately 1.0.

Having values very close to 0.0 in the input is always problematic since those values diminish the effect of any weight in a layer.

51 How is this problem handled?

We make the signal data swing between a low of approximately -0.5 and a high of approximately 0.5.

That way we avoid having values close to 0.0 in the input.

52 Ah, we can achieve that by subtracting 0.5 from the signal!

Correct.

We assume that *morse-xs* is preprocessed in this way. To continue our example, the preprocessed tensor looks like this

$$
\begin{array}{l}
[[-0.76]\ [-0.48]\ [-0.67]\ [-0.50] \\
\ [-0.52]\ [-0.60]\ [-0.47]\ [-0.50] \\
\ [-0.66]\ [\ \ 0.66]\ [-0.63]\ [\ \ 0.47] \\
\ [\ \ 0.51]\ [\ \ 0.43]\ [-0.68]\ [-0.37]]
\end{array}
$$

53 Don't we need to preprocess the *morse-ys*?

No, that is not necessary, since we only use *morse-ys* to produce the loss.

54 Okay.

Now can we train the network?

Let us define a training function to train a network for classifying Morse code signals

```
(define train-morse
  (λ (network)
    (with-hypers
      ((α 0.0005)
       (revs 20000)
       (batch-size 8)
       (μ 0.9)
       (β 0.999))
      (trained-morse
        (block-fn network)
        (block-ls network)))))
```

Here we provide the values for the hyperparameters and then use a helper function *trained-morse* to produce a model from a given network.

Now let us define *trained-morse*.

55 Okay.

We'll be using stochastic gradient for it, correct?

Yes.

Let us use *adam-gradient-descent*.

To make it stochastic, we'll have to use *sampling-obj* with *l2-loss* as the loss function, and the data set

(*morse-train-xs*, *morse-train-ys*)

56 And we'll have to initialize a $\boldsymbol{\theta}$ using *init-*$\boldsymbol{\theta}$.

Here is the definition of *trained-morse*. It accepts a network function *classifier* and a shape list ***θ**-shapes* and produces a model using *classifier* and a trained ***θ***

```
(define trained-morse
  (λ (classifier θ-shapes)
    (model classifier
      (adam-gradient-descent
        (sampling-obj
          (l2-loss classifier)
          morse-train-xs
          morse-train-ys)
        (init-θ θ-shapes)))))
```

57 How did we arrive at those hyperparameters?

Through a grid search, of course.

58 And what is the accuracy of this network?

Let's see

```
▷ (accuracy
    (train-morse morse-fcn)
    morse-test-xs morse-test-ys)
▶ 0.94
```

59 A 94% accuracy.

Is that good?

It's pretty good.

But we can do better.

60 Interesting.

How?

By using *skip* connections.

61 What are skip connections?

Skip connections add the input signal of a block to the output of the block itself.

62 What is the purpose of that?

63

As described in frame 259:43, in very deep networks, as a scalar from the input of a network moves through layers, each layer affects the influence of that scalar on the output.

Yes, it leads to exploding or vanishing problems that cause difficulty in training networks, which is why we have to carefully initialize our network.

64

Correct.

Even when the network is carefully initialized, and training proceeds as expected, some weights still become very small and suppress the scalars in the input.

Adding the input back to the output restores the effect of those scalars, allowing those scalars to have more of an effect on the layers that come after.

This improves the training of the network and makes it more effective at what it is supposed to do.

That sounds great.

How can we add skip connections to *morse-fcn*?

65

Let's begin by defining a function *skip* which accepts a block function *f*, and adds its input to its output

```
(define skip
  (λ (f)
    (λ (t)
      (λ (θ)
        (+ ((f t) θ)
           t)))))
```

Explain this function.

When *skip* is provided a block function *f*, it returns a new block function that adds to the output of *f*

((*f* *t*) **θ**)

the input to the block function

t

Why is this definition dashed?

66 It is dashed because this addition between the input and the output does not work when the respective depths of the input and output are different. For example, the input has the shape

(list n d)

and the output has the shape

(list n b)

and d and b are different.

How do we solve this problem?

---

67 We have to convert the input signal from its shape

(list n d)

to the shape

(list n b)

We can do this by using *recu* itself, by using b filters, can we not?

---

68 The definition of *recu* in frame 8 contains a *rectify*. We don't want to use *recu* directly because this *rectify* might suppress some scalars from the input.

We can, however, use *correlate*, which does not suppress any scalars in the input.

Okay.

What would its filter bank look like then?

---

69 We already know that it needs b filters and the depth of the input signal is d.

We use the value of 1 for m, so that the filters don't merge neighboring values into each other.

What is the shape of this filter bank?

Ah, using filters of width 1 ensures that the overlap is exactly one segment long, so neighboring segments don't affect the output for that particular segment.

The shape of the filter bank is

(list b 1 d)

Correct.

This filter bank, obviously, adds an additional parameter in the $\boldsymbol{\theta}$ for every skip connection.

70 It's time to see some serious magic!

It's coming. Here is the definition of *skip*, which now accepts a second argument j, the number of parameters from $\boldsymbol{\theta}$ consumed by f

```
(define skip                                   ●
  (λ (f j)
    (λ (t)
      (λ (θ)
        (+ ((f t) θ)
           ((correlate θ_j) t))))))
```

How many parameters does the resulting block function consume from $\boldsymbol{\theta}$?

71 It consumes

$$j + 1$$

parameters because f consumes j, and *correlate* consumes an additional one.

The Law of Skip Connections

A skip connection for a block with an input of depth d and an output of depth b requires a bank of shape (list b 1 d) in $\boldsymbol{\theta}$.

Correct.

Here is *skip-block*, that accepts a block *ba*, the depth of the input *d* and the depth of the output *b*. It returns a new block with a skip connection around *block*

```
(define skip-block                              •
  (λ (ba d b)
    (let ((shape-list (block-ls ba)))
      (block
        (skip (block-fn ba) |shape-list|)
        (append
          shape-list
          (list
            (list b 1 d)))))))
```

Explain how the *skip* function is used here.

72 We first give the shape list of *ba* the name *shape-list*.

The function of the returned block uses *skip* to create a skip connection. The first argument to *skip* is the block function

(*block-fn ba*)

and the second argument is the number of arguments consumed by it, which is

|*shape-list*|

Great.

Now explain how shapes of the returned block are determined.

73 We add a new shape for a filter bank for the skip connection

(**list** *b* 1 *d*)

at the end of the shape list of *block*

shape-list

Perfect.

We now define *residual-block*

```
(define residual-block
  (λ (b m d)
    (skip-block
      (fcn-block b m d)
      d b)))
```

Skip connections are sometimes known as *residual* connections.

74 That explains the name.

How do we define our network with *residual-block*?

It is identical to *morse-fcn* except we use *residual-block* instead of *fcn-block*

```
(define morse-residual
  (stack-blocks
    (list
      (residual-block 4 3 1)
      (residual-block 8 3 4)
      (residual-block 16 3 8)
      (residual-block 26 3 16)
      signal-avg-block)))
```

75 And *that* is worth waiting for—pure, unadulterated, beautiful magic.

It also has a much improved accuracy!

▷ (*accuracy*
  (*train-morse morse-residual*)
  morse-test-xs morse-test-ys)
▶ 0.98

That little piece of magic brings us to the end of our straight line to deep learning.

76 But lines have no ends!

Indeed, the learning must never end.

But the rest of this learning journey best begins at the Epilogue.

77 To the Epilogue, then!

What dessert are we leaving with?

Correlated Toys

How about some *jalebis* (जलेबी)?
With a side of clotted cream!

†Thanks, Karen Anne Carpenter (1950–1983), Richard Lynn Carpenter (1946–), and also music arrangers Roger Nichols (1940–) and Paul Williams (1940–).

Any straight path through complex terrain necessarily leaves out the eddies, rivulets and diversions that make the terrain rich and fascinating. Our journey into neural networks has also been such a straight line, and we've deliberately elided many of the features of the terrain that add texture and complexity to the subject. In this epilogue we present a set of destinations that are worth visiting for those interested in exploring further, because in reality, we've only just begun.

1 | Mathematical foundations

Our presentation of deep learning in previous chapters has used a minimal amount of mathematics necessary, but serious studies of existing machine learning literature requires an understanding of the mathematical foundations of the field. The two most relevant fields are Linear Algebra, and Probability and Statistics. These are often accompanied by a healthy dose of Vector Calculus.

Books like *Deep Learning* [1] provide a very condensed presentation of the necessary mathematics, but assume a certain level of mathematical maturity. To develop this maturity, books such as *Coding the Matrix* [2] (for Linear Algebra) and *Bayesian Statistics the Fun Way* [3] (for Probability Theory) are good for learning these subjects from first principles.

2 | Data-generating distributions

Data sets are a curious entity. They appear like there's nothing particularly interesting about them. They just contain a large number of points. But in reality, data sets provide us with a sampling of the outputs of a *data-generating process*. For example, in the Morse code example from chapter 14, we describe how the tensors we use are derived from a physical process of pressing a button on a flashlight.

These data-generating processes can be understood in probabilistic terms. We associate them with an ideal *probability distribution*, which maps each point being generated by the process to the probability of its occurrence. We call this the *data generating distribution*.

The process of learning the $\boldsymbol{\theta}$ of a neural network constructs an internal approximation of this data generating distribution, and applies it to the specific task at hand.

3 | Tasks

Deep learning is all about doing interesting things. The cognoscenti have given a somewhat boring name to these interesting things. They call them *tasks*.

One interesting objective in many applications is predicting prices of things (like stocks, commodities, real-estate) based on a data set collected from prior transactions. In these applications, the task is to predict a single scalar. These types of tasks are known as *regression* tasks.

Chapter 3 shows an instance of regression based on a linear model, i.e., a linear function and its corresponding $\boldsymbol{\theta}$. This kind of model merely implements a mathematical function, but in reality the mathematical function is *modeling* some aspect of the real world, like a price of some asset.

Another set of interesting things to do with neural networks is to identify objects and faces in pictures, identify words in speech or make medical diagnoses from X-ray pictures. These are examples of a task known as *classification*. We encountered classification in chapters 13 and 15.

If we find ourselves in need of language translation services, neural networks can step in and provide such translations. Neural networks have been designed to translate written text from one language to another. Some neural networks additionally can recognize words embedded in pictures and translate them, an application particularly useful in reading signs using the camera on a phone. These kinds of tasks are known as *translation* tasks.

Translation tasks can be applied to pictures too. A particularly fascinating example of such a translation is *style transfer*, where the visual style of an artist is transferred to an input image to produce that same image in the style of that artist.

Another class of applications concerns the *generation* of new points by sampling the data generating distribution the neural network has learned from a data set. For example, we can generate original artistic images or musical compositions that have never been seen before by using specially designed neural networks that have been trained on those types of data sets.

Neural networks are always designed for a specific task that drives the choice of underlying functions and structures. Here we discuss some of the ideas that influence the design space.

4 | Other loss functions

One of the critical decisions while designing a neural network for a specific task is the choice of the loss function. While *l2-loss* is a broadly applicable loss function[4], other loss functions are also used in different types of applications and tasks. Here we explore some of them.

One popular loss function for classification tasks is *cross-entropy* loss. This loss function has two interesting properties. The first is that each tensor[1] argument must sum up to 1.0, and the second is that each element in the tensors[1] represents probabilities for the corresponding class and thus must lie between 0.0 and 1.0. This loss is defined as follows

```
(define cross-entropy
  (λ (target num-classes)
    (λ (xs ys)
      (λ (θ)
        (let ((pred-ys ((target xs) θ)))
          (* −1
            (÷ (• ys (log pred-ys))
               num-classes)))))))
```

When *ys* is a one-hot vector, *cross-entropy* selects the highest class predicted. The multiplication by −1 is because probabilities are always between 0.0 and 1.0, and their *log* is always negative, giving rise to a negative dot product. Since our convention is to have a positive loss, we multiply it by −1.

Cross-entropy loss is usually used in conjunction with a *softmax* decider (we'll see this one soon). In combination, these two functions enable training a network with more accuracy and using fewer revisions.

Here is a loss function that is similar to *l2-loss*, except it uses the absolute value function instead of squaring in order to get rid of negative differences

```
(define l1-loss
  (λ (target)
    (λ (xs ys)
      (λ (θ)
        (let ((pred-ys ((target xs) θ)))
          (sum (abs (− ys pred-ys))))))))
```

This loss function can be used when we don't want outliers in the dataset to disproportionately influence the loss.

5 | More deciders

The only decider in previous chapters is *rectify*. While it has a number of very useful properties and is extremely simple, *rectify* is a rather recent development. Earlier neural networks relied on nonlinear functions, for example, the *logistic sigmoid*[‡] and the hyperbolic *tanh*

```
(define logistic-sigmoid
  (λ (x)
    (let ((ex (exp x)))
      (÷ ex (+ 1 ex)))))

(define tanh
  (λ (x)
    (let ((e2x (exp (∗ 2 x))))
      (÷ (− e2x 1) (+ e2x 1)))))
```

These are still applicable in some special cases, but their usage has dropped significantly in favor of *rectify* and its variants.

Variations on *rectify* include a *leaky* rectify [5] that uses a small non-zero slope for inputs that are less than 0.0. We can define it like this

```
(define leaky-rectify
  (λ (m)
    (λ (x)
      (cond
        ((< x 0) (∗ m x))
        (else x)))))
```

The main benefit of a leaky rectify is that it allows for a small amount of negative gradient to pass through when gradients are calculated. This is useful in deep networks as it speeds up training, and avoids some pathological conditions that *rectify* can sometimes cause in large networks. In this definition, the value for m must be provided as an argument, but other variations exist where m becomes part of the $\boldsymbol{\theta}$ and thus can be learned [6].

Here is another example of a decider that is somewhat limited in where it can be used, but is used widely in those situations. This is the *softmax* function

```
(define softmax
  (λ (x)
    (let ((expd (− (exp x) (max x))))
      (÷ expd (sum expd)))))
```

This function always produces a tensor[1] that meets the criterion of a probability distribution—each element in it is between 0.0 and 1.0, and the elements sum to 1.0. Because of this property, a *softmax* decider is used in conjunction with the *cross-entropy* loss function (which expects a probability distribution), making it ideal for the last layer of a classifier neural network. As an aside, the subtraction of *max* x is necessary to numerically stabilize

[‡]Thank you, Pierre-Francois Verhulst (1804–1849).

the sum so it is never 0.0, but it does not alter the final value of the function.

6 | Higher-dimensional signals

In order to deal with more complex applications that have to do with images and videos, we need to expand our notion of signals. So far we have only dealt with signals that have samples in one dimension (these were our Morse code signals from frame 290:29). Physical quantities like sounds, seismic vibrations, and variability of temperature often give rise to these types of signals, which are useful in many different applications.

Higher-dimensional signals include images, videos, and others, which arise in a very large number of *visual* applications such as the classification of pictures, transformation of photos, and others. The principles of convolutional neural networks such as correlation are analogous in higher dimensions, except they deal with correlating in more than one dimension instead of one. The function *correlate* is then extended correspondingly to more dimensions.

Higher-dimensional signals give rise to networks that have much larger $\boldsymbol{\theta}$s since we're now dealing with a much larger amount of data. It is not uncommon to see $\boldsymbol{\theta}$s containing hundreds of millions of scalar parameters in them. Examples of these networks, like AlexNet [7], ResNet [8], and VGG [9], make for extremely interesting architectural explorations.

7 | Natural language systems

Text-based tasks such as translation and text classification require the processing of natural languages. A neural network designed for natural language processing usually relies on very specific layer structures that allow the network to learn the relationship between words in different parts of a piece of text.

These networks can learn how ideas are threaded through a sequence of sentences and reproduce them as necessary in tasks like translation and summarization. Networks such as GPT-3 [10] carry billions of scalars in their $\boldsymbol{\theta}$s and are able to handle very complex tasks.

Sentences in a text processing system are represented by a sequence of tokens. Text processing neural networks work by building models of the probabilities of one word following another one in a sequence. This is then used for tasks like answering questions, machine-generated conversation (known as *chatbots*), text generation, etc. Text processing neural networks can be combined with speech processing neural networks to enable increasingly common applications like voice assistants.

There are two main kinds of architectures used for text processing. There is a *recurrent* neural network architecture that uses an output associated with a prior token for processing a future token. This allows the network to develop information about the context in which a given token appears.

Recurrent networks are rapidly being replaced by a newer form of network based on the idea of *attention* [11]. The difference in attention-based networks is that they work on whole sequences rather than one token at a time. They include a processing block known as a *transformer* that uses attention to provide a mechanism with which the network can learn how each token in the input sequence influences other tokens.

8 | Generative networks

For applications that require generation, there are two primary types of neural network architectures in use.

The first is known as a *variational autoencoder*. To understand what this does, it is first important to understand what an autoencoder is.

An autoencoder is a neural network that consists of two parts that are trained together, but can be used separately. The two parts are known as the *encoder* and the *decoder*.

The encoder maps every input into a more compact form of the same input. Usually the inputs are tensors consisting of a very large number of scalars. The compact form of the output is usually a tensor[1] consisting of a very small number of scalars. For example, it is possible to have an encoder that can take an image of the letters of an alphabet in a specific font and represent it as a tensor[1] made up of 12 scalars, known as a *code*. By training this encoder on images of different fonts, we can have it produce different codes for each font.

The decoder performs the inverse transformation. It takes the compact form as an input and produces an output that is as close to the original input as possible.

A *variational* autoencoder [12] makes certain that the codes that are produced by an encoder have unique mathematical properties so that they can be treated as samples from a random number generator. Then, by providing new random numbers to the corresponding decoder, new points can be generated that will be similar in characteristics to the original set of inputs the network was trained on.

For example, by providing new random 12-scalar codes to our font decoder, we can produce images of entirely new fonts. The same principles can be used to generate outputs of many different kinds.

The other type of architecture used in generational applications is known as a *generative adversarial network*, or GAN [13]. This type of neural network also consists of two parts.

The first is a generator, which is responsible for converting a random number into an output with the desired characteristics, such as the image of a font. The second is a discriminator, which is responsible for deciding whether the output generated by the generator passes muster. In our example, the discriminator will decide whether or not the image generator is that of a font.

The clever bit about GANs is that their training is designed in a way that both penalizes the discriminator if it is wrong in making a judgment and penalizes the generator if it generates the wrong kind of output.

Training the discriminator and generator together ensures that the generator learns how to produce samples that the discriminator will accept and the discriminator learns to accept only samples that satisfy the application requirements.

9 | Practical things

One of the most important elements of the design of a neural network is its *capacity*, which can roughly be thought of as the number of scalars in its $\boldsymbol{\theta}$. If the network has too few, then it won't learn enough about the training set, a condition known as *underfitting*. If it has too many, then it will learn to be very specific to the training set, a condition known as *overfitting*.

Even if a network has the appropriate capacity, training it with too few *revs* can lead to underfitting, while training it with too many can lead to overfitting.

Either underfitting or overfitting or both might cause the network to not perform optimally. The network will fail to *generalize* to points that lie outside the training set. Selecting networks with the right capacity and choosing the hyperparameters carefully is a very critical part of the network training process.

The concept of the *right* capacity is difficult to define precisely, because design of the network itself influences what "right" means. For example, skip connections can dramatically improve the performance of the network without greatly affecting the number of scalars in $\boldsymbol{\theta}$.

Like many things we have seen here, experimentation leads to the development of heuristics and design rules that help build networks of adequate capacity.

A number of practical tricks are necessary in order to train a network properly for given tasks.

First, it always helps to properly track the metrics of a network as it trains. Tracking the training loss, i.e., the value produced by the loss function at each of the *revs*, helps follow how well the network is training.

Second, using a proper validation set to track the relevant performance metric associated with the network (such as accuracy of predictions) helps determine if the training is proceeding correctly.

Third, techniques like *regularization* are used to manage the effectiveness of training. Regularization is the name given to a technique of adding an additional term to the loss function that influences the direction the gradient descent takes. See Goodfellow *et al.* [1] for examples of regularization. This helps train the network without under- or over-training it, which improves the overall performance of the network for its designated task.

Fourth, initialization of weights is a significant part of training. He *et al.* [6] proposed the initialization scheme used in this book. This scheme is useful with rectifier-based networks. Other schemes such as the one proposed by Glorot *et al.* [14] help with other types of networks.

10 | Onwards, little learners!

This epilogue is a whirlwind tour of the topics and sources for curious readers to pursue. With the understanding of neural networks gained from this book, we hope these topics are less formidable than they would otherwise have been.

À bientôt

Appendix A
Ghost in the Machine[†]

[†]Thanks, Gilbert Ryle (1900–1976) and *The Police*: Andrew James Summers (1942–), Sting (1951–), and Stewart Armstrong Copeland (1952–).

Starting in chapter 4, almost everything relies on the availability of

THE MYSTERIOUS

This appendix and the next, meant for those who are curious about how it is built, present a full explanation. These definitions provide for complete automatic differentiation that provides a semantic foundation for all the programs demonstrated in the *core* of this book, which is chapters 1 through 15.

This is a superset of what is traditionally known in the history of neural networks as *back propagation.* The back propagation algorithm is an instance of *reverse mode* automatic differentiation, which is what we describe here.

The definitions in the core are written in a consciously functional state of mind, carefully avoiding parts of Scheme that can disrupt this state of mind. The generality of automatic differentiation, however, as well as our desire to keep the definitions easy to understand, requires some of the parts of Scheme we have avoided.

Even though these definitions are written in the *metalanguage,* we have attempted to preserve some of the notation from page xxiii, particularly for list members and vector elements. For readers who are attempting to define these functions as they read along, the notations are as follows.

Frame	Metalanguage Notation	Transcription as Scheme
31	$[e\ es\ \ldots]$	`(vector` *e es* `...)`
32	$v\vert_i$	`(vector-ref` *v i*`)`
51	$\dagger v \dagger$	`(vector-length` *v*`)`
51	l_0	`(list-ref` *l* `0)` or `(car` *l*`)`
51	$l_{1\downarrow}$	`(drop` *l* `1)` or `(cdr` *l*`)`
72	(**let²** (⟨*a b*⟩ *E*) *B*)	`(let-values (((a b)` *E*`))` *B*`)`
75	⟨*e1 e2*⟩	`(values e1 e2)`

Symbols like ∇, σ, ρ, κ can be typed in directly as unicode symbols, or they can be spelled out with English letters (e.g. `nabla`, `sigma`, `rho`, `kappa`).

The rest of this appendix is in the frame format, but the style is not the same. Instead of the familiar question/answer style, it is more a comic-book style. It should be read one frame at a time, from left to right within a frame.

1 | Prologue

1

This is the definition of ∇

```
(define ∇
  (λ (f θ)
    (let ((wrt (map* dual* θ)))
      (∇once (f wrt) wrt))))
```

Flummoxed? Fear not.

The goal of this appendix is to fully explain what this definition is about.

2 | Of gradients and things

2

Gradients are *rates of change* of the result of a function with respect to the arguments of the function.

Given a function *f* that accepts one scalar argument, let's invoke it on a scalar *a* like this

$(f\ a)$

3

To understand what the gradient of *f* is, we begin with the method we used in frame 65:30.[†] We invoke *f* on an argument just a little different from *a*, adjusted by a value Δa[‡] that can be made arbitrarily small

$(f\ (+\ a\ \Delta a))$

[†]Except, here we use a more abstract value, instead of the specific 0.0099 in frame 65:30.

[‡]Pronounced "delta *a*."

We expect the result to change by a certain amount as well.[§] We refer to the amount it has changed using

Δf_a

Here, the subscript represents the argument(s) on which *f* is invoked.

[§]We assume that *f* returns a value for this adjusted argument.

4

The gradient of *f* with respect to *a* is the rate of change in the result of $(f\ a)$ with respect to the change in *a*. This makes it the ratio

$$\frac{\Delta f_a}{\Delta a}$$

5

This ratio[†] can be extended to functions of more than one argument such that each argument is treated independently. Let's say g takes two scalar arguments, and we invoke it on a and b.

[†]For those who are familiar with differential calculus: the limits are implicit and expressions using Δa should be implicitly understood to be in the limit as Δa approaches 0.0. For functions that are defined but discontinuous at a, the results of our automatic differentiation are not defined and may be provided with the limit approaching from either the left or the right.

We find the rates of change with respect to a and b independently like this

$$\frac{\Delta g_a}{\Delta a}$$

and

$$\frac{\Delta g_b}{\Delta b}$$

where Δg_a (and respectively Δg_b) is the change in

$(g\ a\ b)$

when a (respectively b) is changed by Δa (respectively Δb).

The gradient of g with respect to a and b is the list[‡]

(**list** $\frac{\Delta g_a}{\Delta a}$ $\frac{\Delta g_b}{\Delta b}$)

[‡]There is an example of this in frame 79:20.

6

Any function that accepts tensors and returns a scalar (such as a loss function) is treated in the same way as a multi-argument function.

Each scalar s within the argument tensors is adjusted by Δs, and the change in the result scalar is observed.

Instead of packing the gradients into a list as we did for g in frame 5, we define the gradient to be a tensor of the same shape as the argument, but with the *gradient* values substituting the scalars in that argument.

7

For example, we let h be a function that accepts a tensor of shape (**list** 2 3) and we invoke it on this tensor.

$$\begin{bmatrix} ax & ay & az \\ bx & by & bz \end{bmatrix}_{(2\ 3)}$$

8

We find the gradients of h with respect to each scalar ax, ay, az, bx, by, and bz, and put them together like this.

$$\begin{bmatrix} \frac{\Delta h_{ax}}{\Delta ax} & \frac{\Delta h_{ay}}{\Delta ay} & \frac{\Delta h_{az}}{\Delta az} \\ \frac{\Delta h_{bx}}{\Delta bx} & \frac{\Delta h_{by}}{\Delta by} & \frac{\Delta h_{bz}}{\Delta bz} \end{bmatrix}_{(2\ 3)}$$

9

A function that accepts lists (of tensors, or of nested lists) is treated similarly, so that the gradient with respect to the list argument is a list with the same structure, but with scalar gradients in the places where the list argument has scalars.

In other words, for a function that produces a scalar, its gradient with respect to a list or tensor argument has the same structure as that argument, but any scalar in the argument is substituted by the corresponding gradient with respect to that scalar.

3 | Primitives, compositions, and chains

10

We have been abstract about gradients, writing them simply as a ratio of two abstract quantities. For primitives like addition and multiplication of scalars (and many others), however, the ratios can be reduced to a fixed formula.†

As an example, consider the gradients of + with respect to two scalars a and b.

†This is what differential calculus is all about.

For +, if we change a (respectively b) by Δa (respectively Δb), the result also changes by Δa (respectively Δb). So we get the gradients of +

1. (**list** $\frac{\Delta +_a}{\Delta a}$ $\frac{\Delta +_b}{\Delta b}$)
2. (**list** $\frac{\Delta a}{\Delta a}$ $\frac{\Delta b}{\Delta b}$)
3. (**list** 1.0 1.0)

The gradients are 1.0 and 1.0 *regardless* of what a and b are.

11

We determine the formulas similarly (although the others are much more involved than this) for all of the primitives we use, so that each gradient is determined by a simple formula based on the arguments to the primitive.

For example, the gradient of $*$ with respect to two scalars a and b is

(**list** b a)

12

In other words, we never really need to explicitly find the ratios of the change in results to the change in arguments.

With these formulas for gradients of primitives, we use a fixed rule to find the gradients of functions that are built from primitives.

13

When the result of the invocation of one function, say g, is an argument to another function, say f, then the result of f is said to arise from the

composition

of f and g.

As an example, let f and g be two functions that each take one scalar argument and produce a scalar result. Applying the composition of f and g to a scalar a is the same as doing this

```
(f (g a))
```

14

We write this in a more explicit way

```
(let ((b (g a)))
  (f b))
```

Let us say that a itself is generated from the application of another function, say h, to another scalar, say 3.72.

We can then "unroll" this invocation of h and add it to our **let**-expression

```
(let ((a (h 3.72)))
  (let ((b (g a)))
    (f b)))
```

15

This **let**-expression is equivalent to

```
(f (g (h 3.72)))
```

Here, we say that f, g, and h form a

chain of invocations

where the invocation of h is the

innermost

and the invocation of f is the

outermost

We can repeat this process of unrolling the component functions all the way until the only functions in the chain are primitive functions.

16

The scalar provided as an argument (here, 3.72) to the innermost function is referred to as

the argument to the chain

And the value produced by the outermost function of the chain is referred to as

the result of the chain

17

The simplest possible composition† of two primitives f and g can be written with this **let**-expression, where the scalar a is a constant

```
(let ((b (g a)))
  (f b))
```

† Also in frame 14.

To find the gradient of the composition of f and g, let's adjust a by Δa.

18

The result of $(g\ a)$ changes by Δg_a. Since $(g\ a)$ is the scalar b, let us give Δg_a another name, Δb. The result of the whole expression now changes by Δf_b.

The gradient of the expression with respect to a is the ratio

$$\frac{\Delta f_b}{\Delta a}$$

19

Let us rewrite this ratio like this

$$\frac{\Delta f_b}{\Delta b} \times \frac{\Delta b}{\Delta a}$$

which is the same as

$$\frac{\Delta f_b}{\Delta b} \times \frac{\Delta g_a}{\Delta a}$$

We recognize a pattern here. The right-hand term is the gradient of g with respect to a, and the left-hand term is the gradient of f with respect to b.

20

So, the gradient of the composition of *f* and *g* with respect to the argument to the chain is

(gradient of *f* w.r.t.[†] its argument)

$\times$

(gradient of *g* w.r.t. its argument)

[†]Short for *with respect to.*

This is known as the

chain rule

It gives us a way of getting the gradient of a composition of functions using the individual gradients of each of the component functions.

21

Now consider a chain with more than two primitives in a composition

(*f0* (*f1* … (*fn a*)))

The gradient is found in a similar fashion

(gradient of *f0* w.r.t. its argument)

$\times$

(gradient of *f1* w.r.t. its argument)

$\times$

…

$\times$

(gradient of *fn* w.r.t. its argument)

22

This can be thought of as walking down the chain while accumulating, using multiplication, the gradient of each primitive with respect to its argument. We refer to the accumulator we use as the

multiplicative accumulator

The starting value of the multiplicative accumulator is 1.0, and we multiply it with one gradient at each step in the chain.

When we're done with the chain, the multiplicative accumulator *is* the gradient of the result of the chain with respect to the argument of the chain.

23

As before, we can generalize this process to include the primitives that accept more than one argument.

For this, we individually accumulate gradients with respect to each scalar argument. Since there are now many scalars with respect to which we find gradients, there are also as many different multiplicative accumulators with each participating only in the chain associated with its scalar.

The definitions in this appendix deal with this full generality, but for this section, we consider only single-argument chains.

Because multiplication is associative, there are two ways to walk this chain. For example, if we have a chain

  $(f\ (g\ (h\ a)))$

The gradient of this composition with respect to a can be found in two ways.

24

For the first way, we start with
  the multiplicative accumulator at 1.0
and multiply it with
  the gradient of h w.r.t. a
then multiply it with
  the gradient of g w.r.t. $(h\ a)$
finally multiply it with
  the gradient of f w.r.t. $(g\ (h\ a))$

In this second way, we start with
  the multiplicative accumulator at 1.0
and multiply it with
  the gradient of f w.r.t. $(g\ (h\ a))$
then multiply it with
  the gradient of g w.r.t. $(h\ a)$
finally multiply it with
  the gradient of h w.r.t. a

25

The first way, starting at h and going to f, is known as

  forward mode

automatic differentiation.

In this mode, we start with a multiplicative accumulator with the value of 1.0.

We then take the innermost primitive in the chain, and multiply its gradient with the initial multiplicative accumulator and continue to process the chain from right to left, carrying the result of the primitive itself, as well as the multiplicative accumulator.

26

In forward mode, we don't need to explicitly construct chains—gradients are found as we determine the results of the primitives.

This works well when the gradients we seek come from functions that have very few scalars in their arguments.

When the arguments to these functions consist of a very large number of scalars, such as those found in tensors and $\boldsymbol{\theta}$s we encounter in neural networks, we have to keep track of a very large number of accumulators. When our chains include binary primitives (and they always do), this causes an unreasonable increase in the number of multiplicative accumulators we must manage.

27

The second way, the alternative to forward mode, is

reverse mode

automatic differentiation.

Here, we walk our chains from left to right, i.e., from the outermost primitive invocation all the way down to the innermost one.

In our example with f, g, and h, this would be how it works in frame 24.

Unlike forward mode, however, this makes us explicitly construct a chain of primitives. We construct this chain while we're computing the result scalar, but start walking the chain only when we actually *require* the gradient.

28

Reverse mode automatic differentiation has the benefit that there is no disproportionate increase in the number of multiplicative accumulators for functions that produce a scalar from compound arguments.

This allows us to maintain a fixed number of multiplicative accumulators, one for each scalar in the argument to the chain, and update those as we walk the chains.

29

The rest of this appendix lays out in detail how reverse mode automatic differentiation is achieved.

It starts with the representation of scalars so that chains of primitives are explicitly constructed, and then describes how compound data structures are handled, and finally how chains are constructed and gradients extracted.

30

Our automatic differentiation happens at run time. We do not attempt to translate functions into their equivalent differentiated forms. Instead, we evaluate the result of a function for given arguments, and then determine the gradient of that result with respect to those arguments.

This means that numerical primitives, such as addition and multiplication, *not only* determine their numerical results, they *also* organize the chain so that gradients can be determined whenever asked for.

31

In order to do this, we need a way to represent scalars that consist of two parts. The first, its

real

part, known as its r, is the numerical value of the scalar. The second, its

link[†]

known as its k, is a function that manages the chain that produced this scalar and is invoked for walking the chain. We refer to this representation as

a *dual*[‡]

[†] The name *link* arises because it is one piece in the chain of primitives that may have produced this scalar.

[‡] Thanks, William Kingdon Clifford. Here, our notion of *dual* is a little different from that introduced by Clifford, but the spirit is similar, so we use the same name.

Each dual is represented by a vector. The function *dual* builds a vector of 3 elements. The 0th element is a tag that is used to distinguish duals from other vectors, the 1st element is the r, and the 2nd element is the k

```
(define dual
  (λ (r k)
    [dual r k]))
```

To provide a unique tag, we use the function *dual* itself as its tag.

In the following, the variable name d and variable names beginning with d all stand for duals.

32

The predicate *dual?* uses this unique tag to test whether a given value is a dual

```
(define dual?
  (λ (d)
    (cond
      ((vector? d) (eq?† d|0 dual))
      (else #f))))
```

†This predicate is true if its arguments reside at the same location in memory. Here, it is true when two functions *are the same.*

The expressions used in the core often include literal constants, for example for hyperparameters or when data sets are read from files. These constants are represented as real numbers. For reverse mode automatic differentiation purposes, however, we treat them as duals.

For an interesting look at *eq?*, see chapter 18, "We Change Therefore We Are the Same!" in *The Seasoned Schemer*, MIT Press, 1996.

33

We *now* refer to both real numbers and duals as

scalars

These are exactly the scalars from the core, as in frame 31:7.

We thus define *scalar?*

```
(define scalar?
  (λ (d)
    (cond
      ((number? d) #t)
      (else (dual? d)))))
```

34

Consequently, we define accessor functions that return the real-part and link from a scalar, regardless of whether it is a real number or a dual.

The function ρ returns the real part of a scalar. It begins by testing if the scalar is a dual. If it is, its real part is returned by reaching into the vector that represents the dual.

If d is not a dual, we assume that d is a real number

```
(define ρ
  (λ (d)
    (cond
      ((dual? d) d|1)
      (else d))))
```

35

Similarly, κ returns the link of a scalar. If d is a dual, its link is returned by reaching into the vector that represents the dual

```
(define κ
  (λ (d)
    (cond
      ((dual? d) d|2)
      (else end-of-chain))))
```

If the scalar is not a dual, there is no chain that produced it. In that case the link should be a function that ends the chain. We refer to this as the

end-of-chain

function and we'll define it shortly.

5 | Differentiable functions

36

The functions that we're interested in finding gradients for usually produce a scalar loss as in frame 59:9. We find the gradients of this loss with respect to the $\boldsymbol{\theta}$ argument of those functions.

For our purposes, we refer to such functions as

differentiable functions

When presented with a batch as in frame 119:12, our differentiable functions produce a tensor[1] of scalars, with one scalar for each element of the batch.

In its full generality, automatic differentiation produces a $\boldsymbol{\theta}$-shaped gradient for each scalar in the result.

37

Here we don't require this generality. So, we make a simplifying optimization. We produce, directly, a single $\boldsymbol{\theta}$-shaped gradient that is the sum of all the individual $\boldsymbol{\theta}$-shaped gradients, without *actually* producing those individual $\boldsymbol{\theta}$-shaped gradients.†

†For those who know what these words mean: we produce a row-wise sum of the Jacobian.

The benefit of this optimization is that it makes it simpler for gradient descent by avoiding the need to keep all the individual $\boldsymbol{\theta}$-shaped gradients.

38

Based on how we construct duals, we should *re-emphasize* here that it is the *dual* itself that carries the chain that has produced it.

Because of this, we are more concerned with the results that are produced by differentiable functions than we are with the functions themselves.

39

Duals, however, get embedded within other structures like lists and vectors (for example, in a $\boldsymbol{\theta}$). These lists and vectors are, in turn, passed in as arguments to differentiable functions and are produced as results of these functions.

We refer to scalars, lists, and vectors as
differentiables
Differentiables are defined as
scalars
lists of differentiables
or
vectors of differentiables

40

We can think of differentiables as tree-shaped[†] structures that have scalars at their leaves. The nodes in this structure are lists and vectors. Further, the scalars at the leaves carry the chains that produced them.

[†] Actually, directed-acyclic-graph–shaped.

We often find the need to traverse the structure of differentiables to reach scalars at the leaves.

41

One useful function for the traversal of a differentiable is map^*. This function produces a new differentiable with the same structure as the argument, but the leaves have other scalars instead.

The first argument to map^* is a function f that accepts a single scalar to produce another scalar. The second argument to map^* is a differentiable y.

Then map^* produces a new differentiable where every scalar, say d, in y is replaced by $(f\ d)$.

42

We define it like this

```
(define map*
  (λ (f y)
    (cond
      ((scalar? y) (f y))
      ((list? y)
       (map (λ (lm†)
              (map* f lm))
         y))
      ((vector? y)
       (vector-map (λ (ve‡)
                     (map* f ve))
         y)))))
```

†*list member*.
‡*vector element*.

This function recursively traverses the structure of y. In the base test, where y is a scalar, we invoke f on y, thus producing its new scalar.

For lists (vectors), we traverse the individual members (elements) recursively.[§]

[§]This definition includes the possibility that vectors may contain lists, even though we don't use vectors like that in the core.

43

This function *dual** converts any scalar to a *truncated dual*. A truncated dual is a dual whose link is always the function *end-of-chain*

```
(define dual*
  (λ (d)
    (dual (ρ d)
      end-of-chain)))
```

Here is an example of how to use *map**. If y is a differentiable

(*map* dual* y*)

produces a differentiable that contains only truncated duals at its leaves. We refer to this kind of differentiable as a

truncated differentiable

44

Now we have some of the machinery to begin understanding ∇

```
(define ∇
  (λ (f θ)
    (let ((wrt (map* dual* θ)))
      (∇once (f wrt) wrt))))
```

The argument f is the function for which the gradient is being sought, and $\boldsymbol{\theta}$ is the argument to f with respect to which we're seeking the gradient.

Since $\boldsymbol{\theta}$ is a list of tensors and since tensors are either scalars or possibly nested vectors, $\boldsymbol{\theta}$ is itself a differentiable.

45

First, we convert $\boldsymbol{\theta}$ to a truncated differentiable

$(map^* \ dual^* \ \boldsymbol{\theta})$

This abandons any prior links that the scalars in $\boldsymbol{\theta}$ might contain. The effect of this is that it restricts the gradient to be determined exclusively on what f performs, and not on the history of $\boldsymbol{\theta}$ prior to the invocation of f on it.

46

This truncated differentiable is named *wrt* to remind us that this is the $\boldsymbol{\theta}$ argument to f

with respect to

which we are determining gradients.

It is worth re-emphasizing that *wrt* is identical in structure to $\boldsymbol{\theta}$, but each scalar from $\boldsymbol{\theta}$ in *wrt* now has become a truncated dual.

Thus, it is also worth pointing out that unlike $\boldsymbol{\theta}$, *wrt always* contains truncated duals at leaf positions.

47

We are now ready to invoke f on its argument, *wrt*, which is really a dressed-down $\boldsymbol{\theta}$. The truncated duals at the leaves of *wrt* become the arguments to chains that get constructed in the invocation of f. In other words, all the gradients of the result of this invocation are determined with respect to these truncated duals in *wrt*.

We invoke the function f on *wrt*. Assuming that this invocation terminates, it produces a differentiable and we then determine gradients for this differentiable with respect to *wrt*.

The actual determination of the gradient is carried out by the function ∇_{once}, which we now describe.

7 | Gradient states and ∇_{once}

48

When we're walking down chains of primitives, we need a structure that keeps track of gradients.

Moreover, this structure needs to remember one gradient for each scalar in the argument.†

†These scalars are a subset of those in *wrt*.

49

We use a *gradient state* to do this. A gradient state associates each scalar d in *wrt* with an accumulator that represents the current gradient of the result of the chain with respect to d.

Technically, it represents the sum of all the gradients of every scalar in the *result* with respect to d as we note in frame 37, but here we ignore that distinction.

50

Gradient states are easily represented as hash tables.

Now we define ∇_{once}

```
(define ∇once
  (λ (y wrt)
    (let ((σ (∇σ y (hasheq))))
      (map* (λ (d)
              (hash-ref σ d 0.0))
        wrt))))
```

Here, we determine a gradient state σ,[†] by invoking ∇_σ on y and an empty gradient state, created with (*hasheq*). Now σ contains the gradients of y with respect to each scalar in *wrt*.

As defined in frame 6, the gradient of y with respect to *wrt* should have the same structure as *wrt*, but with gradients instead of the scalars at the leaves.

So, we use *map** to substitute all the scalars in *wrt* with the corresponding gradient. We invoke *map** on a function that looks up the gradient of a scalar in σ. Here, we use the default value 0.0 when the scalar is not yet present in σ. This produces the gradient of y in exactly the structure we need.

[†]Thanks, Hans Peter Luhn (1886–1964) for the idea of hashtables. This use of σ is the first occurrence of a hashtable.

51

Now we define ∇_σ

```
(define ∇σ
  (λ (y σ)
    (cond
      ((scalar? y)
       (let ((k (κ y)))
         (k y 1.0 σ)))
      ((list? y)
       (∇σ-list y σ))
      ((vector? y)
       (∇σ-vec y (sub1 |y|) σ)))))
```

Here, we traverse the structure of the differentiable y recursively and accumulate gradients in σ.

For lists, we accumulate the gradients from each member by recursively invoking ∇_σ as we traverse the list, using the support function ∇_σ-*list*.

For vectors, we accumulate the gradients from each element by recursively invoking ∇_σ as we traverse the vector, using the support function ∇_σ-*vec*.

52

This brings us to the base test, when y is a scalar. This is where we start walking the chain that produced this scalar.

We first determine the link k of the scalar y

$(\kappa\ y)$

53

The link k takes three arguments. The first is the scalar whose chain we're interested in walking. In this case, this scalar is y.

The second argument is the starting value of the multiplicative accumulator as we begin walking down the chain.

54

Since we're just starting the walk down the chain of y, we provide 1.0, the multiplicative identity, as the starting value for this multiplicative accumulator.

The third argument is the gradient state we'll be updating with gradients.

This invocation returns a gradient state containing the gradients that are obtained from walking the chain.

55

Here is how we traverse lists, one member at a time

```
(define ∇σ-list
  (λ (y σ)
    (cond
      ((null? y) σ)
      (else
       (let ((σ̂ (∇σ y_0 σ)†))
         (∇σ-list y_1↓ σ̂)))))))
```

†This use of ∇_σ is the first occurrence of a mutually recursive invocation, which is a part of Scheme we have not used in the core, as we remarked on page 351.

For vectors we traverse the vector starting at the last element and counting down to the 0th element

```
(define ∇σ-vec
  (λ (y i σ)
    (let ((σ̂ (∇σ y|_i σ)))
      (cond
        ((zero? i) σ̂)
        (else (∇σ-vec y (sub1 i) σ̂)))))))
```

56

We now turn to links. Links, again, are functions that help in the walking of chains of a scalar.

Let's start with the simplest case, when a scalar has the *end-of-chain* link for real numbers and truncated duals.

57

The link *end-of-chain* is always invoked at the end of the chain. By the time we're done walking the chain and reach the *end-of-chain*, we have the gradient associated with this chain in the multiplicative accumulator, which we always refer to as z.

The end of the chain is associated with a scalar, d, which *is* the *argument to the chain*. So, our task at the end of the chain is to remember the gradient z for the scalar d in the gradient state σ.

58

We thus define *end-of-chain*

```
(define end-of-chain
  (λ (d z σ)
    (let ((g (hash-ref σ d 0.0)))
      (hash-set σ d (+ z g)))))
```

In general, a *single* scalar d from *wrt* might actually appear at the end of *multiple* chains that contribute to a *single* result, y. This can happen, for example, when the argument to a function is used more than once.

59

In that case, each occurrence of d at the end of a chain makes its own contribution to the gradient of y with respect to d. The final gradient here is the sum of all these contributions.

So, for example, let us say we have a function f

```
(λ (x)
  (+ x x))
```

60

The result of

$(f\ d)$

is

$2 \times d$

Because x is used twice in the body of f, this counts as two occurrences of d.

The gradient of the result of +, from frame 10, is 1.0 with respect to each argument.

61

Thus, the gradient of the addition with respect to d is

$$1.0 + 1.0 = 2.0$$

62

This requirement is incorporated within *end-of-chain*. We first look up the current gradient g for d in σ using *hash-ref*, with a default of 0.0 if d is not present in σ.

We then add the multiplicative accumulator z to the current gradient g, and remember this sum as the gradient for d using *hash-set*.

63

Let's look at the link of a primitive operation. The addition of two scalars, $+^{0,0}$ from frame 189:40, is defined like this. It accepts two scalar arguments and returns a dual where the real part is the sum of the real parts of its two arguments.

Since $+^{0,0}$ is primitive, its gradients with respect to the arguments da and db are determined by a formula.

Here, $+$ and $*$ are the native arithmetic operations on real numbers

```
(define +^{0,0}
  (λ (da db)
    (dual (+ (ρ da) (ρ db))
      (λ (d z σ)
        (let ((σ̂ ((κ da) da (* 1.0 z) σ)))
          ((κ db) db (* 1.0 z) σ̂))))))
```

Let us now understand what happens when the link here is invoked.

64

We first invoke the link for da, $(\kappa\ da)$, on the scalar

da

the multiplicative accumulator

$(*\ 1.0\ z)$

which we explain below, and the gradient state

σ

to obtain

the new gradient state $\hat{\sigma}$

We next invoke the link for db, $(\kappa\ db)$, on the scalar

db

the multiplicative accumulator

$(*\ 1.0\ z)$

which we also explain below, and the gradient state

$\hat{\sigma}$

finally

the resultant gradient state is returned from the link

65

Now let's look at the multiplicative accumulators. When we walk down the links of *da* and *db*, the multiplicative accumulator is the product of the current accumulator *z* and the gradient of the primitive.

The gradients of addition, with respect to the argument whose chain we are walking down, as in frame 10, are both

1.0

66

So, this link begins the walk down the chains for *da* and for *db* with multiplicative accumulators

(∗ 1.0 *z*) for *da*

and

(∗ 1.0 *z*) for *db*

Also, since this link does not end a chain, we do not need to keep track of any gradients for *d*. Hence, we ignore *d*.

67

We recognize that

(∗ 1.0 *z*)

can be rewritten as *z* to get

```
(define +^{0,0}
  (λ (da db)
    (dual (+ (ρ da) (ρ db))
      (λ (d z σ)
        (let ((σ̂ ((κ da) da z σ)))
          ((κ db) db z σ̂))))))
```

68

We use a similar pattern for exp^0, which is $e^{(\rho\ da)}$ where *e* is the transcendental constant and *da* a scalar. Its gradient is also $e^{(\rho\ da)}$

```
(define exp^0
  (λ (da)
    (dual (exp (ρ da))
      (λ (d z σ)
        ((κ da) da (∗ (exp (ρ da)) z) σ)))))
```

Similarly, we define $*^{0,0}$ in frame 189:41, which is the multiplication of two scalars

```
(define ∗^{0,0}
  (λ (da db)
    (dual (∗ (ρ da) (ρ db))
      (λ (d z σ)
        (let ((σ̂ ((κ da) da (∗ (ρ db) z) σ)))
          ((κ db) db (∗ (ρ da) z) σ̂))))))
```

69

The patterns for defining primitives are very similar, and can be generalized for the definitions of all our primitives.

Let us start with a one-argument primitive. We propose a function *prim1* that can be used to define, for example, exp^0.

```
(define exp⁰
  (prim1 exp
    (λ (ra z)
      (∗ (exp ra) z))))
```

Here, *exp* is the function that will accept one real number argument and produce the real part of the answer, which will be a dual.

70

In this definition, *prim1* accepts two function arguments. The first is the function that defines the real part of the dual. Hence we refer to this as the ρ-function of the primitive.

The second function defines how the body of the link should behave. In other words, it incorporates the formula for the gradient. Hence we refer to this as the ∇-function of the primitive.

71

The second function expects two arguments and is responsible for computing the gradient. The first, *ra*, is the same real argument that is passed when calculating the real part. The second is the multiplicative accumulator that will be passed into the link.

An invocation of *prim1* returns a function that accepts a dual argument and returns a corresponding dual with a properly constructed link.

72

Here's the definition of *prim1*

```
(define prim1
  (λ (ρ-fn ∇-fn)
    (λ (da)
      (let ((ra (ρ da)))
        (dual (ρ-fn ra)
          (λ (d z σ)
            (let ((ga (∇-fn ra z)))
              ((κ da) da ga σ))))))))
```

The two arguments *ρ-fn* (for ρ-function), and *∇-fn* (for ∇-function) are used to produce the real part and the gradient, respectively. It returns a function that accepts one dual argument *da* and produces a dual.

73

The real part of the produced dual is determined by invoking ρ-*fn* on the real part of *da*.

The link of the dual has a body that invokes ∇-*fn* with the real part of *da* and z, and passes the result down the link of *da*.

74

And similarly, here is *prim2*. The biggest difference, aside from the additional argument to ρ-*fn* and ∇-*fn*, is that we use Scheme's multiple-value return feature to receive *two* gradients from ∇-*fn*, one each for *da* and *db*.†

These are then passed down the links for *da* and *db* using $\hat{\sigma}$ as in frame 63.

†See the notation for `let-values` on page 351.

```
(define prim2
  (λ (ρ-fn ∇-fn)
    (λ (da db)
      (let ((ra (ρ da))
            (rb (ρ db)))
        (dual (ρ-fn ra rb)
          (λ (d z σ)
            (let² (⟨ga gb⟩ (∇-fn ra rb z))
              (let ((σ̂ ((κ da) da ga σ)))
                ((κ db) db gb σ̂))))))))))
```

75

We redefine $+^{0,0}$ and $*^{0,0}$ with *prim2*†

```
(define +⁰˒⁰
  (prim2 +
    (λ (ra rb z)
      ⟨z z⟩)))
```

†Each of $+^{0,0}$ and $*^{0,0}$ invokes *prim2*, whose second argument is a function that when invoked, returns two values. See the notation for `values` on page 351.

```
(define *⁰˒⁰
  (prim2 *
    (λ (ra rb z)
      ⟨(* rb z) (* ra z)⟩)))
```

76

To define comparison operations, we use a support function

```
(define comparator
  (λ (f)
    (λ (da db)
      (f (ρ da) (ρ db)))))
```

And then define these

```
(define <^{0,0} (comparator <))
(define >^{0,0} (comparator >))
(define ≤^{0,0} (comparator ≤))
(define ≥^{0,0} (comparator ≥))
(define =^{0,0} (comparator =))
```

9 | Some common numerical primitives

77

```
(define −^{0,0}
  (prim2 −
    (λ (ra rb z)
      ⟨z (− z)⟩)))

(define ÷^{0,0}
  (prim2 ÷
    (λ (ra rb z)
      ⟨(∗ (÷ 1 rb) z)
       (∗ (÷ (∗ −1 ra) (∗ rb rb)) z)⟩)))

(define log^0
  (prim1 log
    (λ (ra z)
      (∗ (÷ 1 ra) z))))
```

```
(define expt^{0,0}
  (prim2 expt
    (λ (ra rb z)
      ⟨(∗ z (∗ z (expt ra (− rb 1))))
       (∗ (∗ (expt ra rb) (log ra)) z)⟩)))

(define sqrt^0
  (prim1 (λ (ra)
           (expt ra 1/2))
    (λ (ra z)
      (∗ (∗ 1/2 (expt ra −1/2)) z))))
```

We refer to this first version of automatic differentiation as System A. In appendix B, we show how to improve System A by redefining some of the functions here.

Appendix B I Could Have Raced All Day†

†With apologies and thanks, Alan Jay Lerner (1918–1986).

"Little" books are all about packaging ideas neatly into little boxes. The automatic differentiation described in appendix A (referred to as System A) is a semantically correct package of ideas for all the programs in the core. Sometimes, however, neat little packages run into trouble with the messy realities of the world outside.

With System A, for example, training networks like *morse-fcn* and *morse-residual* can become prohibitively time consuming. As we try running and training even larger models, it becomes necessary to vanquish these messy realities.

We sometimes like to imagine what Augustin-Louis Cauchy may have mused in 1847, "When my ideas, in the distant future, become well understood, the world will not believe what they can do with my very *clever* algorithms." Well, that distant future is now.

Functions that operate on very large tensors can be a lot more time-efficient by using hardware that executes them "in parallel." These *massively parallel machines*, as they are known, need a little bit of assistance in how our definitions and our data structures are organized, so that they can extract the necessary efficiencies.

In this appendix, we chart a course in our own "Little" style, to meet these demands. We go from the simple package in System A to an evolved package that deftly handles messy realities just as neatly. We'll continue to use the comic-book style and the by now familiar notations from appendix A.

1 | Tensors and their bottlenecks

System A implicitly assumes that tensors of rank higher than 0 are represented with nested vectors. Let's clarify this assumption further.

1

Here's the collection of functions that *allows* us to manipulate tensors of rank higher than 0.

```
(define tref
  (λ (t i)
    (vector-ref t (ρ i))))

(define tlen
  (λ (t)
    (vector-length t)))
```

2

```
(define tensor
  vector)

(define tensor?
  (λ (t)
    (cond
      ((scalar? t) #t)
      ((vector? t) #t)
      (else #f))))
```

3

In addition, we have *ext1* and *ext2*, whose definitions are exactly those given in frames 182:16 and 187:35. Together, these functions form the *abstract interface* to our tensors.

In general, all the scalars in our tensors in System A are duals. Each dual has a real part, which is the value of the scalar, and a link, which contains the necessary information to extract the gradient out of that scalar.

4

When our tensors are large, and our networks are also large (with many layers), the total number of duals and their links that we encounter also becomes large.

Moreover, many of these duals have very long chains, which makes traversal of those chains very time consuming. Having a large number of them slows down System A even more.

2 | Reducing the number of links

5

Let's resolve this bottleneck first and find a way to reduce the number of duals and links in the system. The key observation here is that almost every scalar produced inside System A resides in a tensor.

All of those scalars in that tensor are produced in exactly the same way, usually through an invocation of an extended function.

6

This means that their links are identical in structure. For example, here is how $*^{2,1}$ behaves

1. $(*^{2,1} \begin{bmatrix} 2.0 & 3.0 & 1.1 \\ 1.6 & 2.3 & 4.1 \end{bmatrix}_{(2\ 3)}$
   $\begin{bmatrix} 1.0 & 0.1 & 3.2 \end{bmatrix})$
2. $\begin{bmatrix} 2.0 & \underline{0.3} & 3.5 \\ 1.6 & 0.23 & 13.12 \end{bmatrix}_{(2\ 3)}$

All the scalars in this result tensor will contain the link produced by $*^{0,0}$ which looks like

$(\lambda\ (d\ z\ \sigma)$
$\quad (\textsf{let}\ ((\hat{\sigma}\ ((\kappa\ da)\ da\ (*\ (\rho\ db)\ z)\ \sigma)))$
$\qquad ((\kappa\ db)\ db\ (*\ (\rho\ da)\ z)\ \hat{\sigma})))$

7

The differences between the links are the specific values of *da* and *db*. For example, the underlined scalar 0.3 will have in its link the value of (ρ *da*) as

3.0

And the value of (ρ *db*) as

0.1

The other duals in the tensor will have the corresponding scalars for *da* and *db* in their links.

8

By recognizing this, we can have a representation where the link is associated with the *whole* result tensor, and the equivalent values of *a* and *b* in this link would be the *whole* argument tensors.

So, instead of following individual links in scalars, we could follow a single link for the entire tensor.

3 | Modifying System A

9

This requires us to extend our definition of duals to include tensors in their real part, not just scalars. We refer to duals that are not scalars as *tensor duals*. We refer to the real part of a tensor dual as a *tensor* or sometimes a *non-dual tensor*, to emphasize that it is not a dual.

Our definitions of duals from System A remain the same, but we change some of the other definitions.

We begin with the new definition of *scalar?*—when we have a dual, we check whether its real part is a number

```
(define scalar?
  (λ (d)
    (cond
      ((number? d) #t)
      ((dual? d) (number? (ρ d)))
      (else #f))))
```

10

We define *dual-like?*, which is a predicate that includes checking for vectors, which now allow ρ and κ invocations on them

```
(define dual-like?
  (λ (d)
    (cond
      ((scalar? d) #t)
      ((dual? d) #t)
      (else (vector? d)))))
```

The **else** clause (*vector? d*) allows for the possibility of encountering constant vectors, similar to how we handle constant scalars in frame 361:33.

11

We now modify ∇_σ to also allow for this same possibility of finding constant tensors in the base case by using *dual-like?*. We no longer recursively descend into a vector. We simply expect vectors (i.e., as tensors) to carry their own links, and start traversing the link.

```
(define ∇σ
  (λ (y σ)
    (cond
      ((dual-like? y)
       ((κ y) y (one-like (ρ y)) σ))
      ((list? y) (∇σ-list y σ))
      (else (error)))))
```

12

Unlike our previous definition of ∇_σ, here y can be a tensor dual. So when invoking the link, we pass, for the accumulator, a tensor with the same shape as

$(\rho\ y)$

but with 1.0s in it.

And we generate this tensor using *one-like* whose definition we'll see soon.

13

The other big difference that we encounter once we allow for tensors inside duals is that a gradient state σ no longer maps duals only to scalars.

The purpose of σ is to map a dual to its gradient. When our duals contain tensors, the gradients corresponding to those duals will also be tensors of the same shape.

14

This means we need a slightly modified definition of *end-of-chain*

```
(define end-of-chain
  (λ (d z σ)
    (let ((g (hash-ref σ d 0.0)))
      (hash-set σ d (+ρ g z)))))
```

In this definition, $+^{\rho}$ is an extended function that simply adds two (non-dual) tensors together, similar to the extended version of + described in frame 49:11, but with a few differences. We'll look at its definition shortly.

15

We similarly update *map**

```
(define map*
  (λ (f y)
    (cond
      ((dual-like? y) (f y))
      ((list? y)
       (map (λ (yi)
              (map* f yi))
         y))
      (else y))))
```

That was the easy part.

Now, we consider the implications for extended functions of wrapping tensors inside duals.

4 | Extension functions with tensor duals

16

Our definitions of *ext1* and *ext2* in Interlude V expect tensors in which each nested scalar is a dual. This is what allows us to find the gradients of extended functions easily.

Now, however, since these tensors are wrapped inside duals; both *ext1* and *ext2* are updated to produce a tensor dual where the link has a well-defined way to walk down the chain of tensor duals.

17

Let's handle this problem first. We begin with renaming our existing definition of *ext1* to $ext1^{\rho}$ and of *ext2* to $ext2^{\rho}$. The ρ superscript reminds us that this extension will be used to produce the real part of a tensor dual.

As this suggests, $ext1^{\rho}$ and $ext2^{\rho}$ are the real paths of *ext1* and *ext2*, respectively, where the real part of a dual is determined. Here are the redefinitions.

18

```
(define ext1ρ
  (λ (f n)
    (λ (t)
      (cond
        ((of-rank? n t) (f t))
        (else (tmap (ext1ρ f n) t))))))
```

```
(define ext2ρ
  (λ (f n m)
    (λ (t u)
      (cond
        ((of-ranks? n t m u) (f t u))
        (else
         (desc (ext2ρ f n m)
           n t m u))))))
```

19

The rest of the definitions of the support functions remain identical to those in Interlude V.

In the definitions of these functions, *t* and *u* are *non-dual* tensors, i.e., they are the real part of tensor duals, and they produce tensors that are non-dual as well, i.e., they produce only the *real* part of a resultant tensor dual.

20

Let's tie up a couple of loose ends now. We define *one-like* using $ext1^{\rho}$

```
(define one-like
  (ext1ρ (λ (s) 1.0) 0))
```

And $+^{\rho}$ using $ext2^{\rho}$

```
(define +ρ
  (ext2ρ + 0 0))
```

5 | Modifying extension functions

21

Let us now look at what *ext1* and *ext2* turn into, and beginning with *ext1*.

The function *ext1* expects, as before, a function *f* to extend, and the base rank *n*. Here, we expect *f* to accept a dual and return a dual.

22

Then, *ext1* returns a function that accepts one *tensor dual* argument *da* (of rank *n* or greater) and returns a dual whose real part is determined by using $ext1^{\rho}$.

Here is its skeleton

```
(define ext1
  (λ (f n)
    (λ (da)
      (dual
        ((ext1ρ [      R      ] n) (ρ da))
        (λ (d z σ)
          (let ((ga ([      N      ] da z)))
            ((κ da) da ga σ)))))))
```

23

The link of this returned dual is responsible for determining the *extended* gradient of *f*. We do that using *N*, which returns a function that will determine gradient *ga* using *da* and the multiplicative accumulator *z*. We pass along *ga* to the link of *da* to continue walking the chain.

We'll explain what an extended gradient of a function means soon.

The interesting part here is that this function is structurally similar to invoking *prim1* on *R* and *N*! We can now define *ext1*

```
(define ext1
  (λ (f n)
    (prim1 (ext1ρ [      R      ] n)
      [      N      ])))
```

6 | Primitives come to play

24

Our task now is to determine *R* and *N*. When using System A, the argument *f* of *ext1* could be *any function* that takes a single tensor of rank *n* as an argument and returns a single tensor of any rank as a result.

In the tensor dual system, however, we make an additional restriction. This restriction is that we can extend only *primitives*, i.e., we can extend functions that are produced using either only *prim1* or *prim2*.

25

This is not overly restrictive since most of our extensions have been only of primitive functions so far.

Secondly, since our definition of *ext1* is an invocation of *prim1*, functions extended with *ext1* automatically comply with this restriction.

26

A primitive can be considered to have two sub-functions: its ρ-function, which is the first argument to *prim1*, and its ∇-function, which is the second argument to *prim1*.[†]

[†]This also applies to primitives of two arguments and *prim2*.

For extended functions, each of these sub-functions is extended separately.

27

The extension of the ρ-function is invoked for the real part of a tensor dual. We see a glimpse of this when we invoke *ext1*$^\rho$ to get the ρ-function of *ext1*.

The extended gradient from frame 23 is determined by extending the ∇-function and invoking it on *da* and *z*.

28

We stipulate the existence of two *accessor* functions *ρ-function* and *∇-function*, which extract the ρ- and ∇-functions, respectively, from any given primitive. We'll define them shortly.

Now, we can see that *R* is

```
(ρ-function f)
```

So we can fill in some of *ext1*'s skeleton

```
(define ext1
  (λ (f n)
    (prim1 (ext1ρ (ρ-function f) n)
      [          N          ])))
```

29

Just as we have *ext1*$^\rho$ for the ρ-function extensions, we assume a function *ext1*$^\nabla$ for ∇-function extensions.

So, *N* looks something like

```
(ext1∇ [     G     ] n)
```

30

Since *ext1*$^{\nabla}$ extends the ∇-function of f, we have

G

is

(∇-*function* f)

We can now complete *ext1*

```
(define ext1
  (λ (f n)
    (prim1 (ext1^ρ (ρ-function f) n)
      (ext1^∇ (∇-function f) n))))
```

7 | Adding accessors to primitives

31

We now have our work cut out for *ext1*.

We need to define the accessors

ρ-function and ∇-*function*

and the extender

ext1$^{\nabla}$

Let's begin with *ρ-function* and ∇-*function*. The arguments to these two functions are always a *primitive* function generated using *prim1*.

32

Since a primitive created using *prim1* is a function, the only operation possible on it is *invocation*.

Here is *ρ-function*

```
(define ρ-function
  (λ (prim)
    (prim ρ-function)))
```

And here is ∇-*function*

```
(define ∇-function
  (λ (prim)
    (prim ∇-function)))
```

33

But wait, primitives are not defined to accept functions as arguments.

They expect only tensor duals.

So, let us fix that by redefining *prim1* so that primitives can also accept the functions *ρ-function* or ∇-*function* as an argument.

34

Here is a revised definition of *prim1*

```
(define prim1
  (λ (ρ-fn ∇-fn)
    (λ (daf)
      (cond
        ((eq? daf ρ-function) ρ-fn)
        ((eq? daf ∇-function) ∇-fn)
        (else
         (prim1-dual ρ-fn ∇-fn daf))))))
```

When invoked with ρ- and ∇-function arguments, *prim1* returns a function that tests its only argument.[†]

[†]The design of this function is intended to build what might be recognized as a *funcallable instance* which can also be written in some languages as a record that can be invoked or an object that inherits from a function class.

35

If *daf* is the function

ρ-function

it returns

ρ-fn

If *daf* is the function

∇-function

it returns

∇-fn

36

If the argument is neither, it performs what the original *prim1* function does, which is to produce a dual that invokes the necessary sub-function as needed. We capture that as an invocation of the function *prim1-dual*.

Here is the definition of *prim1-dual*

```
(define prim1-dual
  (λ (ρ-fn ∇-fn da)
    (let ((ra (ρ da)))
      (dual (ρ-fn ra)
        (λ (d z σ)
          (let ((ga (∇-fn ra z)))
            ((κ da) da ga σ)))))))
```

This definition behaves identically to *prim1* from frame 371:72 once it has received its arguments *ρ-fn*, *∇-fn*, and *da*.

We give the real part of *da* the name *ra* and use it in both the real part of the dual and its link.

37

Now we define *ext1*$^{\nabla}$

```
(define ext1∇
  (λ (∇-fn n)
    (λ (t z)
      (cond
        ((of-rank? n t) (∇-fn t z))
        (else
         (tmap (ext1∇ ∇-fn n) t z))))))
```

It accepts two arguments ∇-*fn*, which is the ∇-function of a primitive, and n, the required base rank of ∇-*fn*.

38

It returns a function that accepts t, a *non-dual* tensor, and z, and results in a tensor that represents the gradient of the extended version of f.

This definition is similar to *ext1*$^{\rho}$, but the main difference here is that ∇-*fn* expects two arguments to produce a gradient: an element of t at a given index, and the element from z at the same index.

39

Similar to *ext1*$^{\rho}$, if the rank of t has met its base rank n we invoke

∇-*fn* on t *and* z

This produces a gradient value of f at t.

The recursive case is analogous to *ext1*$^{\rho}$ where we invoke *tmap* using

(*ext1*$^{\nabla}$ ∇-*fn* n)

on every element of t and z, and assemble their results into the new gradient vector.

40

The definition of *ext2* is analogous to that of *ext1*

```
(define ext2
  (λ (f n m)
    (prim2 (ext2ρ (ρ-function f) n m)
      (ext2∇ (∇-function f) n m))))
```

We need, however, the definitions for *prim2* and *ext2*$^{\nabla}$ to complete this definition.

41

For our next definition, we need *variable-arity functions.*[†] Such a function can be invoked with any number of arguments, which are collected into a list and passed into the function.

Here is an example.

```
(define bizarre
  (λ xs
    |xs|))
```

The *xs* after λ has no parentheses.

[†]This is another part of Scheme that does not occur in the core that we alluded to on page 351.

Here we invoke *bizarre* with 3 arguments and then 5 arguments

```
(bizarre 17 45 81)
3
```

```
(bizarre 83 22 16 41 94)
5
```

42

We can start with *prim2*

```
(define prim2
  (λ (ρ-fn ∇-fn)
    (λ ds
      (let ((daf ds_0))
        (cond
          ((eq? daf ρ-function) ρ-fn)
          ((eq? daf ∇-function) ∇-fn)
          (else
           (prim2-dual ρ-fn ∇-fn
             daf ds_1)))))))
```

And *prim2*'s support, *prim2-dual*

```
(define prim2-dual
  (λ (ρ-fn ∇-fn da db)
    (let ((ra (ρ da))
          (rb (ρ db)))
      (dual (ρ-fn ra rb)
        (λ (d z σ)
          (let^2 (⟨ga gb⟩ (∇-fn ra rb z))
            (let ((σ̂ ((κ da) da ga σ)))
              ((κ db) db gb σ̂))))))))
```

43

The function returned from *prim2* is a variable-arity function because it would get only a single argument if it were invoked from *ρ-function* or *∇-function*, but would get two arguments if it were invoked as a primitive.

The function *prim2-dual* also behaves identically to *prim2* from frame 372:74 once it has its 4 arguments.

44

That brings us to the definition of *ext2*$^{\nabla}$. We can see by analogy to the similarity of *ext1*$^{\nabla}$ to *ext1*$^{\rho}$, that *ext2*$^{\nabla}$ should be similar to *ext2*$^{\rho}$, but will need to allow for the additional z argument.

Here is how we define *ext2*$^{\nabla}$

```
(define ext2∇
  (λ (∇-fn n m)
    (λ (t u z)
      (cond
        ((of-ranks? n t m u) (∇-fn t u z))
        (else
         (desc∇ (ext2∇ ∇-fn n m)
           n t m u z)))))))
```

45

When the rank of t meets n and the rank of u meets m, we produce a pair of gradients by invoking

(∇-*fn* t u z)

Otherwise, we descend into one or both tensors. We do this by invoking *desc*$^{\nabla}$, which is structurally very similar to *desc* from frame 188:37. The main difference here is that *desc*$^{\nabla}$ additionally accepts a multiplicative accumulator z.

Here is how we define *desc*$^{\nabla}$

```
(define desc∇
  (λ (g n t m u z)
    (cond
      ((of-rank? n t) (desc-u∇ g t u z))
      ((of-rank? m u) (desc-t∇ g t u z))
      ((= †t† †u†) (tmap2 g t u z))
      ((rank> t u) (desc-t∇ g t u z))
      (else (desc-u∇ g t u z)))))
```

46

There are three support functions here that we haven't seen

desc-t$^{\nabla}$

desc-u$^{\nabla}$

and

tmap2

Let's look at *tmap2* first.

It maps g over t, u, and z

```
(define tmap2
  (λ (g t u z)
    (build-gt-gu †t†
      (λ (i)
        (g t|i u|i z|i)))))
```

47

Here g produces two gradients at each invocation. These gradients are assembled into two separate vectors to produce two gradient tensors, one with respect to each of t and u.

This is handled by *build-gt-gu*, which is invoked with the size of the gradient vectors needed (here the length of t) and an initialization function that produces two values for each index i.

48

We define *build-gt-gu*

```
(define build-gt-gu
  (λ (tn init)
    (let ((gt (make-vector tn))
          (gu (make-vector tn)))
      (fill-gt-gu gt gu init (sub1 tn)))))
```

Here we first create two vectors *gt* and *gu* each of length *tn* where each element has some default value (usually 0).

Then, *fill-gt-gu* invokes the function *init* with the index i to get the value for $gt|_i$ and $gu|_i$ and replaces the default values there. It finally returns *gt* and *gu*.

```
(define fill-gt-gu
  (λ (gt gu init i)
    (let² ((⟨gti gui⟩ (init i))
      (vector-set! gt i gti)†
      (vector-set! gu i gui)
      (cond
        ((zero? i) ⟨gt gu⟩)
        (else
          (fill-gt-gu gt gu g (sub1 i)))))))
```

† We use the side-effecting *vector-set!*, and the body of the **let²** is evaluated in sequence. Some may find this shocking, but it is justified here as a one-time initialization of previously uninitialized vectors. We are satisfied that *build-gt-gu* presents an abstraction that is free of side effects, even though its implementation might not be. A side-effect-free version can be defined using *list→vector*, at the expense of more memory allocation.

49

Let us now define *desc-t*$^\nabla$

```
(define desc-t∇
  (λ (g t u z)
    (build-gt-acc-gu |t|
      (λ (i)
        (g t|i u z|i)))))
```

When descending into t, but not u, we handle the gradients returned by g differently. We do this by invoking the support function *build-gt-acc-gu* which, again, is invoked with the length of the vector we need to build, and an initialization function that produces two values when given an index i.

50

The *whole* of *u* is used with each element of *t* when we descend into *t* but not *u*. This means *u* is repeated for each element of *t*.

Because of this repeated use, we add the *gu*s produced at each *i* together, similar to frame 368:60.

51

In other words, we *accumulate* the *gu*s. This is why our support function here is called *build-gt-acc-gu*.

And here is its definition

```
(define build-gt-acc-gu
  (λ (tn init)
    (let ((gt (make-vector tn))
          (gu 0.0))
      (fill-gt-acc-gu gt
        init (sub1 tn) gu))))
```

52

It takes two arguments, *tn*, the length of the vector being built, and the initialization function *init*. It then creates a vector *gt* of length *tn* where each element, again, has some default value.

For the purposes of accumulation, we begin with *gu* being set to 0.0. We then invoke *fill-gt-acc-gu*, which repeatedly invokes *init* for each index *i* and sets each element of *gt* while accumulating *gu*.

53

Here is how *fill-gt-acc-gu* is defined

```
(define fill-gt-acc-gu
  (λ (gt init i gu)
    (let^2 ((⟨gti gui⟩ (init i))
      (vector-set! gt i gti)†
      (let ((ĝu (+^ρ gu gui)))
        (cond
          ((zero? i) ⟨gt ĝu⟩)
          (else
           (fill-gt-acc-gu gt
             init (sub1 i) ĝu)))))))
```

It is similar in structure to *fill-gt-gu*, but we accumulate *gu* with $+^{\rho}$ instead of setting the values in a vector.

†The framenote in frame 48 applies here as well.

54

The remaining function, *desc-u*$^\nabla$, is very similar to *desc-t*$^\nabla$, but the support function accumulates *gt* instead of *gu*

```
(define desc-u∇
  (λ (g t u z)
    (build-gu-acc-gt ∤u∤
      (λ (i)
        (g t u|i z|i)))))

(define build-gu-acc-gt
  (λ (n init)
    (let ((gu (make-vector n))
          (gt 0.0))
      (fill-gu-acc-gt gu
        init (sub1 n) gt))))
```

Here is the definition of *fill-gu-acc-gt*

```
(define fill-gu-acc-gt
  (λ (gu init i gt)
    (let^2 (⟨gti gui⟩ (init i))
      (vector-set! gu i gui)†
      (let ((ĝt (+^ρ gt gti)))
        (cond
          ((zero? i) ⟨ĝt gu⟩)
          (else
           (fill-gu-acc-gt gu
             init (sub1 i) ĝt)))))))
```

†. . . and here.

55

With these changes, our definitions for scalar primitives and their extensions remain identical to those seen in the core and in appendix A.

Non-scalar primitives, or primitives accepting tensors of rank higher than 0, e.g. sum^1 and $argmax^1$, are redefined to respect the restriction in frame 24.

9 | Non-scalar primitives

56

We begin by redefining sum^1 as the ρ-function $sum^{1\,\rho}$

```
(define sum^1ρ
  (λ (t)
    (summed^ρ t (sub1 ∤t∤) 0.0)))
```

Here is $summed^\rho$

```
(define summed^ρ
  (λ (t i a)
    (let ((â (+^ρ a t|i)))
      (cond
        ((zero? i) â)
        (else
         (summed^ρ t (sub1 i) â))))))
```

57

There is a corresponding ∇-function $sum^{1\nabla}$

```
(define sum^1∇
  (λ (t z)
    (tmap (λ (t) z) t)))
```

This function is the predetermined formula for the gradient of a sum of scalars within a tensor^1.

58

We can now define sum^1[†]

```
(define sum^1
  (prim1 sum^1ρ sum^1∇))
```

[†]Other vector operations are defined similarly, with their predetermined formulas for the ∇-functions determined individually. We refer the reader to

www.thelittlelearner.com

and extend it as usual, since it is now a primitive. We get both *sum* and *sum-cols* from it

```
(define sum
  (ext1 sum^1 1))

(define sum-cols
  (ext1 sum^1 2))
```

59

These new definitions for *ext1* and *ext2* are fully capable of handling tensors inside duals so as to reduce bottlenecks by many orders of magnitude for programs like *morse*.

We now look at another optimization that further improves the performance of our models.

10 | Flat tensor representation

60

The layout of the tensors in memory is a crucial factor in determining how quickly the scalars in these tensors can be retrieved for operating on them.

In most cases, the hardware favors tensors that are "contiguous" when laid out in memory, meaning that all the scalars in the tensor appear in contiguously placed memory locations.

61

In most real-world problems for deep learning, we work with very large tensors.

In such cases, it pays to organize our tensors for contiguous representation in memory, including for massively parallel hardware.

62

The tensors we have here, using the vector representation, are not contiguous.

Since we use a nested representation, different parts of the same tensor (when higher than rank 1), could be found in various non-contiguous locations within memory.

63

Here, we provide an overview of a different representation of tensors that skirts nesting altogether, and relies on a single, fully contiguous section of memory to represent the whole tensor.

We call this a *flat tensor representation.* Here we provide insight into this representation and refer the reader to the definitions that can be found at

www.thelittlelearner.com

Hybrid representations that combine flat and nested tensor representations are possible, of course, and sometimes make sense on certain kinds of massively parallel hardware. Here, however, we limit ourselves to completely flat tensor representations.

64

A *flat tensor* has three parts that define it. The first is its *shape*, which is a list, identical to the shape of any given tensor seen in the core.

Unlike the naturally recursive definition of *shape* in frame 39:37, which traverses the nesting of a tensor, here we provide the shape of the tensor *when it is constructed.*

65

The second part is a *store*, which is a contiguous section of memory for all elements of the tensor.

All the scalars in the tensor (which are now just real numbers) are kept contiguously in this store.†

†This is similar to *arrays* found in languages like Fortran and C.

66

The third is an *offset*, which is a natural number indicating how many locations into the store this tensor begins.

This is necessary to be able to select sub-tensors out of a given flat tensor without having to copy elements of the original store into a new store.

67

As an example, here is a tensor[3]

$$\left[\begin{bmatrix}1 & 2 & 3 & 4\\ 5 & 6 & 7 & 8\\ 9 & 10 & 11 & 12\end{bmatrix}\ \begin{bmatrix}13 & 14 & 15 & 16\\ 17 & 18 & 19 & 20\\ 21 & 22 & 23 & 24\end{bmatrix}\right]_{(2\ 3\ 4)}$$

In a nested representation, this is how this tensor is constructed

```
(vector
  (vector
    (vector  1  2  3  4)
    (vector  5  6  7  8)
    (vector  9 10 11 12))
  (vector
    (vector 13 14 15 16)
    (vector 17 18 19 20)
    (vector 21 22 23 24)))
```

68

Its flat representation is

```
(flat (list 2 3 4)
  (store 1 2 ... 24)
  0)
```

Here, the function *store* allocates a contiguous memory segment and fills it with the values provided.

69

Let us temporarily give a name to this store

```
(define t-store
  (store 1 2 ... 24))
```

And now we define t as the tensor[3] from frame 68 using *t-store*

```
(define t
  (flat (list 2 3 4)
    t-store
    0))
```

70

How can we represent the various sub-tensors of this tensor? For example, say we want the sub-tensor given by

$t|_1$

This would be the tensor

$$\begin{bmatrix} 13 & 14 & 15 & 16 \\ 17 & 18 & 19 & 20 \\ 21 & 22 & 23 & 24 \end{bmatrix}_{(3\ 4)}$$

With the flat tensor representation we can reuse *t-store* for this purpose

```
(flat (list 3 4)
  t-store
  12)
```

The offset argument 12 indicates that this tensor begins at the 12th position in *t-store*. We refer to the portion of the store that is occupied by the scalars in a tensor as its *extent*.

Here, the extent of this tensor begins at the 12th position and goes up to the 23rd position (we assume, of course, that the numbering of positions begins at 0).

71

The function *shape* now simply returns the shape associated with the flat tensor.

Here, then, is this familiar definition of *rank* from frame 41:42

```
(define rank
  (λ (t)
    |(shape t)|))
```

72

Extension operations *ext1* and *ext2* over flat representations are also simpler, because no descending into sub-tensors is necessary.

For example, take a scalar extension, such as *log*. The function $ext1^{\rho}$ now allocates a new store and fills it by traversing the extent of the tensor and invoking the ρ-function of log^0 on the corresponding input element.

73

We refer to this type of traversal as *looping*. The number of elements processed at each step is known as a *stride* of the loop. For scalar operations the looping occurs with a stride of one element. This looping is used primarily to fill in the right values for pre-allocated tensor stores.

For extended functions, such as *sum*, $ext1^{\rho}$ will need to invoke the ρ-function of sum^1 with a stride of the length of the tensor^1 that needs summing.

74

It is this simplified traversal that gives us the speed advantages for massively parallel machines.

We need to, of course, have a corresponding $ext1^{\nabla}$, which is the mirror operation of $ext1^{\rho}$, but it invokes the ∇-function.

75

For $ext2^{\rho}$ and $ext2^{\nabla}$, the shapes of the argument tensors determine the pattern of looping and the strides necessary for each argument, as well as the shape of the output tensor being filled.

For example, when one of the argument tensors, say t, is repeated because it has met its base rank, but the other tensor, say u, hasn't, then the looping pattern continues to traverse u, but starts again for t everytime the end of t has been reached.

76

Because extensions in the flat tensor representation need to pre-allocate stores, it becomes necessary for primitives to be able to report the shapes their outputs will require.

For example, sum^1 produces only one scalar everytime it is invoked but requires a $tensor^1$ to produce that scalar. Similarly $+^{0,0}$ produces one scalar for one scalar in each of its inputs, but one of the inputs may be used repeatedly.

77

In order to support this pre-allocation of stores, we now require primitives to also have a *shape function.* A shape function for unary operations takes an input shape (of its base rank) and produces an output shape.

For example the shape function of sum^1 is

```
(define shape-sum¹
  (λ (st)
    (list)))
```

which says the shape of the output of sum^1 for any given input shape of rank 1, is the empty list, which means the output is a scalar.

78

Similarly, the shape function for all scalar primitives of two arguments is

```
(define shape⁰,⁰
  (λ (st su)
    (list)))
```

The shape function for $*^{2,1}$ is

```
(define shape*²,¹
  (λ (st su)
    st))
```

This definition says that the output produced by $*^{2,1}$ has the same shape as its rank 2 argument, *st*.

79

Primitives are now defined with their shape functions. For example

```
(define sum^1
  (prim1 sum^{1ρ} sum^{1∇} shape-sum^1))

(define +^{0,0}
  (prim2 +
    (λ (ra rb z)
      ⟨z z⟩)
    shape^{0,0}))
```

Both *prim1* and *prim2* will correspondingly require a test for the argument *shape-fn*, defined thusly

```
(define shape-fn
  (λ (prim)
    (prim shape-fn)))
```

80

Since *ext1* and *ext2* are also defined as primitives, we need to provide shape functions for these as well. These, however, can use the shape functions of their primitives and automatically derive a shape function for the extension.

The definitions of shape functions for *ext1* and *ext2* both mirror the structure of $ext1^{\rho}$ and $ext2^{\rho}$ but instead of producing tensors, they produce only shapes.

12 | And lastly ...

81

We have purposely been abstract about how stores are represented. A simple way to represent them in Scheme is to use *vector*

```
(define store
  vector)
```

Some languages allow for native libraries, usually known as *foreign function interfaces*, that enable stores to be represented in operating system native representations that are much friendlier to the underlying hardware.

82

Many massively parallel machines provide such native libraries which can be used for the benefit of efficient parallelized execution.

This path to massively parallel machines also requires careful reconstruction of *ext1*, *ext2*, and all the primitives to take advantage of the parallelism, but we leave that as homework for you!

83

Well, that's that, then.

Now that we've met every character without skipping chapters, it is time to end our *little* journey here. We leave with another poem.

You will see light in the darkness
You will make some sense of this
And when you've made your little *journey*
You will find the fun you've missed.[†]

[†]With apologies and thanks, Sting.

Acknowledgments

Guy Steele and Peter Norvig were exactly the right contributing authors for the forewords. They understood exactly what we were trying to say and they each captured its spirit beautifully. Our only regret is that our words can only *approximate* how thrilled we are to include their elegantly phrased stories of this journey.

Qingqing Su's drawings have a brand new style that is inspired by illustrations from prior "Little" books, but her creations have their own unique personality. Our gratitude goes to her for the skill with which she produced these drawings.

We are grateful to Suzanne Menzel and Mitch Wand, who have been involved with "Little" books for a long time. They each let us know exactly what was wrong, confusing, or could be improved in the gentlest of ways, which led to many significant improvements. Our appreciation and thanks go to Julie Sussman who stepped in at the penultimate hour to rescue this book from more shortcomings in the writing than we had anticipated.

Our early readers, Steve Betzold, Ron Garcia, Nick Faro, and Richard Otten, gave us the confidence to continue trying to think harder about what we were doing. We want to especially thank Jason Hemann whose review at the time was a joy to read. Thanks also to Parker Mores and Zach Wilkerson, who used an early variant of the notation page xxiii, which convinced us to keep using that page style.

We would like to thank Nick Drozd, Shriram Krishnamurthi, Weixi Ma, Zack Seiliger, Adithya Selvaprithviraj, and Michael Vanier for their patience, reading, and feedback. Qingyi Ji was instrumental in helping us develop compassion for our readers, especially in the early chapters. Jon Rossie was an enthusiastic supporter who showed us how to help some readers who are often overlooked.

We are especially thankful to Darshal Shetty and Chanikya Vmmanagari, not only for being readers but also for their work on helping us improve the accompanying code. We also thank Yafei Yang, whose keen eye has caught some very subtle errors at the twilight of completion.

We thank Matthias Felleisen and the entire Racket team who have carried the spirit of Scheme forward in Racket. We admire this enormously successful, continuing, multi-decade effort. And a very special thanks to Dorai Sitaram for his creation of SLaTeX.

Our team at the MIT Press of Elizabeth Swayze, Matthew Valades, and Jay Martsi has earned our gratitude and appreciation for making the process as painless as possible. Thanks also to Alex Hoopes for her initial involvement in the process.

We also thank Yuzhen Ye, Lynne Mikolon, Benita Brown, and Charles Pope, who have made life at Indiana University much easier than anyone has a right to expect. For the inspiration that arose from the discussions and Tech Talks, we thank Christine Lao, Raunak Vijan, and Jonathan Wu, as well as Spencer Ballo and Amogh Batwal, who were also early readers.

And finally, we thank our families for their encouragement, patience, and strength in tolerating endless video calls between Dan and Anurag, and all the weekends and weeknights consumed by our passion.

Dan thanks Mary, his amazing wife; Robert (an early reader) and Shannon and their children, Samantha and Chase; Rachel and Joseph and their daughter, Willow; and Sara and Travis and their children, Brooklyn, Aria, and Wyatt.

Anurag thanks Aruna, his wonderful wife, and their two daughters, Rishma and Aria Nina (also an early reader).

References

[1] I. Goodfellow, Y. Bengio, and A. Courville, *Deep Learning.* MIT Press, 2016.

[2] P. N. Klein, *Coding the Matrix: Linear Algebra Through Applications to Computer Science.* Newtonian Press, 2013.

[3] W. Kurt, *Bayesian Statistics the Fun Way.* No Starch Press, Inc., 2019.

[4] L. Hui and M. Belkin, "Evaluation of neural architectures trained with square loss vs cross-entropy in classification tasks," in *9th International Conference on Learning Representations, ICLR 2021*, OpenReview.net, 2021.

[5] A. L. Maas, "Rectifier nonlinearities improve neural network acoustic models," 2013.

[6] K. He, X. Zhang, S. Ren, and J. Sun, "Delving deep into rectifiers: Surpassing human-level performance on imagenet classification," in *Proceedings of the IEEE International Conference on Computer Vision (ICCV)*, December 2015.

[7] A. Krizhevsky, I. Sutskever, and G. E. Hinton, "Imagenet classification with deep convolutional neural networks," in *Advances in neural information processing systems*, 2012.

[8] K. He, X. Zhang, S. Ren, and J. Sun, "Deep residual learning for image recognition," in *IEEE Conference on Computer Vision and Pattern Recognition (CVPR)*, 2016.

[9] K. Simonyan and A. Zisserman, "Very deep convolutional networks for large-scale image recognition," in *International Conference on Learning Representations*, 2015.

[10] T. Brown, B. Mann, N. Ryder, *et al.*, "Language models are few-shot learners," in *Advances in Neural Information Processing Systems* (H. Larochelle *et al.*, eds.), vol. 33, Curran Associates, Inc., 2020.

[11] A. Vaswani, N. Shazeer, N. Parmar, *et al.*, "Attention is all you need," in *Advances in Neural Information Processing Systems* (I. Guyon *et al.*, eds.), vol. 30, Curran Associates, Inc., 2017.

[12] D. P. Kingma and M. Welling, "Auto-Encoding Variational Bayes," in *2nd International Conference on Learning Representations, ICLR 2014, Banff, AB, Canada, April 14-16, 2014, Conference Track Proceedings*, 2014.

[13] I. Goodfellow, J. Pouget-Abadie, *et al.*, "Generative adversarial nets," in *Advances in Neural Information Processing Systems* (Z. Ghahramani, M. Welling, *et al.*, eds.), vol. 27, Curran Associates, Inc., 2014.

[14] X. Glorot and Y. Bengio, "Understanding the difficulty of training deep feedforward neural networks," in *Proceedings of the Thirteenth International Conference on Artificial Intelligence and Statistics*, PMLR, 2010.

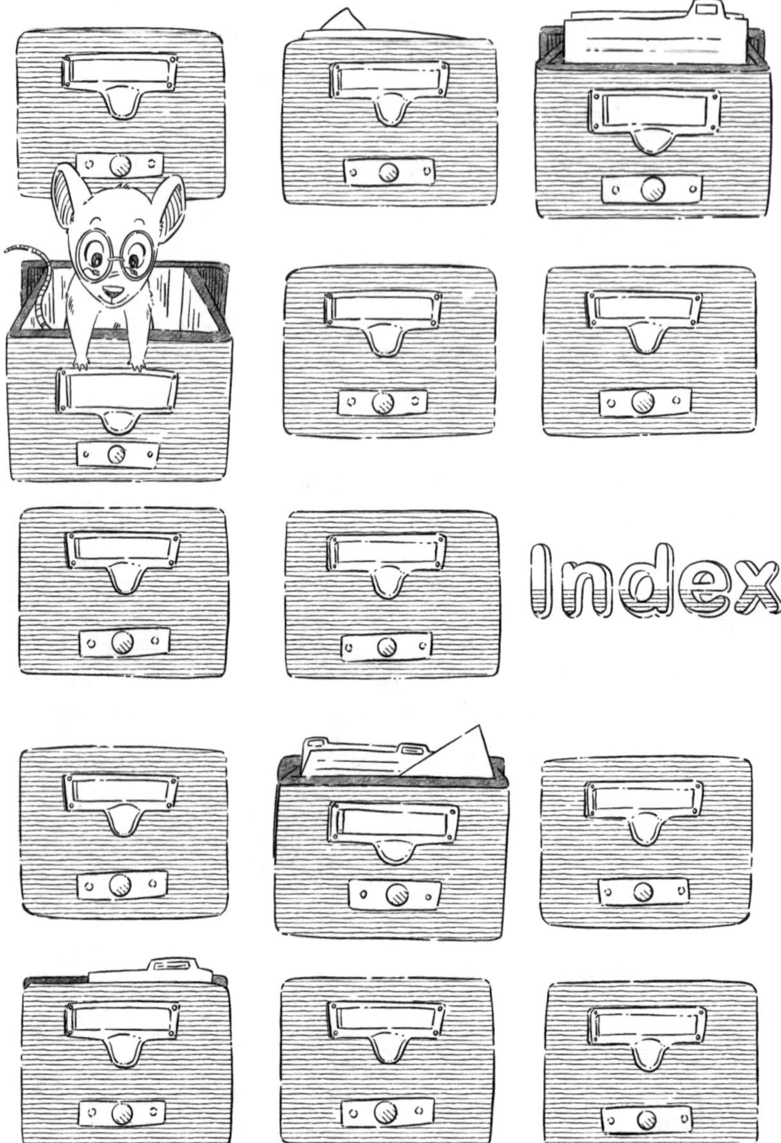
Index

Index